Consulting the Public

Guidelines and good practice

John Seargeant and Jane Steele

Policy Studies Institute
LONDON

PSI PUBLISHING

The publishing imprint of the independent
Policy Studies Institute
100 Park Village East, London NW1 3SR
Tel. 0171 468 0468 Fax. 0171 388 0914

ISBN 0 85374 727 X
PSI Report 849

A CIP catalogue record of this book is available from the British Library.

PSI publications are available from: Grantham Book Services Ltd, Isaac Newton Way, Alma Park Industrial Estate, Grantham NG31 9SD

Orders: (tel) 01476 541080 (fax) 01476 541061

Books will normally be dispatched within 24 hours. Cheques should be made payable to Grantham Book Services Ltd.

Booktrade representation (UK and Eire): Broadcast Books,
24 De Montfort Road, London SW16 1LZ Tel. 0181 677 5129

PSI subscriptions are available from PSI's subscription agent:
Carfax Publishing Company Ltd, P O Box 25, Abingdon, Oxford OX14 3UE

Typeset by Policy Studies Institute
Printed in Great Britain by Page Bros, Norwich

Consulting the Public

Policy Studies Institute (PSI) is one of Europe's leading independent research organisations undertaking studies of economic, industrial and social policy and the workings of political institutions.

PSI is a registered charity, run on a non-profit basis, and is not associated with any political party, pressure group or commercial interest.

PSI attaches great importance to covering a wide range of subject areas with its multidisciplinary approach. The Institute's researchers are organised in groups which currently cover the following programmes:

Crime, Justice and Youth Studies – Employment – Ethnic Equality and Diversity – Family Finances – Information and Citizenship – Information and Cultural Studies – Social Care and Health Studies – Work, Benefits and Social Participation

This publication arises from the Information and Citizenship Group and is one of over 30 publications made available by the Institute each year.

Information about the work of PSI and a catalogue of publications can be obtained from:

Publications Department
Policy Studies Institute
100 Park Village East
London NW1 3SR

Contents

Abbreviations

ABSA	Association for Business Sponsorships of the Arts
ACW	Arts Council of Wales
ADC	Association of District Councils
ASD	Analytical Service Division
BA	Benefits Agency
BBSRC	Biotechnology and Biological Science Research Council
BCHT	Bradford Community Health Trust
BHA	Bradford Health Authority
CAB	Citizens Advice Bureau
CBHA	Community-Based Housing Association
CBI	Confederation of British Industry
CBMDC	City of Bradford Metropolitan District Council
CCT	Compulsory Competitive Tendering
CE	Chief Executive
CIH	Chartered Institute of Housing
CLD	Commission for Local Democracy
CPAG	Child Poverty Action Group
CRE	Commission for Racial Equality
CRT	Customer Relations Team
CSB	Customer Services Branch
DBT	Danish Board of Technology
DoE	Department of the Environment
DSS	Department of Social Security
ESG	Estate Steering Group
FBHO	Federation of Black Housing Associations
GIS	Geographical Information System
HACT	Housing Associations Charitable Trust
HAT	Housing Action Trust
INLOGOV	Institute of Local Government Studies
LGMB	Local Government Management Board
LSC	Locality Sensitive Commissioning

NACAB	National Association of Citizens Advice Bureaux
NICOD	Northern Ireland Council of Disabled
NAG	New Art Gallery
NCA	National Customer Survey
NDPB	Non-Departmental Public Body
NHF	National Housing Federation
NIHAS	Northern Ireland Hospital Advisory Service
NPL	National Physical Laboratory
SCODA	Standing Conference on Drug Abuse
SRB	Social Research Branch
SSD	Social Services Department
TEC	Training and Enterprise Council
VAN	Voluntary Arts Network

Acknowledgements

Our colleague, Gillian Bull, a Senior Research Fellow at PSI until September 1996, made a major contribution to this research. She played a large part in the earlier stages of the study and carried out a substantial amount of the fieldwork.

This book would not have been possible without the generous help of all the case study organisations and the participants in their consultation projects. Very many people shared their knowledge and experience with us, gave us their time and contributed to the work in a spirit of openness exactly in keeping with the aims of the research.

The work was funded by the Cabinet Office and the Economic and Social Research Council, through the Whitehall Programme. We are grateful for their support.

While many people were involved in this work, the views expressed are entirely our own.

PART ONE

Guidance

Introduction

Consultation by public service organisations has grown in popularity and use in the past decade. The interest in involving consumers, customers, service users and 'citizens' in public service organisations has been expressed centrally through initiatives such as the Citizen's Charter and the Code of Practice on Access to Government Information. Many government departments, executive agencies and non-departmental public bodies (NDPBs) have gained considerable experience in the use of consultation as a tool for service or policy development.

Some local organisations – notably local authorities – took the road of consumer consultation in the 1980s, and have in the 1990s moved towards consultation with residents as 'citizens'. Indeed social services departments have been attempting to reflect the needs and wishes of service users in their work for much longer than this. Health authorities and trusts have sought both service user and local community views on their services through a series of initiatives stretching back to the early 1990s.

It seems therefore timely to stand back and reflect on the achievements of consultation and its contributions to public services and public policy. This document considers how consultation may be done most effectively.

We use the term 'consultation' as a convenient way of describing a range of activities concerned with involving the public. This guide encompasses many different types of involvement, including consultation exercises with differing degrees of intensity, depth, and participation in decision-making.

This guide

We draw on a wide range of experience to give guidance to those responsible for consulting the public, and the guide presents a sequence of stages. However, because public consultation is a complex and difficult activity, we suggest that you read the whole document first. It is intended to help you think about why you want to consult, how to do it, and how to make it worthwhile. The different stages will then give you guidance as you move through the process.

Origins of the guide

This guide to consultation was commisioned by the Cabinet Office as part of an ESRC research programme into the working of central government – the Whitehall Programme – the aims of which were, broadly, to describe and develop understanding of both recent and long-term changes in the nature of British government.

The guide was written following research into specific consultations commissioned and carried out by public service organisations. It relies on studies made during 1996 of a selection of consultation exercises by public bodies across the United Kingdom. These studies are appended to the guide, as essential examples of the rich diversity of possibilities which consultation embodies. They are a fascinating record of the hard work and achievements of staff in the commissioning organisations.

The lessons we draw here from the difficulties encountered in practice by the organisations commissioning consultations are far outweighed by the evidence of achievements and of problems overcome in reaching conclusions of benefit to organisation and consultees alike. The reader will see that consultation is not a straight road, and that even partial success may be achieved only after a change of route, or even after starting again, in a different direction.

Does consultation work?

We found that many writings on consultation have tended to concentrate on the processes. But the question which public service providers are much more likely to want an answer to is 'Does it work'? We set out, therefore, to examine the detail of and relationships between the different stages of consultations, and to assess how these may influence both the products of consultation, and its outcomes.

In doing this, we have been able to assess the possible usefulness of different methods of consultation in contributing to improvement in public service policy and practice.

Methodology

This work is based entirely on study of real consultation exercises. From a large trawl of over one hundred possible exercises, we selected 14 which between them covered as many consultation methods as we had found. The selection procedure was designed to identify those projects which were most likely to provide examples of good practice and effective consultation.

The 14 commissioning organisations included local authorities and health authorities, executive agencies, government departments, and NDPBs. The 'subjects' of the consultations were as varied as possible, bringing in addition a good range of consultees. A variety of types of issue – policy, planning, services – was ensured. Consultations whose methods were prescribed by statute – such as planning enquiries – were excluded.

We examined each of the 14 exercises in detail, through interviews with participants and study of relevant documents from as many sources as possible. Some organisations had carried out their own analyses and these were most useful. One of our principal concerns was that as a process which brings together individuals or groups from different environments, consultations might well be understood, interpreted, and appreciated very differently by the participants. Identifying differences of perspective and understanding was therefore a key task.

Key findings

Our research was not an evaluation of specific consultations, but of the factors which go to making up successful consultation for different purposes, in different organisational settings, and covering different issues. We identify the *method* of consultation as the most important feature of consultations, and this leads us to try to answer the question 'Which method is best suited to what?'

The answer to this question lies in several aspects of the consultation, and this is explained in Stages One to Four. We found that the method needs to be selected to meet the purpose of the consultation – some methods are better suited to, say, policy issues than to service provision issues. Different methods may be appropriate for contributions by different consultees, who may have a range of relationships with the consulting organisation, and with the issues. The sorts of results and outcomes sought by the consulting organisation must be matched with the method. Finally, the traditions, experience and capacities of the commissioning organisation must be examined to assess how effective the organisation is likely to be using particular methods.

After the method, the other main issue is how well the consultation is carried through. Much of this falls into the domain of good project management, but there are many specific issues which arose in the consultations which we draw out in the sections on process. This is described in Stages Five to Eight.

The benefits of consultation

Consultation and participation (we use the single term 'consultation' throughout this guide), used appropriately in public service organisations can improve decision-making, and by association, improve services. This is the quality which makes consultation appealing to service providers. In a period of concern for customer and public contributions to services, consultation and participation are excellent vehicles for securing that contribution.

Consultation can make a useful contribution to the decision-making of a public service organisation because it provides mechanisms which bring the organisation into contact with outsiders. These outsiders may be users of services, interest groups, other service providers, or various members of the general public. Consultation may also, in theory, bring one part of an organisation into contact with another.

Many specific examples of the specific benefits of consultation exercises are provided in the guide and the case studies appended to it. In more general terms, consultation can offer a fresh perspective on issues, policies and services; can enable service providers to uncover the needs and preferences of users; can reveal dissatisfactions and other problems with public services; can improve the internal workings and culture of public service organisations; can raise the profile and status of both the organisations and the issues on which they are consulting; can provide the public with a means of both giving voice to and practising its own wishes for involvement and being listened to; and, can lend authority to decision-making in a wide variety of contexts.

Some of these advantages are specific and practical, others relate more to the sorts of values and beliefs which tend to accompany a willingness to encourage consultation. All are in their different ways valid, although in the guide we are at pains to warn against undeclared motives and impractical exercises which lead to no substantial conclusion and no discernible changes.

The limits to consultation

The meeting of different perspectives in a consultation exercise is an opportunity for the commissioning organisation, but it may also be a threat. It can be difficult for organisations to listen to others, and consultations can fail if a perceived threat is not recognised and managed. Similarly, organisations often contain contending interests which may find it hard to reach agreement amongst themselves, and some of these interests may not be entirely compatible with the organisation's publicly expressed overall aims.

It is unlikely that a consultation exercise will lead to, or encourage, a sudden surrender of the positions taken in the past, or of the influence over decisions which different groups have held. Consultations are therefore unlikely of themselves to transform public services. But over a long period, the development of a tradition of effective consultation will enhance the decision-making of an organisation, and help to change its internal culture.

Further, any consultation exercise may encounter widely divergent views amongst its consultees. However, because consultation is primarily between provider and user, between public services and the public, with the idea of arriving at an agreed and supported way forward, as an approach to public involvement it is not especially suited to resolving disputes amongst consultees.

In circumstances where consultees disagree both fundamentally and sharply, most consultation methods will not iron out these differences, and alternatives such as mediation and negotiation may have to be considered. In some cases the disagreements may only be resolvable by decision-making at higher levels within the service, including at the political level. Both negotiation and mediation are separate activities which are not examined here.

Popular methods

Some methods are currently better regarded than others, and we were wary of the temptation to choose a particular method because it is much discussed. Developing expertise in consultation inevitably involves trying different methods. But popularity or fashion is not a very good guide to which method to use, and we feel obliged to caution against such an approach. It is probable that organisations who are enthusiastic about consultation will want to develop their capacities and experiment with 'new' methods. Indeed there are two case studies which experiment with a new method as a key purpose of their consultations. However, different methods are suitable in different circumstances, and settling on a method on a sound basis is essential. In practice, successful consultation often borrows from several methods.

DEMOCRACY, ACCOUNTABILITY AND CONSULTATION

In the 1970s consultation and participation were seen as components of community involvement in public affairs, and this concern has returned in the 1990s. Consultation and participation are currently identified as 'democratic' activities by some local authorities. Interest in consultation has been renewed in a general context of concerns about democracy, accountability and openness.

Some of the consultation exercises which form the basis of this guide were explained to us in these terms by the commissioning organisations. These links between consultation and other, wider social concerns are an essential part of the motivations of commissioning organisations, and in part account for the growth in interest in consultation. But the success of some of the consultations in this study was not primarily sustained by the beliefs of the organisations, but by the systematic and careful hard work which went into making the consultation exercises work. Concerns about democracy and accountability are important motivators, but of themselves they cannot guarantee success. Successful consultation needs specific aims. This was very clear from the 14 studies.

STAGE ONE

Purposes of Consultation

INTRODUCTION

Our research shows that the purpose of the consultation needs to be matched to the method(s) used, if a successful conclusion is to be reached. Purpose is therefore one of the three key steps which together should determine choice of method (the other two are defining the consultees and organisational traditions and capacities).

There are two related aspects to purpose, which although similar, play distinct roles in the choice of method: what drives the consultation – what it is about; and the goals and products sought in the consultation. These are closely related but need to be considered separately to ensure that both aspects of purpose are included in the decision on which method to use.

The drivers of consultation may be issues about policy, services, or plans. But consultation may also be driven by the desire to raise issues, to educate, by beliefs in democracy, and many similar motives. Finally, it may be about exposing disagreements, resolving disputes, or being seen to be active and participative. All of these may come into play in a consultation exercise.

The goals of consultation may vary from wanting a decision to be made by consultees, to wanting general soundings to inform debate – with many shades of outcome sought in between. The products may be statistics, opinions, voting results, indications of satisfaction or of preferences, and so on.

The purposes brought to consultation will be those of the commissioning organisation, the consultees and those whose responsibility it is to implement the results of consultation. All three groups need to be considered in selecting method. The different aspects of purpose may conflict or contradict each other, and this too requires assessment. Differences may arise because the commissioning organisation want a number of things at the same time, or because other participants – consultees or joint commissioning organisations – have brought different motives and desired outcomes to the process.

DRIVERS OF CONSULTATION

We found a number of different types of driver in consultations, some being more obvious than others, with different degrees of influence in shaping the process and the outcomes. In considering what consultation is about, you must be as clear as possible about all of the possible drivers which may be in play during the consultation.

We identified three types of driver, which we describe as:

- specific, explicit;
- contextual, background;
- instrumental, by which we mean related to other agendas or needs.

The 14 case studies were guided for the most part by specific drivers but in some cases other drivers exercised a strong influence.

Specific drivers

The influence of purpose on the choice of method can be clarified mainly by understanding the nature of the specific drivers about which you are consulting. The explicit purpose of a consultation exercise will be found in the matters about which you need to consult. Different matters may suggest different methods.

It has been many years since public service organisations began to adopt explicitly rational approaches to the planning of their work. There is in general an established habit of detailed forward planning of services over long periods, and widespread familiarity with the devising of plans and the language of 'mission statements' 'goals', 'objectives' and so on. To this has been added, perhaps more recently, the language of customer care, of citizenship and charters, of openness. In general a high value is now placed on these consumer/citizen/community perspectives, at least when organisations are expressing their intentions or their aspirations.

Unsurprisingly, the organisations in this study experienced little difficulty in expressing their desires to consult within a 'rational' framework which included the specific purposes of the consultation. Purposes were usually set out in the presentation of the need or the intention to consult, both internally and in presentation to outsiders. A commissioning organisation may present its purposes with differences of emphasis for internal and external consumption. These should of course be compatible.

Specific drivers and organisations

In the research we identified four types of specific driver about which organisations wanted to consult:

- the needs of service users, non-users and so on;
- policy, plans or strategies;
- service priorities;
- service performance.

Some of the 14 case studies encompassed more than one type of specific driver. Although there are no automatic single choices of method inherent in these types of driver, there are strong indications which we can provide as a guide to which method is best suited to each.

The needs and wants of users, non-users or potential users

By this we mean an exploratory process of uncovering need, of trying to find out what users might want in a situation where an organisation is undecided about the direction, emphasis, or culture of its general service development. We do not include in this consultations about choices, priorities plans or policies offered as part of specific proposals for future action.

Methods should allow for the abstract nature of questions about need by creating opportunities to explore ideas and problems in a safe, supportive environment – discussion groups, focus groups, small meetings. The option of some sort of long-term involvement, which can allow for the development of expressions of need, should be considered. Surveys can be used, but only where it is reasonably certain that users are already clear about what they want.

It should be noted that if users are organised in campaign groups, consultation methods may not be productive – see Stage Two.

Walsall Art Gallery wanted to find out what facilities and services the public wanted when the new art gallery opened. A range of methods were used – exhibitions, workshops, visits to schools and a postal survey – to cope with the need to explain the possibilities, to give the public the chance to develop ideas about what it wanted, and to discover the views of as many residents as possible.

Tate Gallery Liverpool wanted to learn more about what younger people wanted from the gallery. The method was long-term involvement of a group of 20-30 young people in the work of the gallery.

Waltham Forest Housing Action Trust (HAT) wanted an all-round understanding of residents' needs and views across the board (and long-term input to policy and practice). The main method was long-term tenant representation on key committees and groups.

Policy, plans or strategies

By this we mean long-term or large-scale matters concerning policies, planning, or strategies. These are likely to be complex in their detail, in the amount of prior knowledge which may be required, and in the length of time consultees may need to devote to responding. Methods which allow for imparting of a lot of information, or providing face-to-face explanations, or which provide written materials and time to respond are likely to be needed – exhibitions and events, deliberative methods, discussion groups, evidence-taking groups, or written drafts.

Lewisham Council sought residents' views on how to act to lessen the effects of illegal use of drugs on the community. The method was a citizens jury.

The Arts Council of Wales sought to develop a national framework for increasing participation in the arts. The method was an enquiry by a specially convened group which first took evidence from interested parties and then produced a draft consultation document, which when finalised was circulated widely for written response.

Devon and Cornwall Police Authority sought the views of the public on the annual police plan. The method was presentation and discussion at a series of public meetings.

The Eastern Health and Social Services Board offered a series of options for strategic development of specialist services for people with learning disabilities. The method was presentations at meetings with service users to discuss and elicit views.

The Housing Corporation wanted to assess reaction to its new proposals for its approach to black and minority ethnic housing needs. The methods were discussion meetings with interested parties, and an invitation for written comments on a draft framework document.

The Science Museum wanted to obtain the views of non-specialists on a complex and technical general public policy driver – plant biotechnology. The method was deliberative – a consensus conference of a lay panel, which heard evidence and then reached its conclusions.

Service priorities

By this we mean drivers about specific choices offered about some specific aspects of a service where immediate development or actions are at stake. We do not include more abstract longer-term drivers, which we would place under the heading of policy.

There is a choice to be made from two sorts of methods for service priorities drivers. Some matters will be well-known and publicly discussed – in which case survey methods and public meetings, with voting, can work well. With others there may be little knowledge about a service priorities matter, and methods will therefore need to emphasise explanation, information, discussion. Finally, some drivers relate to priorities which affect only small groups of users, in which case small groups or meetings, using discussion, seeking consensus, are better.

The Highways Agency wanted to re-examine the views of interest groups and others about proposed routes for a road development. The method was a conference of interested parties to produce a report to the Department by the independent chair.

Mid-Lothian (Edinburgh) Council wanted a road repair service which would be responsive to the needs and priorities of the local population. The method was a well-publicised dedicated freefone service for all street repairs, which was able to inform changes in repair priorities and systems for carrying out repairs. This example differs from others, in that a customer-responsive system was the method. The characteristic of this system which underlies its effectiveness is that receipt of the customer complaint, and understanding of the customer's priorities, can both be derived from the one system.

Service performance

By this we mean attempts to discover how well a service is performing in the eyes of its users, potential users, or the public in general. We include consultations designed to ensure future performance for new services. We do not include more abstract assessments here – for example, about whether having a National Health Service is a good thing. These we would place under the policy heading.

The most appropriate method will depend on the familiarity and frequency of use of the service by the target consultees. Services which are used routinely and frequently are likely to be assessable using survey methods. Those used infrequently will require more discussion in order to elicit useful views – in groups.

The Benefits Agency wanted a developing knowledge-base about how well their services were performing in the eyes of claimants. The method chosen was a National Customer Satisfaction survey, of a statistically representative sample of customers, carried out annually over a five-year period.

The Inland Revenue wanted to develop a usable and cost-effective system for self-assessment of income tax liability. This involved both discovering the needs of future users and tailoring a new system to meet these. A large range of methods were used, mostly emphasising interaction, discussion, 'homework', and some practical exercises in the use of new systems.

Bradford City Council and its partners wanted to routinely discover residents' views on local services. A residents' research panel was recruited to be a statistically representative sample of the population, responding regularly to questionnaires.

Specific drivers and consultees

The specific matters which are the subject of consultations do not usually originate with consultees. If the terms of the consultation are well set out by the commissioning organisation, consultees generally respond rationally, by contributing their opinions, knowledge, experience, skills and time to the process and its products.

However, assessment of any other drivers which are likely to sustain consultees' involvement is an important part of setting the method. There will always be some guesswork in this, as in many cases little may be known about consultees in advance (see Stage Two for more on this).

The specific drivers which motivate consultee participation and which we describe here are drawn from the observations of the commissioning organisations and from direct discussion with consultees. We found three different consultee-related specific drivers:

1 To contribute to improvement of a service:

Panel members of the Bradford Metropolitan Council research panel;

Participants in the Inland Revenue's multi-method development of self-assessment forms.

2 To influence a particular policy or practice:

Participants in the Highway Agency's round table conference.

3 To let service providers know what is needed:

The families of users of learning disability services provided by the Eastern Health and Social Services explained their needs for support.

Contextual drivers

It is important to explore the contextual, background drivers at play in a consultation, alongside the more explicit ones. Contextual drivers may be less transparent than explicit ones, and will involve more abstract ideas and notions. Contextual drivers are embedded in the situation in which the consultation takes place – they are in a sense intrinsic to it. They are therefore likely to be influential in the consultation process.

Awareness of contextual drivers will enable you to allow for their influence, and to take steps, if necessary, to diminish any potential for disruption which they may occasion. Some contexts will of course be strengths, and these will be of benefit.

Contextual drivers are not mysterious, and are quite easy to identify and assess. They tend to occur in the patterns indicated below.

Contextual drivers for organisations

Contextual drivers are likely to relate broadly to an organisation's general role and culture, its broadly defined interests, or its beliefs or philosophy. In the case studies we have identified four different organisational drivers which we describe as contextual:

Belief in the value of consultation

Many of the organisations studied expressed a commitment to consultation in general terms, beyond its practical benefits. Typically, they described themselves as having a tradition of, or experience in, consulting, in customer-friendly service delivery, or in the promotion of involvement by the public or by service users. These beliefs can be a source of enthusiasm and therefore of great help to consultation, whatever the method chosen.

The desire to reach a consensus

The assumption that a consensus could be promoted by consultation underlay some consultations. In situations where there is disagreement about the subject of the consultation, either within the organisation, or amongst users or the public, there is no real basis for assuming that consultation will produce consensus.

The influence of an approach based on consensus will therefore depend on how likely it is that such agreement can be reached. Awareness of underlying assumptions that people will reach agreement permits consideration of the possibilities for disagreement in the consultation. Such possibilities can then be allowed for in considering what method(s) to select. For example, the development of coherent responses through discussion will be more difficult if participants take strongly opposing positions in advance. Separate meetings with committed groups, perhaps as one stage in a consultation, may therefore be more effective in allowing different views to contribute to the consultation.

In the Eastern Health and Social Services Board and Council consultation, a range of options for a service development strategy was offered to participants in open meetings, without indications of the Board's preferences. This approach was useful for some service users, but others, who saw the consultation as an attempt to close down their hospital, responded with a campaign which inhibited discussion and prevented the development of ideas in the meetings. The consultation process reproduced pre-existing differences, and a further process, which excluded the campaign group, was needed to reach a decision on a service development strategy.

The Highways Agency Round Table planning conference was an attempt to reach a consensus on the route for a major road. This was not achieved. Local people had already expressed strong preferences in an earlier exercise. Further, it was not possible to reach a decision which would not be seen as very detrimental to at least one group's immediate concerns. No compromise was possible.

Developing greater 'ownership' amongst consultees

The belief that consultation can bring consultees closer to an organisation, or perhaps to the subject of the consultation, appears to be well-founded. Participative consultation can be a sort of launch platform for continuing involvement, and therefore for an improved contribution to an organisation's work. Participation can promote ownership of the subject of the consultation.

Consultation in which participants are engaged in discussions, meetings, and generally in active participation are those which develop this best. You should however note that some consultations by their nature require a response from uninvolved and distant participants – for example statistical surveys of representative samples of the general population – and the possible negative side of a growth of commitment must be monitored with care.

Consultees' 'distance' (see Stage Two) may be from either the subject of the consultation, or from the commissioning organisation, or both. When a non-involved or non-expert view is sought from participants, their involvement will of itself shift them into greater engagement, and therefore away from the position which gave them their initial value as consultees. This is most likely with highly participative methods, but will occur with all long-term involvements – committees, special groups, long-term panels and so on.

The young people involved in the Liverpool Tate developed considerable understanding of the gallery and its services, and a loyalty to the Tate which was sustained through all criticism.

Members of the Lewisham citizens jury were motivated to seek further involvement in community drivers by the experience of jury membership

Members of the Bradford research panel expressed the desire to be more involved, and felt that their time on the panel had equipped them to make a better contribution. If magnified, this sense of being 'on the inside' would inhibit their representativeness.

Waltham Forest HAT's programme of tenant involvement is informed by the belief that empowerment of tenants promotes ownership of the entire process of creating a high quality housing environment.

Securing public support for a proposal

Some organisations approached consultation with a contextual aim of securing support for their proposals for change. The exposure which consultation offers to proposals does of course improve the chances of their being considered by audiences outside of the organisation. The openness and enthusiasm which is often a feature of consultation exercises can enable the proposals to be presented in a positive framework, and favourably.

The risks of this contextual driver are mainly that the exposure becomes the main purpose, and the consultation itself produces no identifiable outcomes. Consultees will then perceive the exercise as a failure and may associate this with a perception that the proposals themselves are defective, or that the organisation was wasting their time.

Methods which allow for presentations and exhibitions will actively publicise proposals, and the vividness and immediacy of these may well be of help in developing public support. Display methods tend to offer relatively simple models, with options or alternatives, and this clarity is a strength. However, to avoid the risk of providing little other than publicity, display options must be substantial and realisable, and the feedback from them to consultees must be transparent about any influence flowing from the consultation.

Discussion-based methods will also encourage support because they involve interactions where the public's ideas are heard by the organisation. As with displays, discussions must be seen to have specific conclusions which are inclusive of the viewpoints expressed or developed. Conclusions reached must have a clear relation to the discussions.

Experiments with methods

Some consultations had an experimental aspect, in that one of the drivers was to expand organisational capacities and knowledge by testing particular methods. This occurred in two cases, and in both the choice of subject came after the choice of method. We classify these drivers as contextual rather than specific because they are part of some organisations' general approaches and beliefs about the role of participation in democratic processes.

Both the Lewisham citizens jury and the Science Museum's Consensus Conference were experiments in assessing how well a group of non-experts might cope with a complex subject, and in how useful the conclusions of such a lay group could be for policy-making.

In Lewisham the choice of a specific driver came after the decision to hold a citizens jury, enabling the link between specific driver and method to be very explicit. The breadth of the drugs issue, its status as a matter of public concern, and the need for education about it before views could be expressed, were the characteristics which governed its selection.

In the Science Museum the choice of specific driver also came after the decision to hold a lay panel, and the Science Museum's choice of specific driver was motivated by its suitability for the method. Plant biotechnology was identified as an issue of public concern which required a deliberative method if useful conclusions were to be reached by a lay panel.

Contextual drivers and consultees

The contextual drivers brought by consultees are likely to relate to what is described as the interests of a group of consultees. In the case of individual consultees, it may well be impossible to assess in advance any likely contextual drivers, as these may depend on the personal characteristics and experiences of the individual.

We found three different consultee drivers which we would describe as contextual. As with specific drivers for consultees, these are closely associated with motivations for taking part and commitment to staying involved.

Performing a public duty

Ideas about public duty and service to the community – 'doing my bit' was the most clear expression – were common amongst different consultees. It was expressed by:

- *members of the Science Museum lay panel;*
- *members of the Lewisham citizens jury;*
- *members of the Bradford research panel;*
- *tenant representatives of the Waltham Forest HAT committees.*

Representing the ordinary person

Some consultees saw themselves as representatives of the person in the street, taking an opportunity to tell the experts what the ordinary person thought. Although this is in reality a kind of populist delusion, it is important to recognise its force as a driver of consultee involvement. (For an examination of consulting organisations' approaches to the driver of 'representativeness' see Stage Two and Stage Four.)

Members of the Bradford research panel and members of the Lewisham jury stressed the importance of the 'ordinary' citizen being heard.

Interest groups and lobbying

Some groups of consultees will use consultation as an opportunity to put across their views as an interest group, and this will influence the style of their participation and therefore the choice of a suitable method. Some interest groups may want to make points or raise matters which are not entirely relevant, and different interest groups may express contradictory views.

In considering method, you will need to allow for the involvement of such groups. Some methods are more suited to accommodating lobby-type groups than others, and some can allow for strong disagreement more readily. There is a further decision – about how to deal with the raising of non-relevant matters. Dealing with these problems is explored in Stage Two and and Stage Six.

Instrumental drivers

We describe instrumental drivers as those which seek to achieve something quite different from the apparent or explicit purpose of the consultation. Like contextual drivers, they are often intrinsic to situations. But unlike contextual drivers, they may be unrecognised, undeclared or even covert.

Instrumental drivers can damage consultation exercises because they may well be more powerful drivers than specific, explicit drivers. Instrumental drivers may be introduced by the commissioning organisation, or by consultees, or both. At their most influential, they can prevent a useful outcome.

Because instrumental drivers are likely always to be present in consultations, it is essential, as far as is possible, to discuss them openly, to ensure that their force is understood and their influence allowed for in selecting the consultation method.

Instrumental drivers and organisations

In the research we came across a number of drivers which fall into the instrumental group in the behaviour of consulting organisations. We found it reassuring that in every case the commissioning organisations were aware of these drivers – sometimes in retrospect – and had sought to accommodate them, although not always successfully.

Resolving disputes/avoiding difficult decisions

It can be tempting to use consultation as a tool for resolving internal disputes or for avoiding facing differences of view within the commissioning organisation itself. The research showed that consultation will not automatically resolve disputes or avoid difficult decisions. If there are disagreements between service providers these are quite likely to remain after the consultation. They may even be reproduced in the responses from the consultees.

> *The London Borough of Lewisham and the local Health Commission did not agree on the questions to be put to the citizens jury. The Council found the citizens jury's views on community education a useful spur to service and policy development, but the jury's views on drugs treatment were rejected by the Health Commission.*
>
> *Views held by different local groups before the Highways Agency round table on the A259 became more entrenched during the consultation process, as they saw what they thought were decisions reopened for debate.*

Insuring against future challenges, legal or otherwise

Consultation is increasingly a requirement for public service organisations, and in some cases a legal requirement. Failure to consult adequately can bring the risk of challenge through a number of mechanisms – in particular judicial review. Avoidance of challenges is therefore an important consideration. A concern to avoid challenges can have a negative effect on consultation, such that the appearance of a proper process takes over from substance. 'Going through the motions' is a good colloquial expression.

Compliance with legal frameworks or the requirements of influential others

The risk with this as a driver of consultation is that organisations may concentrate on conformity to the detriment of substance. There were no examples of this occurring in the 14 case studies, perhaps because of our filtering process in selecting them. A number of the organisations in the studies were required to consult – usually by law – but without prescribed formats, but in one case only did this contribute to a doubt about the purpose of the consultation.

The Housing Corporation is in general obliged to consult, and did so when its second five year strategy for meeting the needs of black and minority ethnic tenants ended. However, the substance of the new policy was decided before the consultation, and the purpose of the consultation was therefore not as obvious as might have been the case.

Promotion of the quality of the organisation

Seeking to promote the quality and value of a service can be a useful minor driver of consultation. But if promotion becomes a dominant driver, it will inhibit acceptance within the commissioning organisation of the doubts and criticisms expressed by consultees.

Educating the public or service users

Education, as part of the process of consultation, is likely to form a necessary part of some methods, and a largish part of deliberative methods. Education may also be one of the specific drivers of consultation – although alone it would not suffice. However, if it is deployed instrumentally, as an undeclared driver, it is likely to inhibit the success of the exercise.

> *The Devon and Cornwall Police Authority consultation sought to educate the public as well as obtaining input to the police plan. The confusion of these drivers impeded adequate use of the inputs obtained.*
>
> *Waltham Forest HAT's involvement of tenants necessitates a programme of training for tenant participants. Because the training aims specifically to enable participation, it does not cause confusion about the purpose of the consultation.*

Instrumental drivers and consultees

We identified two instrumental drivers brought to consultations by consultees.

Exercising a habit of negative complaint

Consultations about service provision are prone to attracting criticism of services. This is a key part of a successful consultation about services, but it can also occur as a theme in itself, and become an instrumental driver for some of the consultees.

Table 1 Organisational drivers of consultation

Specific drivers	*Case study*
Needs of service users	Inland Revenue; Tate Gallery Liverpool; Walsall Metropolitan Council; Waltham Forest HAT
Policy plans or strategies	Arts Council of Wales; Highways Agency; Devon & Cornwall Police Authority; Eastern Health & Social Services Board & Council; Housing Corporation; London Borough of Lewisham; Science Museum
Service priorities	Bradford Metropolitan Council; Devon & Cornwall Police Authority; Eastern Health & Social Services Board & Council; Edinburgh City Council; Waltham Forest HAT
Service performance	Benefits Agency; Inland Revenue; Bradford Metropolitan Council; Waltham Forest HAT
Contextual drivers	*Case study*
Belief in the value of consultation	All case studies expressed this
The desire to reach a consensus	Eastern Health & Social Services Board & Council; Department of Transport
Developing greater 'ownership' amongst consultees	Tate Gallery Liverpool; London Borough of Lewisham; Waltham Forest HAT
Securing public support for a proposal	Devon & Cornwall Police Authority; London Borough of Lewisham
Experiments with methods	London Borough of Lewisham; Science Museum
Instrumental drivers	*Case study*
Resolving disputes/ avoiding decisions	Eastern Health & Social Services Board & Council; Highways Agency
Insuring against future challenges	Eastern Health & Social Services Board & Council; Housing Corporation
Compliance with the requirements of others	Housing Corporation
Promoting the quality of the organisation	None identified
Educating the public or service users	Devon & Cornwall Policy Authority

This is most likely to occur with interest groups who are accustomed to oppositional stances and the experience of not being listened to or of failing to influence.

Our society appears to have two contradictory cultural traditions – one of complaint and the other of the expression of high levels of satisfaction. In practice we found that for most individuals involved in consultation the complaint tradition is very likely to give way quickly to more constructive engagement. This is less likely in the case of groups or organisations, and methods should allow for groups with a track record of negative complaint.

Table 2 Consultees' drivers of consultation

Specific drivers	*Case study*
To contribute to improvement of a service	Bradford Metropolitan Council
To influence a particular policy or practice	Arts Council of Wales; Highways Agency; Housing Corporation
To let service providers know what is needed	Devon & Cornwall Policy Authority; Eastern Health & Social Services Board & Council; Tate Gallery Liverpool; Walsall Metropolitan Council
Contextual drivers	*Case study*
Performing a public duty	Bradford Metropolitan Council; Devon & Cornwall Policy Authority; London Borough of Lewisham; Science Museum; Waltham Forest HAT
Representing the 'ordinary' person	Bradford Metropolitan Council; London Borough of Lewisham
To lobby as an interest group	Arts Council of Wales; Eastern Health & Social Services Board & Council
Instrumental drivers	*Case study*
Exercising a habit of negative complaint	None identified
Using the consultation as a campaign platform	Eastern Health & Social Services Board & Council

Using the consultation as a campaign platform

Some consultees will use a consultation exercise as an opportunity to campaign for what they want, but some methods of consultation are unable to accommodate campaign organisations which use campaign methods. There are few methods with which campaigns can easily fit, and they will need to be accommodated in particular ways. Methods which include meetings as forums for open discussion and the development of ideas through exchanges of views cannot usually sustain campaign methods. (This is explored in more detail in Stage Two and in Stage Four.)

Goals and products of consultation

A few key points about the goals and products of consultation need to be considered when selecting a consultation method. Goals – what you want out of the consultation itself – are an important part of the purpose of consultation. The goals sought for the specific drivers of consultation are not necessarily the same as the goals of the consultation process itself. For example, an organisation may ultimately be seeking a new policy, but in consulting on that policy may only want ideas which feed in to future discussions of that policy. These two goals are different.

Goals may involve broader social or political considerations, usually related to the contextual drivers of consultation. For example, if a contextual aim is to demonstrate that a thorough consultation process has been undertaken, then one goal will be satisfactory levels of publicity for both the process and the commissioning organisation.

Products may or may not be linked closely to methods. Some methods produce specific types of products – commentaries, statistics, opinions, and so on. Others may be more flexible in the possible outputs which they can provide. Whichever is the case, the product which is sought by the commissioning organisation must be matched with a suitable method.

The products of the consultation can also play a role in the achievements of its goals, and the product must be capable of delivering the goal of the consultation.

Goals

It is unusual for the goal of a consultation to consist of full decision-making on the subject of the consultation. Most organisations are reluctant to cede control over decision-making to outsiders, however 'representative' of communities they may be deemed to be. In any event, many organisations carry statutory responsibilities for their own decision-making, through their boards and committees.

Much more likely is a desire to consider the products of the consultation as part of the development of the new policy. The goal of the whole process, of which the consultation is only one element, may be the policy. The outcome of the consultation is a contribution to be assessed and pursued by the organisation as it sees fit.

In this way the goal of the consultation itself is separate from the goal sought for the specific driver. If you want to develop a new policy, it is still necessary to decide on the role of a consultation exercise in shaping the policy. What this comes down to is the influence over decisions which the output of the consultation can have.

Some consultations do of course wholly determine outcomes – democratic elections, shareholder votes, and juries in the legal process are common examples. But we have not found any examples of full decision-making powers being handed to consultees. Notions of contributions, advising, bringing perspectives, informing debates and so on are much more likely.

Commissioning organisations need to be both realistic and honest about this. Fudging of the uses to be made of outputs, and therefore of the desired goal of the consultation, is a source of frustration and disillusion both to the consultees, and to the staff in organisations who have tried hard to make difficult processes work.

Products

The products of consultation have the same range or variety as any other review or assessment of services, policies or plans. Some methods result in specific products – for example, surveys produce statistics, group discussions produce summaries and notes, voting produces counts, inviting comments on drafts produces written observations. The detailed relation between these is explored in Stage Four.

Some products are suggested by some desired goals, although there are no absolutely necessary links. The most obvious example is the need for statistically valid information if you want to base improvements to services on the problems experienced by large numbers of service users. Similarly, if you need to sound out views on a complex matter on which you have to make a decision, then discussions and responses to written/oral presentations will provide the necessary level of thought and reflection you are seeking. Conversely, if you want the public to make a decision, then you will consider methods which involve voting.

These links between products and goals break down when organisations, say, collect statistically valid information and decide on something not in the responses, when meeting votes are ignored, or when soundings are taken but never again mentioned. Consultees who have devoted time and energy to generating the products find that no related goals are achieved.

Implementers of change

The goals of both the specific drivers and the consultation process may require implementation, and the purposes of those who implement need to be considered in selecting the method. Implementers may be in the same or other organisations as those commissioning the consultation. If they are in the same organisation then they are best involved in the process – see Stage Five.

Within organisations, implementers are often at regional and local levels, and their experience of the practical aspects of the services delivered is likely to be the main influence on the drivers which they bring and the goals which they seek. Some drivers – such as the improvement of services, or decisions about practical priorities for service delivery – may be of greater perceived relevance to implementers. This can make them more likely to see the pitfalls, as well as to be more creatively involved in the process.

Joint commissioning

Purposes may also vary if consultation is commissioned by more than one organisation. In these cases it is important to try to identify the drivers brought by all of the commissioners and to accommodate these in the selection of methods. Failure to do this at an early stage brings the risk of uncertainty and disagreement about both the processes of consultation, and about the meaning of any results. Ensuring that this happens is discussed in Stage Five.

Three of the case studies were joint consultations, with some differences between drivers.

Bradford Metropolitan Council's research panel was set up jointly with other local organisations – the Training and Enterprise Council (TEC), and health organisations. The agreement was for one individual survey each, per annum, as well as joint surveys. The purposes and expected outcomes were explored carefully in setting up the panel.

In the Eastern Health and Social Services Board and Council consultation the Council's purpose was to lend its consultation skills to the entire process in the context of an important strategic service driver. The Board saw the exercise as related to its own strategic development decisions, with the Council's role limited to facilitating the public meetings. Despite the strongly shared driver of the strategic development of learning disability services, the differences were sufficient to produce different assessments of the conduct and outcomes of the exercise.

The Lewisham Citizens Jury was led by the local authority, with the Health Commission, police and others taking part in the steering group. Although considerable efforts were made to ensure that the jury was jointly owned, the Health Commission expressed serious reservation about the jury process and the jury's views on specific drug treatments.

STAGE TWO

Defining the Consultees

INTRODUCTION

One of the three key assessments in selecting the consultation method is the identification of the consultees. This step is as important as the other two. (The other two are the purpose, and the commissioning organisation's organisational traditions and capacities.)

Consultees are almost always outsiders to the commissioning organisation, and it is likely to be very difficult for an organisation to allow outsiders to influence its development or its decisions. Realistic expectations of consultees will improve this, and careful identification of consultees will help to set achievable goals for a consultation and to use methods which will deliver those goals.

The experience of organising a public meeting which attracts very few attenders, of despatching questionnaires which fail to return, of obtaining views or opinions which are at best of marginal use and at worst idiotic and harmful, is all too common. These pitfalls may well be less easy to avoid at present, given that consultation is generally seen to be 'a good thing' and that the opinions of different populations and groups are thought almost automatically to be of use.

Consultees and method

On the one hand organisations may have a detailed understanding, in advance, of who they are consulting with. On the other, consultees may be entirely self-selecting. In between there is a need to be as clear as possible about the types of people you want to involve.

If consultees are defined in advance, it is important to match the method with an assessment of the geographical location, interests, abilities and capacities of potential consultees. This assessment may rule particular methods in or out. Specific consultation exercises may also be aimed at more than one group of consultees, requiring more than one method.

Individual and organised consultees

If consultation with organisations with which you have a relationship does not go well, there will be opportunities to recover over time. With individuals with whom you have no organised relations, or with organisations you are not routinely in touch with, poor consultation can cause longer-term harm. As it is likely to be more difficult to develop a picture of individual consultees than organisations, this issue should be considered with care.

Understanding consultees

There are four closely related questions to ask about potential consultees:

1 who are they?
2 what is their relation to/involvement in the consultation?
3 what do you think they can bring/contribute to it?
4 what will they want/get from the process and its outcomes?

In answering any one of these you may well answer the others. However, each of the four questions is an important factor in understanding who you want to consult with, and therefore in selecting the method. By themselves none of these questions implies any particular method. But by combining an assessment of all four, certain types of method will be suggested.

Main difficulties in defining consultees

Some of these questions may not have an answer – this too is important. It may be difficult to develop an assessment of the target consultees, for a number of reasons:

- you may not know who you need to consult with;
- you may know little about them;
- there may be popular ideas about consultees within the organisation which are not based on adequate knowledge;
- consultees may be greatly varied in abilities, interests etc, and a clear/simple idea of them may not be possible.

All of these factors should be weighed up in selecting the method.

Who are the consultees?

We have identified seven possible categories of consultee:

1 the general public, the local population, the community;
2 service users and their relatives and friends;
3 people the service is aimed at, but who do not use it;
4 population groups perceived as affected or interested, or whom you want to interest;
5 selected specific organisations/individuals;
6 self-selected organisations/individuals;
7 staff/groups within your own organisation/branches/sections (but only in the context of external consultations – this guide is not about employer/employee relations).

What is their relation to the consultation?

Consultees' relation to a consultation will depend on how close they are to it. Distance from the consultation can take two forms – physical and social. Both are important.

Physical distance

The physical distance of consultees both from the commissioning organisation and from each other has specific implications for methods. A wide geographical spread of individual consultees, such as a county-wide, regional or national spread will require methods which can match the spread. This will involve either postal methods and samples, large numbers of meetings in different locations (and therefore substantial resources), or the designation of individuals as representatives of large numbers/specific areas and so on. A wide geographical spread of local and/or national organisations may not have the same requirements, in that organisations may be more readily able to despatch representatives to specific meetings, or to respond to postal surveys or draft proposals.

Social distance

The degree of social distance can be roughly predicted by identifying the nature and frequency of the involvement with the drivers of the consultation. Potential consultees who are socially close to a consultation driver are likely to be:

- groups and organisations with a special interest;
- people who use a service regularly and frequently;
- individuals from the general public if the driver is socially important or popular and well understood.

Socially close consultees will be able to respond to methods where a viewpoint is obtained with minimal contact, or without a strong information input before seeking responses. Postal and face-to-face questionnaires and written response to draft proposals will be more practical for this group, than for more distant groups.

Potential consultees who are moderately socially distant from a consultation are likely to be:

- people who use a service infrequently;
- specific groups/categories from the public who you are trying to develop a service for, but who do not yet receive it;
- groups and organisations whose interests are very broad.

Moderately socially distant consultees will respond most effectively to methods which provide a degree of initial information and input before they are required to respond. This suggests face-to-face methods – meetings, group discussions – where presentations can be made and options set out are more usable. If drivers are complex and detailed (see Stage One) then written proposals are likely to prove helpful.

Potential consultees who are socially distant from a consultation are likely to be:

- individuals who do not use a service, and at whom it is not aimed;
- individuals when a consultation driver is not socially prominent;
- individuals when a consultation driver is intellectually complex;
- individuals if a driver is subject to popular prejudices or tabloid-type opinions.

Potential consultees who are socially distant may find it difficult to make a useful contribution. Large-scale consultations with such general populations may produce opinions which are not helpful to decision-making, and are probably not useful. It may therefore be better to consider smaller-scale methods – group discussions, small meetings – perhaps selected for different population groups – in order to get a feel for what might be a larger-scale input later.

Depending on the amount of information which needs to be conveyed before a useful response can be obtained, deliberative methods may be appropriate. Deliberative methods, which consist mainly of discussion, absorption of knowledge and then decision-making or expressions of 'findings' by consultees, will also be needed where popular prejudices or tabloid-type opinions predominate.

What can potential consultees contribute?

This question is difficult to answer, but it is important to develop realistic expectations which can be matched to a method. Some organisations are obliged by law, by custom, or by their superiors to consult with specific groups, and if this is the case then this question may not seem relevant. However, the requirement to consult rarely includes prescription of the method, and in asking what consultees can contribute you will enhance understanding of the best method to use.

Judgement about the contribution consultees can or should make is in part a decision about what the commissioning organisation will agree to their making. These are separate judgements, but they need to be set against each other to ensure there is no strong discrepancy. For example, involving highly knowledgeable and motivated consultees and then ignoring their views (however elliptically this is done) is harmful to long-term relations with them.

Solid experience and reflection

Some consultees will have been involved in a service, will have organised themselves into groups, will have discussed the subject of the consultation over long periods. In these cases, the commissioning organisation will get the benefit of sound experience from an essential perspective. Effective and useful proposals about plans, policies and services may be obtained.

The views of the 'people'

Large populations, whether local, regional or national, can provide indications of problems with and preferences for the details of routine public service provision, or initial reactions to proposed changes. Comparisons of the views of involved and uninvolved members of the population can be useful.

Sounding boards

Groups of individuals not involved in a service can be useful for sounding out proposals and ideas in some depth.

The 'non-expert' view

Consultees can contribute to matters which are the subject of disagreement or uncertainty amongst experts, as non-experts. Such exercises involve a lot of effort from consultees, and involvement of consultees in this way should involve specific advance commitments about what will be done with non-expert views once obtained, to avoid consultee disillusionment. Note here the likely failure of attempts to resolve disputes through non-expert viewpoints (see Stage One).

A range of different views

Consultations of all kinds can identify differences in viewpoints, preferences and priorities. Identification of such differences may be a key component of decision-making.

Selection of options

There are circumstances where consultees can choose between options and therefore make the decision.

Legitimation of proposals

Obtaining the views of consultees can legitimate proposals which are controversial, disputed, or unpopular. However, if this is a purpose care must be taken not to carry out an unconvincing consultation, and to be prepared for a different result.

Adding to debates

This applies mainly to methods which involve meetings, discussions and deliberation. Consultations can give ordinary people the chance to contribute to public debate, without any specific changes envisaged. However, care must be taken to specify the lack of outcome intended from the start.

What will consultees want/get from the process and its outcomes?

Both what consultees may want out of consultation, and what they can realistically get out of the specific consultation is also important. The drivers of consultee involvement are explained in Stage One. There is some overlap with the purpose, but here we examine the practical outcomes which may be sought by or available to consultees. Some are obvious, others less so.

A new policy, service plan

Some consultees will expect the results of the process to be a set of specific changes. This is most likely with consultees who are close to a service, involved in it and with worked-out views. In these cases the consultation process must include the development of the new aspects to the plan, policy or service.

Better understanding/acknowledgement of their concerns

Better understanding of the concerns of consultees may be sought in circumstances where there are no specific proposals for change on the table, or where change is longer-term. Consultees most likely to take this view are those who are close to a service, or where the consultation is about a socially popular subject on which they hold reasoned views.

Improvements

We list this separately from expectations of specific changes because the desire for improvements can cover a wide range of consultations. It relates primarily to negative experiences either of services or of less tangible social drivers – for example crime.

It may well be expressed as a desire for prevention, or as ceasing to do something harmful or of poor quality. This type of outcome is very hard to accommodate, as it may well be that the commissioning organisation itself has little idea how to make improvements.

Consultation about such difficult outcomes is rarely effective from the consultees' viewpoint.

To make a contribution

This may relate to purpose, but is different. It addresses the broad notions of acting as a good citizen, representing the community, being heard as an individual and so on, but if these are desired outcomes there will be no other outcomes expected. As an outcome, making a contribution requires no other consequences.

However, if a consultation is prolonged, then it is unlikely that consultees will maintain this as their sole desired outcome. New wishes are likely to emerge as the consultation progresses. One-off consultations of short duration are most likely to allow this outcome to remain the only one desired.

Positive and negative outcomes

The possibility of positive and negative outcomes for different consultees must be weighed up. Some consultees may seek to prevent something happening, others may want some specific option to win the day. Where consultees can see the possibility of a positive gain as a result of the consultation, their reactions to the process are likely to be more constructive and open.

> *It became clear during the Arts Council of Wales consultation that additional funding from the National Lottery would become available for organisations working in the area covered by the consultation. This removed some of the concerns about scarce resources and promoted more constructive involvement.*

There are two points to make here:

1. the possibility of positive outcomes enhances involvement;
2. a mixture of positive and negative may suggest the need for different methods.

Where consultees are likely to want to prevent an outcome, then campaign methods may well be used by them. Campaign methods and presentations, discussions and so on are not usually compatible, and the excitement generated by a campaign may prevent discussion.

Exchanges of views, reflection and compromise are also unlikely outcomes where there are mixtures of positive and negative, for different groups. Skilful handling of meetings can facilitate presentation of opposing views, but compromise on the whole is not negotiated by consultation.

Who is it legitimate to consult?

Consultation with individuals, groups, and other organisations, will often raise concerns about who should be consulted. The commissioning organisation may be uncertain about this, and there may be disputes amongst consultees about the legitimacy of consulting with particular groups or individuals, and about the relative weight to be given to different consultees. Clarity about this is essential, as well as awareness that the commissioning organisation's view of legitimacy may not be shared by all.

In assessing legitimacy, you should consider:

- Who is affected by the proposed consultation?
- Are there different groupings/degrees of being affected?
- Are there different effects – especially positive and negative?
- Are there different views on legitimacy amongst potential consultees?

In the Highways Agency round table road planning exercise there were differences of view on who was entitled to be consulted, and these differences were a source of tension and difficulty in the whole process. Particular controversy surrounded the weight to be given to local views (and how these should be defined) and to national interests.

Consultees and campaigns

Consultation with organisations may include campaigning organisations, with public and fixed positions on the drivers the organisation is consulting about. Mixing campaigning consultees with individual consultees is likely to prevent the views of individuals from surfacing. Different methods may therefore be required in the same consultation.

The Eastern Health and Social Services Board (felt that) it was obliged to consult on a matter which, it was already known, would produce campaigning fervour by both the families of service users, and by interest groups employed in a Health Trust. A consultative model which relied on presentation, discussion, and exchange of views was in part swamped by campaign and public demonstration activities.

Consultees as representatives

When consultation is about finding out what unknown, undifferentiated, large or divergent populations think, want or aspire to, then the idea of consultees as 'representative' of larger populations assumes a particular importance.

Representativeness is often alleged in popular or journalistic descriptions of social events, activities, and individuals, when, for example, images of one or two people carrying out an activity, or comments from one or two individuals (selected at random) will be taken to represent the activities or views of very large numbers of people. In particular, the less which is actually known about the group being described, the easier it becomes to make the claims of representativeness. Often such claims tell us more about those making them than about the individuals described as 'representative'. These journalistic uses are to be expected, but should be avoided in ascribing characteristics to consultees.

Representativeness is a notion which may be used in a number of ways by consulting organisations. We consider that there are two valid uses of the term – statistically representative samples, and elected representatives – and two possible fudged uses – special interest groups, and where the notions of 'representative' and 'ordinary' citizen are merged.

Representativeness as a quality in consultees does not stand above other consultee qualities. But commissioning organisations do need to be clear about whether it is a characteristic which they would like consultees to have.

Statistically representative samples

Some methods of consultation rely on the involvement of a large enough selection of individuals from a particular population, selected using reliable sampling methods, to make it possible for the results of the consultation to 'represent' the views of the whole population.

The Benefits Agency National Customer Survey relied on a representative sample of customers for the reliability of the information obtained through the survey. The Agency was therefore able to identify a number of national problems and trends on which it could rely for the development of its services.

The Bradford Metropolitan Council 'Speak Out!' panel recruited a representative sample of local residents using a quota sampling technique.

Judgement about the numbers needed, and how many of each category of the population, are specific statistical judgements which require advice from qualified researchers.

Statistical reliability should not be confused with the quality or value to the consulting organisation of the responses. A survey which is of a representative sample of service users may only provide limited information, or even information of little use (see Stage Four). However, where a representative sample is claimed, it must be statistically valid.

Elected representatives

There may be a need to involve elected representatives in consultation, and the fact of their election gives authority to their claims to speak on behalf of others, although often they may be expressing only their personal views, or the views of their political party. This problem of who represents the people or the community is often in evidence in consultation, and usually requires careful negotiation.

Tenant members of the Waltham Forest HAT were elected by the tenants.

Special interest groups

Representativeness may well be claimed by interest groups involved in consultation, and such claims must be weighed and assessed, and possibly negotiated. Many specific groups will of course have perspectives on issues which others outside of those groups could not bring – for example groups of people with disabilities, groups from minority ethnic communities. But it is not automatically the case that such groups represent the totality of views in their constituencies.

Campaign groups in particular may well represent only one possible viewpoint in a consultation, but may present this as a general view. Such negotiation is often political and may involve mediation (see Stage Four).

The 'ordinary' citizen

Some consultees may be presented as capable of representing the views of 'ordinary' people because they are non-experts. This can happen particularly where the views of 'ordinary' people are sought by methods which involve discussion and deliberation. It may be tempting to ascribe to a small group the opinions of a much larger one, but there is no reasonable justification for this.

The force of a small group's views in influencing policy can only lie in the process itself – for example by deciding in advance to implement findings.

The Lewisham citizens jury, with its 16 members, was presented as in some way 'representative' of the local population of around 250,000. However, the findings of a group of 16 people can represent only their own views.

Consultees who depend on the organisation

If consultees depend on an organisation for a service, for funding or other support, then there will be an incentive to take part in consultation. At the same time, there may be a bias towards positive endorsement of the organisation's own views.

The power relationship in consultation is almost always in favour of the commissioning organisation, and the dependence on it by consultees may well inhibit adequate input. Methods must take both into account.

Consultees and keeping to the point

Consultation processes may be made more difficult in some cases by the behaviour of consultees. Although the commissioning organisation is the originator of the consultation, the consultees who agree to take part may not really accept that the consultation is the most suitable or timely contribution to their concerns. Interest groups are especially likely to want to pursue their own concerns regardless of the content and purpose of the consultation. You may find some consultees seeking to steer the consultation on to different ground.

This can be very frustrating for all concerned. The commissioning organisation will not get the feedback it is seeking, and participants who are motivated by the explicit purposes of the consultation may not get the opportunity to contribute.

If this happens, it is clear from the case studies that acknowledging and dealing with it as quickly as possible is by far the best way to ensure the effectiveness of the consultation.

Groups of anti-road lobbyists came to the Highway Agency's round table road consultation meeting after the basic rules were agreed, and flouted them. The Chair physically left the meeting to let the delegates decide whether they would continue to abide by the agreed rules, or whether he would leave permanently.

The Tate Gallery Liverpool recruited a voluntary group of young people who wanted an active role in development of a display. Initially there was a lot of teenager-type behaviour, which the staff dealt with by enforcing a set of ground rules.

Alternatives for consultees with other agendas

If you find that some consultees are unable or unwilling to take part on the terms set, or to stick to the explicit agenda, it is best to seek alternative methods suited to them as quickly as possible.

Some examples will involve groups and organisations who want in the main to state their general case, or other concerns. If these are relevant to the commissioning organisation, they do not present any real difficulties, and special meetings with the commissioning organisation, at the appropriate level, can be organised without too much extra cost. At these meetings, the commissioning organisation should listen, note, and treat the inputs as part of the consultation.

Alternative consultations: mistakes by the commissioning organisation

It is possible that the matter about which you are consulting is not the driver the consultees think is the most important or relevant one. If you discover this half-way through, it may be either that the method can accommodate the 'real' driver, or that you need to switch to a different method.

In either case, open acknowledgement of the need to change, and an explicit change of direction or emphasis will be needed to make it work (see Stage Six).

STAGE THREE

Organisational Traditions and Capacities

The method chosen for the consultation depends in part on the purpose and on who the consultees are. But success in consultation will depend in part on the commissioning organisation's past experience and traditions, and the skills and resources which can be deployed. Before going on to select a method of consultation and begin the process of planning it, you will need to reflect first on your organisation's traditions and capacities, the levels of experience available to you internally and how easily you can get access to this.

Here we provide a framework for general thinking about traditions, capacities, experience and your choice of method. The details of what may be required to carry out an effective consultation are explored in sections on devising and managing the process, and are not repeated here.

THE TRADITIONS OF THE ORGANISATION

Embarking on consultation from within an organisation with no traditions of external consultation is difficult – the main problem being not knowing what you do not know. It is prudent to begin with a relatively modest exercise. For a first consultation, sister organisations with whom you enjoy friendly relations should be a first point of contact, if they have relevant experience. Guidance may also be available from associations and other bodies.

ORGANISATIONAL CAPACITIES

Who has the skills needed?

In selecting the appropriate method for consultation, the commissioning organisation needs to match the demands of each method to its available skills and experience, and to decide whether any deficiencies can be remedied by buying in the necessary skill, or by collaboration in a joint venture.

Many skills are simply those of effective project management, and are not discussed here. But it is very common for staff who know nothing of a particular set of skills to have no idea that these are needed. Failure to progress a consultation can be caused by inadequate or inappropriate skills.

Those which are specific to consultation are of four kinds:

1 research skills – to enable the selection of suitable techniques and approaches to information-gathering and analysis;

2 communication and listening skills – for presentations at meetings, for discussions, for explaining results;
3 community work/community development skills – for identification of audiences, encouragement to participate, and for feedback and ending;
4 education skills – to assist consultees to learn as part of their responses.

Large organisations may have all of these. Some may need to be borrowed either locally, or through the purchase of services. It is very important to list the portfolio of skills needed as thoroughly as possible.

> *The Benefits Agency, through a mix of in-house skills and contractors, ensured that the National Customer Survey was carried through with the project management, research, and policy skills required.*

Who has the relevant experience?

Experience is likely to overlap with skills but it is identified through a slightly different process. Basically this involves identifying individuals or sections within an organisation who have done similar exercises in the past. This sounds straightforward, but in practice it may be difficult for the consulting team to know of other relevant work or individuals. Finding out about them can short-cut the process of selection of a method.

What resources are there?

Some methods involve greater resources than others. Some depend on the scale of the consultation (see Stage Four). It is important to consider the driver of resources when settling on a method. There is a basic distinction between direct expenditures and staff resources/overheads, and these need to be considered separately.

If consultation is a designated part of the activities of a particular team or section, then the decisions about resources will be determined by the team's available time and budgets. But if a consultation is proposed as a specific exercise, then separate estimates of staff time available will be necessary.

STAGE FOUR

Choosing the Method

INTRODUCTION

Selecting an appropriate method or methods for consultation is the crucial single decision you will need to make. In Stages One and Two we have explained the main factors governing the choice of method – the purpose of the consultation and the nature of the consultees. A third factor – your organisation's capacities, experience and resources – was also identified as an important (though less difficult) driver to deal with before selecting a method.

The aim of this section is to explain the available methods and their characteristics, and then to offer guidance on how to choose a method, using information already provided about Stages One and Two.

We do this first by providing a brief description of the methods in each case study, secondly by describing the modes which different methods fall into, and thirdly by describing methods using four scales: cost, interaction, types of information, and reliability of results. Finally, a series of tables, and a chart at the end, relate these factors to the components of purpose and consultees explored in earlier sections.

It is important to bear in mind that although a sound understanding of the method(s) chosen, and an appreciation of what each may and may not deliver is vital, there will always be overlaps in the elements of methods. Also, some parts of one method may be combined with parts of another. Whilst there are key characteristics to each method, adherence to a strict formula is not recommended.

HOW DIFFERENT ARE DIFFERENT METHODS?

Some differences between methods are stark and self-evident. For example, large-scale surveys are very different from small discussion groups, not only in their format, but also in their outputs. Surveys produce quantitative information – large numbers, expressed usually in percentages, which provide information divided into clear categories; whereas discussions produce qualitative information – detailed and rich accounts of views, of shifts of view, of the reasons for views or beliefs, and of behaviour in interactions with other.

On the other hand, distinctions between methods can sometimes be artificial. Sometimes the names given to methods can make them seem different, when they are similar. Some methods do not have names which adequately describe their characteristics. Often methods share characteristics or activities, but do not necessarily describe them in similar terms. In selecting methods, you will need therefore to look behind the names or appearance and understand the key features of each method. This is in fact quite straightforward, although a little lengthy to convey.

THE CASE STUDIES

The studies of consultation which are in Part Two were intended to be of 14 different methods of consultation. In selecting these, we sought to include at least one of each contemporary method.

There are in addition some methods which we know of, but which were not actively in use at the time of the study and which could not therefore be included. These are named below.

Methods in the 14 studies

The 14 case studies are both analysed and summarised in Part Two. Some exemplify a single method, others consist of a mixture, or take elements from different methods. The possibility that several methods may complement each other for a particular consultation must always be considered. Each case study outlines the main features of each consultation, including strengths and difficulties. The 14 are:

1 a citizens jury;
2 a 'consensus conference';
3 a freephone-based complaints system;
4 the consultative relationship between a Health and Social Services Board and the 'permanent' consumer body, a Health and Social Services Council, studied through a consultation based on public meetings;
5 exhibitions and displays to discover local preferences for aspects of a new local art gallery;
6 focus groups for aspects of a government department's development of new procedures, as part of a wider programme of consultation;
7 an informal (round table) conference of interested parties around a road proposal;
8 an investigative group at an Arts Council, followed by a consultation paper;
9 a long-term advisory group of young people at a major national art gallery which is a non-departmental public body;
10 a National Customer (satisfaction) Survey of a statistically valid sample of customers by a major Next Steps Agency;
11 permanent tenants' representatives on a Housing Action Trust's Committees;
12 public meetings organised by a police liaison committee to inform the new policing plan;
13 a 'research' panel of the residents of a city, selected to be statistically representative of the local population, who agree to complete questionnaire surveys regularly;
14 'listening meetings' with interest groups, followed by written comments on a draft policy on black and minority ethnic housing needs, by a large non-departmental public body.

Table 1 Case studies using mixed methods

Case study	*Method(s) studied*	*Other methods used*
Arts Council of Wales	Meetings with interest groups	Draft report for written comments
Eastern Health & Social Services Board & Council	Public meetings	Draft report for written comments
Inland Revenue	Focus groups	Surveys, workshops, pilot testing
Housing Corporation	Draft document for written comments	Meetings
Tate Gallery Liverpool	Long-term advisory group	Education, workshops
Waltham Forest HAT	Tenant representation on committees	Surveys, meetings
Walsall Art Gallery	Exhibitions and displays	Surveys, meetings
Benefits Agency	Customer satisfaction surveys	Forums, a national conference, focus groups, mystery shopping
Bradford Metropolitan Council	Survey panel	Forums, focus groups, referenda

Mixing methods

Table 1 illustrates the mix of methods used in the case studies. Many consultations in the study involved either substantial mixing, or had small elements of other methods in them.

Six basic modes

Table 2 illustrates modes and main methods in each case study. Methods of consultation use a range of mechanisms, which are fewer in number than the names of each method might suggest. The characteristics of each method are in part determined by the mechanism which it uses. We describe the mechanisms as modes of consultation, to distinguish the mechanism from the title of the method. The 14 methods on which this guide is based fall into six modes, which we describe in common-sense terms as:

1 written comments on documents;
2 meetings;
3 surveys;
4 discussions;
5 response to complaints;
6 visuals and presentations.

Three of the six modes are sub-divided by frequency, who is involved, and so on. These sub-categories also influence the characteristics of the method.

Meetings

- One-off meetings with interest groups:
  - *Highways Agency Round Table conference;*
  - *Arts Council of Wales – a series of one-off interviews.*

Table 2 Methods and modes

Method title	*Case study*	*Mode*
Citizens jury	London Borough of Lewisham	Deliberative discussions
Consensus conference	Science Museum	Deliberative discussions
Round table conference	Department of Transport	One-off investigative meeting
Consultative relationship examined through public meetings	Eastern Health & Social Services Board & Council	Routine/regular meetings as a permanent activity, examined through dedicated one-off meetings
Complaints system	Edinburgh City Council	Response; feeding in to policy
Exhibitions and displays	Walsall Art Gallery	Visual presentation of options
Focus groups	Inland Revenue	One-off discussion groups
Investigative groups	Arts Council of Wales	One-off meetings with interest groups
Listening meetings with interest groups and written comments	Housing Corporation	One-off meetings; circulation of draft for written comment
Long-term advisory group	Tate Gallery Liverpool	Routine and regular meetings as a permanent activity
Permanent representation on committees	Waltham Forest HAT	Meetings with long-term representation and shared decision-making
Public meetings	Devon & Cornwall Police Authority	Routine/regular meetings with varying attendance
Survey panel	Bradford Metropolitan Council	Valid sample of population with regular surveys
Survey of customer views	Benefits Agency	Large-scale satisfaction survey by interview

- One-off meetings with the public or service users:
  - *Eastern Health and Social Services Board and Council consultation on a special services strategy for people with learning disabilities though public meetings across the region.*
- Routine/regular meetings, hosted as a normal or permanent activity by an organisation with service users as individuals and/or in interest groups, or with the public as individuals and/or in interest groups:
  - *Devon and Cornwall police liaison meetings;*
  - *Tate Gallery Liverpool Young Tate groups.*
- Individuals as permanent members of an organisation's decision-making or influential committees or groups. The inclusion of outsiders, often as 'representatives' of outside bodies, allows for routine input to discussion and decision-making:
  - *Eastern Health and Social Services Council membership of the Board;*
  - *Waltham Forest HAT tenants' representation.*

Discussions

- Deliberative methods. These involve a process of evidence and information-giving to groups which then express views:
  - *Lewisham citizens jury;*
  - *Science Museum consensus conference.*
- Focus groups held with either the public or service users or potential users who discuss a matter and express their opinions on it:
  - *Inland Revenue self-assessment tax form consultation.*
- Discussions at public meetings:
  - *Eastern Health and Social Services Board and Council*

Other possible methods

Some methods were not included in the case studies because we were unable to discover contemporary examples.

Meetings

- 'Shadow' committees and conferences. These are set up alongside an 'official' body, to consider the same drivers as that group, often in the same time frame, but consisting of different individuals and groups.

Discussions

- Deliberative opinion polls. These are polls of samples of the public which take place before and after discussion and information-giving.
- 'Parliaments'. An attempt to create a forum for debate and expression of views amongst particular sections of the public. Current interest focuses on 'Children's parliaments' and experiments by Save the Children and others are in development.

Four variable factors

Alongside the mode into which a particular method falls, there are four variable factors which need to be allowed for when choosing a method of consultation:

1. cost;
2. the amount of interaction which the method requires from all parties;
3. the type of information-giving and gathering the method is suited to;
4. the reliability/replicability of the results.

Different methods score high and low on these factors, and some are in the middle. Three factors are on the whole constant within each method. The fourth – cost – can be varied for some methods, according to the scale of the consultation, but some methods are inherently expensive in comparison with others.

Cost

The details of what costs to include and their balance are discussed in Stage Five. Actual costs are as far as possible given in the case studies in Part Two.

Cost can depend importantly on scale – for example a national remit for a consultation is likely to be more costly, and involve more events, people, and preparation. The Benefits Agency survey, with its national remit, was more expensive than, for example, the Bradford research panel.

High cost

The largest item of cost is usually staff time, and in general terms, deliberative methods are likely to be more expensive in terms of staff time. Deliberative events may be contracted out to specialist organisations, but if there is no substantial staff input to preparation and follow-up from the commissioning organisation, this will also have to be bought from the contractors. Any attempts to conduct trials and dummy runs amongst future service users as part of consultation are also very costly.

These two are closely followed in cost terms by preparation of documents for comments, and any groups or meetings which involve detailed preparation. In both cases costs are incurred because staff spend considerable time in preparation. If drafts were required regardless of whether there was a consultation, then these costs can be 'piggy-backed' and therefore discounted. Methods involving other specially prepared presentations – visuals and exhibitions – are also likely to involve high costs.

Finally, joint consultations – involving more than one commissioning organisation – are costly in terms of staff time in building the consensus and then in keeping everyone involved.

Low cost

Meetings with groups which are well-versed in the issues are usually low cost, as are focus groups where the main cost is the facilitator. Public meetings with little preparation are likely to be cheap, but feedback is usually poor.

Meetings which are routine aspects of organisational activity may add little to existing costs. The inclusion of permanent members of other bodies or groups in decision-making meetings can have a high initial cost – selection, induction, training etc – but will settle into a lower-cost framework after the initial period.

Surveys can be low cost if routine and supported by in-house expertise. However, analysis of results can be time-consuming and therefore expensive.

Interaction

Types of interaction and method in each case study

Interaction between the participants is part of some methods and not others. The degree of consultee contribution varies widely and is sometimes set on a scale from active to passive. This variation is one which in practice affects all participants, not only consultees. Table 3 illustrates the levels of interaction for the different methods used in the case studies.

Table 3 Levels of interaction for different methods

Case study	*Method*	*Level of interaction*
Arts Council of Wales	Investigative group	High
Benefits Agency	Survey of customer views	Low
Bradford Metropolitan Council	Survey panel	Low
Devon & Cornwall Police	Public meetings	Medium to low
Eastern Health & Social Services Board & Council	Consultative relationship examined through public meetings	High for the relationship, medium to low with the public
Edinburgh City Council	Customer-responsive freephone	Low
Highways Agency	'Round table' conference	High
Housing Corporation	Listening meetings with interest groups, draft report	Medium
Inland Revenue	Focus groups	Medium
London Borough of Lewisham	Citizens jury	High with the issue; medium with staff
Science Museum	'Consensus' conference	High with the issue; medium with staff
Tate Gallery Liverpool	Long-term advisory group	High
Walsall Art Gallery	Exhibitions and displays	Low
Waltham Forst HAT	Permanent representation on committees	High

Interaction also encompasses the relations between the participants during the process of consultation. Strong interaction is most often, although not necessarily, face-to-face. Written consultation exercises with other stages to them may well be set in an interactive framework.

Highly interactive methods are strong in dealing with complexity and for promoting change and development as part of the consultation. Methods with low interaction are suited to uncovering pre-existing responses or for settling on preferences already held to.

High interaction

Deliberative methods are highly interactive, involving extensive inputs to the consultees and complex and sustained responses from them. Consultees' interactions with the staff of the commissioning organisation may be at a low level because of the independent element in deliberative methods (see Stage Six). But consultees' interactions with each other and with the issues will be at a high level.

Methods which involve long-term membership of committees and other groups by consultees are similarly highly interactive. Other methods share some of this, although in general are less interactive than long-term involvements or deliberative methods. These are any methods involving discussion, including focus groups and public meetings at which presentations are made and ideas aired.

Low interaction

The lowest form of interaction is the postal survey, where the questions generally require selection of responses from a list of options.

Other low interaction methods include public meetings of a routine or general nature, where presentation and discussion are unlikely to take place, and one-off meetings or events which are not repeated.

Type of information-giving and gathering

Table 5.4 illustrates the different types of information activity and methods for each case study. Some methods are better suited to collecting some types of information than others. The drivers of the consultation will determine the nature of the information exchange, and information type is therefore tied to these drivers.

There are two questions to ask about information both to be given and to be received during a consultation:

1 Is it quantity, quality, or both which is offered and sought?
2 How complex is it to convey, how complex is the desired feedback?

Some methods will always involve particular types of information. Others can vary.

Quantity and quality

Quantity and quality are not used here to suggest that one is better than the other. The task is to match the type of information to the purpose, the consultees, and the available resources and experience of the organisation. Some consultations will be about quantities – how many think this, how many that. Others will be about quality: what is the range of preferences, what complexities do consultees' ideas contain, how strongly are views held, is there a common ground to be reached?

The information provided to consultees will shape strongly the information received, so that a consultation which offers many small items of information will want many small responses, collated into percentages and other descriptive statistical forms. Consultations which ask perhaps only one or two general questions will want discussion and development of ideas – possibly from large numbers of respondents, but often not. Consultations about specific services are more likely to have the offering and receipt of quantitative information as a key element. Consultations about policy and planning are unlikely to involve quantitative information, unless this is in support of general options or proposals.

Methods suited to conveying and receiving qualitative information are those which involve discussion and exchange of views – described as interaction above.

Quantitative information is always produced by surveys. Voting is another way of obtaining quantitative information (although voting is also a decision-making tool, and can involve small numbers only) in cases where, for example, large numbers of public meetings have been held. Quantitative information is not therefore uniquely featured in less interactive methods, as may often be thought. The deliberative poll method (not studied here) is an attempt to combine interaction and quantitative information.

Table 4 Types of information in different methods

Case study	*Information giving*	*Information gathered*	*Reliability**
Arts Council of Wales investigative group	Complex	Qualitative, complex	High – in-depth views of relevant groups obtained
Benefits Agency survey of customer satisfaction	Simple	Quantitative, complex	High – statistically reliable sample
Bradford Metropolitan Council survey panel	Simple	Quantitative, complex	High – statistically reliable sample
Devon & Cornwall Police Authority public meetings	Complex	Qualitative, simple	Low – meetings attended by self-selected small numbers
Eastern Health & Social Services Board & Council consultative relationship examined through public meetings	Complex	Qualitative, complex	Medium – information from many participants, but through partly unsuccessful mechanism
Edinburgh City Council customer-responsive freephone	Simple	Simple	Two assessments: high reliability because of public selection of problems and large numbers; but a passive method which can miss other problems
Highways Agency Round Table conference	Complex, intensive	Qualitative, complex	High – in-depth views of relevant groups obtained
Housing Corporation listening meetings with interest groups, and a draft report	Complex	Qualitative, complex	High – in-depth written response from main organisations
Inland Revenue focus groups	Complex	Qualitative, complex	High – large-scale exercise, across the country
London Borough of Lewisham citizens jury	Complex	Qualitative, simple	Low – small groups of a very large population
Science Museum consensus conference	Complex, intensive	Qualitative, complex	Low – small groups of a very large population
Tate Gallery Liverpool long-term advisory group	Complex	Qualitative, complex	Low – small groups of a very large population
Walsall Art Gallery exhibitions and displays	Complex	Qualitative, simple	Difficult to assess – depends on how many responses
Waltham Forest HAT permanent tenants' representatives on committees	Complex	Qualitative, complex	Low, unless representatives are routinely polling the tenants

* Reliability of the information collected refers only to whether the information can reasonably be interpreted as being the information which would have been obtained if the entire population of consultees had been involved. This does not indicate good or bad consultation.

Quality and quantity – a trade-off?

In terms of quantitative and qualitative information, there is often a trade-off between obtaining responses from a large enough sample of consultees to get statistically reliable results, and the depth and quality, and therefore the usefulness, of the responses. Consulting in small group discussions is likely to provide more detailed and thought-through responses than will a postal questionnaire. But a questionnaire can be sent to a sufficiently large number of individuals to ensure that they are a representative sample of the views sought. Small group discussions are usually far too resource-intensive to allow for a large sample of a population to take part.

Simplicity and complexity

Complex information will require a method which either allows for the opportunity to explain, answer questions, and discuss, or which provides a written text as the basis of the consultation, or both, if useful responses are to be obtained from consultees.

If complex information is already well-known to intended consultees it can be conveyed with a different method from a subject which is little known or is subject to tabloid-type opinions. In the former case, circulation of a written draft for comments can work. In the latter, explanation and discussion through face-to-face methods will be needed, including in some cases deliberative methods.

Consultations which involve imparting only simple information are not necessarily about simple matters. Consultations with groups well-versed in an issue may not require much in the way of information. Responses may well be readily understandable and pre-digested in terms easy to interpret, because the groups have a history of involvement, and in this context quite complex matters may be considered through simple information exchanges. One-off discussions can therefore cope with either simple information or complex information, according to who the participants are.

Long-term relationships accommodate complex information exchanges routinely, but will work just as well with only simple information inputs and responses.

Reliability of the results

The problem of reliability is about whether the results can give a true picture of what all of the potential consultees, had they been involved, might think or want. The degree of reliability sought is a matter of choice which depends on what the commissioning organisation wants and needs.

Some methods seek statistically representative samples of populations, or in some cases try to consult with an entire population (all service users, all residents of a locality etc), and it can reliably be said that these methods offer the chance to find out what everyone thinks or wants. Other methods may be described as involving representatives of particular groups or populations, when they do not do so in the sense of providing a reliable guide to what the entire population thinks. Misplaced use of the notion of 'representativeness' can have odd consequences (see Stage Two for more on 'representativeness').

High reliability

Statistically valid samples of large populations produce reliable results, although the information obtained by surveys, panels or opinion polls may be less 'rich' than by other methods. High reliability can also be achieved by using several methods and comparing results.

Carrying out more of a method can also enhance reliability. For example, holding a whole range of focus groups or meetings is likely to give better results than one or two. In circumstances where all consultees are reasonably identifiable, then encouragement of maximum involvement in meetings, written responses and other discussions will also promote high reliability.

Low reliability

Low reliability is likely where consultees are a tiny fraction of the total target population, or where selection of consultees is not well-related to the driver and the total of potential consultees. This can occur with many methods.

Highly interactive methods can also produce results with a risk of low reliability, because of the risk of the consultees taking on the perspectives of the commissioning organisation. Long-term groups and deliberative methods can both carry this risk, whether the involvement is of a large number (for example in Bradford), or a small number (for example the Tate Gallery Liverpool). In the case of deliberative methods, independent control of the practicalities of the consultation, and independent decision-making by consultees, will help to remedy this.

Low reliability is also a risk with meetings with self-appointed spokespeople or representatives, unless they can be seen to be backed by organisations and large numbers. The presence of campaign-type organisations, who generate heat, may serve to mask low reliability by force of presentation. A strongly-held response is not however necessarily representative of anything other than the individual respondent's views.

THE PROCESS OF CHOOSING A METHOD

In selecting a method, you will need to consider the mode, and each of the four factors, and match these to the two key indicators already identified: the purpose; the consultees. The organisation's resources, capacities and experience will also need to be taken into account.

Steps in the selection of the consultation method

The three steps summarised here cover the main decisions in selecting a method of consultation. Step 1 is to decide what the consultation is about – what is specifically driving it – and to assess which method(s) will work best. Step 2 involves checking that this method(s) is suited to the identified contexts driving the consultation. Step 3 involves checking that the method matches the consultees.

You will of course have to consider skills and resources, and the organisation's experience of consulting, in making the final selection.

Step 1 Match specific drivers and methods

Specific drivers	*Suitable methods*
Needs	Two approaches: surveys of individuals; meetings/discussions, including focus groups
Policy	Three approaches: methods which impart information – deliberative methods, written reports for circulation; long-term involvements in organisational bodies; displays and events
Priorities	Three approaches: discussions, including focus groups, or written reports; long-term involvements in organisational bodies; displays and events
Performance	Surveys, complaints-based systems, discussion

Step 2 Check contextual drivers and the match with method

Contextual drivers	*Suitable methods*
Value	Any
Consensus	Two approaches: decision-making discussion meetings or deliberative methods; and voting methods
Ownership	Involvement is the key – by discussion, meetings, votes
Support	Two approaches: involvement – discussions, meetings, votes; public profile – displays, events

Step 3 Check consultees against proposed methods

Consultees	*Suitable methods*
If involved in the issues	One-off meetings, surveys
If uninvolved in the issues	Methods requiring explanation and discussions: at meetings, through displays, through deliberative methods
If tabloid-type views predominate	Deliberative methods, or a strong educational element
Geographical closeness	The issues are scale and cost, matched against budgets and organisational abilities
What contribution can they make?	This can vary from decision-making to sounding-out. The method must match the intended contribution, which should be clear at the start.
What are their motivations?	These may be practical or related to public service. Public service motives must be matched by methods which are seen to be participative and community-based. Practical motives must be matched by methods which give a clear result.
What do they hope for?	The main issue is whether there are positive and/or negative outcomes, and whether these affect different groups in different ways. The potential for a positive outcome encourages participation.

STAGE FIVE

Planning the Process

INTRODUCTION

In Stages One to Four we discussed the purpose of consultation, who to consult, organisational traditions, and the method to use. Having settled these fundamental questions, an organisation is only partly prepared to begin the project. It is important also to plan the whole process in advance, right through to the analysis and use of the results.

In this section we discuss those aspects of the process which the research showed it was particularly important to consider before beginning the consultation itself. They fall into three groups: creating commitment and credibility; project planning; and completing the process. The case studies demonstrated their importance: it was common for projects to falter because they had not, for example, considered people's likely attitudes to the consultation or motivations for taking part, assessed all the skills that would be needed, or set up procedures for considering the results.

COMMITMENT AND CREDIBILITY

Consultation exercises require the commitment of all the different groups involved. The exercises have to be credible in the eyes both of those taking part and those you seek to influence with the results.

Ownership

Ownership means having a sense of responsibility for and obligation to the process, and a commitment to fulfil those responsibilities and obligations. Ownership is necessary if people are to participate fully in the process. The case studies showed that the process can be designed in ways which create and enhance a sense of ownership by different groups. In most cases, ownership must be shared between three groups of people:

1 Those who commissioned the work or decided it needed to be done, along with those organising and carrying out the consultation. This may be a small number of people but quite a large number may be involved, perhaps drawn from different parts of the organisation, or different organisations. Creating a sense of involvement and commitment for all of them is important.

2 Those who will use the outputs and findings. If those who can make decisions as a result of the work are not involved in it from an early stage, the outputs may ultimately be regarded as less significant or important, or even irrelevant. This group will include those at the most senior level in the organisation where decisions have to be made at that level.
3 The consultees. The degree of ownership which you need to foster amongst consultees varies with the purpose and method of consultation. Where people are involved in the most passive or transitory ways (in a postal survey, for example) ownership is needed to the extent of encouraging a good rate of response. But where continuing contact is required or where methods are intense and participative, such as in a consensus conference, ownership is vital.

It is not possible or desirable for any one group to own the process completely, and the right balance should be sought. The 'right' balance will depend on the purpose and method, as explained above. Whatever balance is struck, it is important that each group understands the others' roles. This is discussed below in the section 'Making the process and purpose clear'.

Particular approaches to ownership are required for different settings, as discussed below.

In large organisations

Large organisations and/or complex or multi-faceted projects present particular difficulties. Many different individuals will be involved, so good communication and liaison arrangements will require more effort. Each person or group may be responsible for a fairly specific task, and if this is so it will be more difficult to create in them a sense of ownership of the whole process.

National organisations may plan exercises at their headquarters which they want to be taken up at regional or local level. 'Next Steps' principles actively seek to empower local and regional managers, and to sustain a sense of ownership of a national project.

The Inland Revenue treated consultation with its own regional and local staff as an important part of its overall programme of consulting the public and conducting market research with users.

The Benefits Agency encouraged and supported customer surveys at district and local levels at the same time as its launch of the National Customer Survey.

With diffuse groupings

If a consultation project is being undertaken by a diffuse group from across different parts of an organisation, then multi-disciplinary or inter-departmental working groups, steering groups, planning groups and so on can help enhance the sense of ownership by all of the different elements.

The Walsall Art Gallery project drew on the expertise of a number of different departments and organisations. A structure of various inter-disciplinary groups ensured that those carrying out the consultation and those working on the wider development of the gallery were in close contact.

Elected members

Elected and appointed members of committees and boards should be involved in and informed about the process. In the case studies, there were a number of instances of members expressing reservations about the validity of public consultation. They were concerned that consultation, particularly the more participative methods, encroached on their own responsibility for representing the public and deciding policy. Securing their commitment at an early stage makes a difference to their commitment later on, as does involving them in the consultation activities

The Lewisham citizens jury and the consultation about the new art gallery in Walsall both received firm political support. Police authority members in Devon and Cornwall attend public consultation meetings on a regular basis.

Partnerships

Consultation is often carried out by partnerships of organisations. It may be cheaper for each organisation to do it this way, or the partnership may be a way of enhancing or affirming a working relationship. Perhaps both organisations have an interest in the results. Whatever the reason, it is necessary for both or all organisations to have a sense of ownership, although some will have a more prominent role than others. Establishing ground rules for the relationship can help.

Partners may choose to underplay their distinct roles in public in order to enhance the partnership or to avoid displaying potential tensions in their relationship. But this may not always be helpful to the consultees, who need to understand the respective roles, particularly if one organisation has responsibility for or authority over the other.

In Devon and Cornwall, the police force and the police authority carry out their consultation sessions jointly. This is intended to demonstrate their constructive working relationship. However, some members of the public and the authority felt that the independence of the authority should be made more explicit, and that this might encourage people to be more open and direct in stating their views.

Corporate plans and objectives

Consultation linked to important corporate plans or specific objectives is more likely to be owned and noticed at the highest level in an organisation.

In the Arts Council of Wales, the decision to carry out the exercise arose from the priorities of the corporate plan. The report on the exercise went back to the Council. In the Inland Revenue, the fundamental importance of self-assessment to the work of the Revenue meant that reports were made, and resources secured, at Board level.

Ministers took part in press conferences on the work. At the Benefits Agency, the National Customer Survey was one element in the strategic development of the service, led by the Chief Executive. Tenant involvement at Waltham Forest HAT is on several levels, including representation on the Board, which thereby has oversight of the entire approach to involvement.

Continuity

It is very helpful to have continuity between those responsible for the process, for presenting the results and for making decisions on the basis of the results. Without this, understanding and impetus are easily lost.

The Arts Council of Wales project was conducted, reported and presented to Council by the Director, who led the project. In contrast, the report on the consultation by the Eastern Health and Social Services Board and Council was presented by a Director who had not been involved in the exercise. In the former we can trace a very clear route from the consultation through to policy decisions, whereas in the latter, a second process was put in place in order to achieve a result.

Leadership and enthusiasm

Our research provided evidence of the importance of clear and enthusiastic leadership for consultation projects and of this being supported by, if not directly provided by, the most senior level of management. Enthusiasm from consultees will also be a constructive influence. Leadership and enthusiasm can be encouraged in a number of ways:

- By the project leader him/herself. The case studies provide a number of examples of enthusiastic, skilled, even charismatic, people in key roles throughout the life of a project.
- By political or management figures giving initial support and continuing endorsement.
  - *The Bradford panel and the Clarence help line both received the public support of all political parties.*
  - *In Devon and Cornwall, senior police officers, including the Chief Constable and Deputy Chief Constable, attend public meetings from time to time.*
- By considering the motivation of consultees. Why might they be willing to take part? This will depend on their level of personal interest in the subject and the likelihood of a positive outcome for them. Showing consultees that you appreciate their effort will make them more enthusiastic and may increase their commitment. Where significant demands are made on members of the public it is usual to pay them expenses and, sometimes, a token amount for their time.
  - *Participants in the workshop on the Walsall Art Gallery commented enthusiastically on the organisation of the event and the attention to detail which made them feel personally valued.*

- *Jurors in the Lewisham citizens jury were invited to attend and speak at the meeting of the Council Committees which discussed and adopted jury recommendations. Jurors also attended a reception after the meeting with councillors and the Chief Executive*

See Stage Two for more on the motivation of consultees.

Objectivity and independence in the process

Objectivity and independence are important in two ways: to obtain honest answers and to obtain independent recommendations.

Obtaining honest answers

The carrying out of consultation is often contracted out by the organisation which wants answers to its questions. This increases the chance of getting honest responses from respondents who might, for example, be reticent about voicing criticisms of current provision to those on whom they depend for services.

Obtaining independent recommendations

Consultation methods include processes which can sustain, at one extreme, maximum independence for the consultees and, at the other, maximum involvement by the commissioning organisation. Most consultation processes lie between these two.

To obtain independent recommendations or conclusions it is necessary to maximise the distance between consultees and other groups (organisers and policy-makers). But this limits the ownership felt by these other groups. However, independence from involvement with the commissioning organisation does not imply any distance from the issues during the consultation.

Some consultation exercises aim to support a group of people to reach conclusions and make recommendations independently of any of the stakeholders or key players in the field. This is usually the case with deliberative methods such as consensus conferences or citizens juries which seek to understand the viewpoint which might be held by informed lay people. The ultimate aim is for policy to be influenced by this, and not only by expert or specialist views, which may, in any case, conflict with one another.

Examples such as this face a particular difficulty of ownership: how to engage the commissioners and policy makers sufficiently to create the sense of ownership and commitment which is necessary for the process to work well, while enabling the consultees both to be well informed and to take as much control as possible of the process and its outputs.

However, independence of consultees is not appropriate where, for example, an organisation is developing a policy which will affect the very organisations it is consulting. Such a purpose can only be served by discussion. Although the process may raise some difficulties about players' abilities to be open with one another, a process which involves exchanges between the various participants is essential.

Tensions in such a process may be eased by bringing in other people with the skills, knowledge or personal authority which can supplement that of the organisers. A transparent process also helps to alleviate suspicions.

The Arts Council of Wales had one 'outsider' on its working group, all the other members being Council staff. This person was able to act as a catalyst by bringing in new information and knowledge and challenging established positions. Successive drafts of the consultation document were published, enabling consultees to see that their input had an influence, and giving them an opportunity to comment further.

The Eastern Health and Social Services Board invited the Eastern Health and Social Services Council to chair all of the public discussion meetings, to ensure and demonstrate the objectivity of the process through the independence of the chair.

In between these two ends of the spectrum are a range of consultation methods and purposes which demand a certain amount of distance between consultees and those who seek to consult them, during the process. For example our case studies involve exercises where those organising the consultation have taken a supporting or facilitating role. They have sought to provide their consultees with the resources and confidence to form and express their views. Examples include, in particular, the coordinator of the Young Tate in Liverpool.

Where independence is the goal, attention should be paid to different stages of the process:

- Conveying knowledge to the consultees. The choice of witnesses and experts was a difficult driver for the consensus conference and the citizens jury. Ideally, members should have the time to make the selection themselves, but this may not be wholly practical. In any case, they are likely to need initial guidance on the range of viewpoints which are available to them.
- Deciding on the subject and the questions. A truly independent process will involve the consultees setting their own agenda. The lay panel at the consensus conference decided on the specific questions they wanted to pursue, within the broad topic of plant biotechnology. The breadth, and practicality, of the topic are also important considerations. Too broad a topic may make it impractical for the consultees to specify questions.
- Formulating the report and the recommendations. A truly independent process will involve the consultees formulating their conclusions and recommendations without any assistance or support by the event's organisers. Lay panel members became concerned about their perceived independence, or lack of it, and went into closed session to produce their report. The citizens jury's report was drafted by external consultants and the jury's recommendations were presented to the jury for their agreement, not written by them.
- A steering group drawn from a broad range of interests can help to safeguard the impartiality of the process. But membership of the group must be carefully balanced and may still be criticised where different groups hold strong views.

PROJECT PLANNING

Organisational deadlines and timing

If the results of a consultation are needed to inform a particular action or decision, for which the date is firmly set, the process has to be planned well ahead and, if necessary, tailored to fit the timetable. Even where this is not the case, a firm timetable is a good discipline. This has the additional benefit of giving a clear indication to participants of what to expect, and when.

The Inland Revenue had an absolute deadline for the introduction of self assessment and this determined the dates by which forms and systems had to be ready, staff and agents trained, and taxpayers prepared. The evolving programme of consultation began more than three years ahead of this deadline. The flexibility of the contractors within this programme was crucial, in order to respond to changing needs and circumstances, and emerging findings.

The Devon and Cornwall Police Authority has an annual cycle of public consultation. Its methods are determined partly by the need to fit a region-wide consultation into a fairly short period before the drafting of the plan begins.

The Benefits Agency survey was conducted annually for five years, and was subject to a detailed timetable each year.

However, there may in some circumstances be clear benefits of not being committed to a rigid schedule.

The Arts Council of Wales was able to extend its deadline to take account of the consultation on the new funding scheme from the national lottery. And the planning conference on the A259 was able to adjourn for new route proposals to be studied.

Consultation may be seeking to influence decisions to be made by an outside body. It is particularly difficult to do this if the consultation topic or method requires a long period of planning and preparation and/or dates for decisions are not yet fixed.

The Science Museum's consensus conference took a year from the beginning of the planning stage to the actual events. The Danes, who have extensive experience of the method, can complete a consensus conference within six months. However, this sort of timescale may be longer than that used in planning parliamentary or political decision making, which may therefore be difficult to influence through this method.

Some topics will be of more interest to consultees at different times, and timing will help to determine how fruitful a consultation is, and how smoothly it runs.

The planning conference on the A259 was a second attempt by the Highways Agency to consult on this road scheme. The public had already expressed their views and were surprised to find a second consultation taking place. Views had become entrenched by then, making the consultation, which aimed at consensus, less productive than it might have been if it had taken place earlier.

The Housing Corporation was carrying out other consultations at the same time, involving some of the same consultees, causing some confusion for some of the participants.

Responsibilities

What are the different functions required? Who will be responsible for what? What are the management, reporting, liaison and communication structures? These are important elements of the planning of a consultation project, as much as in any other project. Dealing with these issues requires standard management skills and tasks, which are not discussed here. However, there are examples in the case studies of key responsibilities not being allocated and projects faltering as a result, so it is important not to overlook them.

Additional considerations apply to partnership ventures. Formal agreements on terms of reference or ground rules were found to be useful in these relationships.

There is a key responsibility which does merit specific discussion in the context of planning a consultation exercise: the responsibility of consultees. Where a degree of contact and involvement is expected, you are obliged to make clear to consultees your expectations and their responsibilities. In a number of our case studies, organisations had found it helpful to introduce ground rules or codes of practice for conduct and behaviour.

Those attending the A259 planning conference were asked to register as delegates. The use of this term brought the expectation that they would attend for the whole of the time the conference was sitting, to enable discussion to develop. They were allowed to speak for as long as they held the other delegates' attention, but not to repeat themselves. The word 'conference' implies reaching a conclusion which all are party to, and a duty to produce an end result.

Tate Gallery Liverpool ascribes part of the success of its display group to the ground rules laid down at the start of the group by Tate staff, and agreed to by the young people involved. These rules provided a framework for controlling teenage-type behaviour and helping the young people to develop new ways of thinking and expressing themselves

Resources

The case studies contain all the information we were able to obtain about the costs of the different consultation exercises. It is indicative of a general problem that we were not always able to obtain complete information on costs.

Most commonly, organisations were unable to determine or even estimate with any accuracy, the amount of staff time involved, especially where staff took on new activities for the duration of the project. But there was widespread agreement that the work had taken more staff time than had been envisaged at the beginning. It is important, therefore, to consider not only the staff time that will be needed, but the implications this will have for other work not being done, and the need for temporary or replacement staff.

Other costs will include: accommodation and catering; travel; communication; contractors (surveys, facilitators and so on); and computer analysis.

Skills

It is in the nature of consultation that many people doing it are inexperienced in the work, because they have done it infrequently or not at all. Consultation tends to be something that organisations do from time to time; while large organisations have some specialist staff with some of the skills involved, no organisation is likely to have extensive experience of all the stages and activities involved. However, many of the skills which are involved are required for other types of work as well.

The following skills are commonly required: chairing; listening; management of projects, staff and budgets; teamwork; planning; research skills; analysis; communication; writing; administration; policy development; facilitating; negotiation; community development; and knowledge of the subject, the organisations and drivers involved.

Some of these skills may need to be bought in from outside the organisation because:

- the organisation does not have them in-house;
- they may exist in-house but are not available to the project;
- there is value in having particular skills provided by an outsider, such as independent facilitator or a person who can challenge established views.

There were a number of examples in our research of the personal skill and manner of a key individual making a significant difference to the success of the process. In other cases, the key skills of a small group were important components of success.

Consultees need skills too, depending on what you are asking of them. Above, we discussed the need for information and briefing sessions for the more participative methods of consultation. Skills may be enhanced through training.

Waltham Forest HAT, for example, expressed its intention to achieve empowerment through providing tenants with the skills, knowledge and training they required.

Tate Gallery Liverpool embarked on an initial education and induction programme into the workings of the gallery and basic knowledge about the professional practices involved.

You should think also about how to deal with consultees with different levels of skill.

The delegates to the A259 planning conference had a wide range of experience and skill in important areas, including public speaking, lobbying, advocacy and organising support. Here, the skill of the chair became even more important as he had to minimise the advantages of the experienced and professional over the inexperienced and amateur.

Making the process and purpose clear

A clear understanding of the process and purpose are vital ingredients of a constructive discussion and productive consultation exercise. The aim should be for organisers, users and consultees to share an understanding of what the consultation is for, and how it will be conducted. The case studies include a fairly high incidence of misunderstanding, which probably made the processes less productive.

It may be harder to achieve this understanding than organisers expect, as a result of:

- people's previous experience of consultation, which influences their expectations;
- different use of language – one person's plain English may still be another person's jargon;
- a level of unfamiliarity with the roles of organisations, their processes and policy making, amongst consultees, which organisers fail to appreciate;
- set views or positions which people want to advocate, even if this is not appropriate for the particular context;
- the inherent complexities of the processes and objectives you are trying to explain;
- commissioning organisations and those responsible for the work failing to identify and describe the purpose and process clearly for themselves;
- a deliberate lack of clarity, to suit organisations' own purposes;
- people not absorbing information which is made available to them, perhaps because it is in an inappropriate format or does not seem relevant at the time.

Devon and Cornwall Police Authority has two objectives: to inform the public and gather information from them. Both activities take place concurrently, but only the latter is stated as an objective to the public. This influences the methods they use, which have to involve interaction with the public. If only the second objective existed, it is possible that other methods would be appropriate.

In the Science Museum's consensus conference, the respective weight of the two objectives (to inform public debate and to test the consultation method) were not made clear. This has made it difficult for anyone to evaluate the conference. The terms and language used are also imprecise. Words such as 'public' and 'consensus' have been variously interpreted.

For the A259 planning conference the purpose was clearly stated in a pre-conference meeting and publicity material, but was not widely understood. People failed to realise its scope in relation to the geography of the area and previous decisions. Also, the process was a new and unfamiliar one. Many participants had previous experience of planning enquiries and the role of the inspector there. The Chair of the planning conference found he had to restate his role (which was quite different from an inspector's) and position frequently.

Completing the Process

Planning how to process the results

The method of consultation you choose will determine the form of the results and output. It is important to envisage this and think through the next steps. What physical form will the results take? What will you have in your hands at the end of the consultation, and how will this be transformed into something upon which decisions about changes can be made?

Quantitative methods produce data which is, in a way, more straightforward to deal with than the more diffuse material that results from qualitative work. For both, people with research skills will be needed to analyse and interpret the results. Without this, organisations run the risk of not gaining the maximum benefit from their work, or of drawing ill-founded conclusions.

Qualitative research in general, and certainly the qualitative methods used in the case studies, are characterised by the absence of explicit statements about the processes used to move from information gathering to results and conclusions. This is not helpful in demonstrating the credibility or integrity of the exercise, or to others who want to use a similar approach. The aim should be for an explicit or transparent process which enables people to see a clear link between input and output and, eventually, outcomes.

The Arts Council of Wales produced several successive drafts of its consultation document. The influence of contributors was evident in each version. Towards the end of the process a draft was circulated more widely for comment. The final published and adopted policy was closely related to this.

The Housing Corporation included a summary of all responses to its draft framework document as an appendix to the final document.

Following through to the end

There are likely to be several 'ends'. The completion of the actual consultation exercise should not be an end as the further essential stages are the consideration and use of the findings for decision making, and, later, monitoring and evaluating the impact of those decisions. Following through also involves providing feedback to the consultees.

It is at this stage that many of the case studies faltered. The consultation was not always followed through properly, or at all, rendering the exercise largely or entirely a waste of time. However, it was possible to identify a number of common, critical factors which made it more likely for an exercise to be followed through:

- Those who were in a position to make decisions were involved in the work from the beginning, and felt a sense of commitment and interest in it.
- The work was credible in the eyes of those who could act on it – they accepted its purpose, methods and legitimacy.
- There was continuity of staff between those carrying out the consultation and those making decisions on the basis of it.

- There was a clear route and institutional framework for using the results to influence decisions.
- The timing of the work was right for the work to be able to influence relevant decisions.
- The results were broadly acceptable to those required to act on them.
- The environment had not changed dramatically since the consultation began.
- Results were presented in a form that was accessible and meaningful to those intended to use them.

STAGE SIX

Managing the Process

INTRODUCTION

Having planned the process of consultation, including the use of the results and the monitoring of their impact, it is time to consider how to manage the process. In this section we concentrate on those aspects of management which relate to managing consultation in particular. We do not attempt to repeat what is already known about good practice in management generally, or to give guidance on effective project management, although both of these are important.

The emphasis in this section is on managing the relationships with the wide range of people involved in a consultation exercise. It is these relationships which are a critical factor in achieving a smooth running and productive consultation exercise, and which will help to maximise its impact.

An important principle is to establish the relationship before the consultation activity itself begins, and to pay attention to it once that period of contact has finished. You need the commitment of many people to make the consultation work, and this means involving them before and after the events themselves.

WHO DO YOU HAVE A RELATIONSHIP WITH?

The consultation will involve you (the individuals or group responsible for carrying out the consultation) in relationships with some if not all of the following:

- other parts of your own organisation;
- partner organisations, doing the consultation together;
- those who will act on the results (at policy and operational levels), both inside and outside the consulting organisation;
- organisations with whom you have a permanent relationship, such as that between an executive agency or NDPB and its sponsoring department;
- contractors doing work on the consultation;
- other participants, such as experts and witnesses;
- consultees.

The relationship with consultees is of fundamental importance and considerable complexity. We discuss this in a separate section below.

It is clear from this list that the pattern of relationships involved in a consultation is not straightforward. Further, many of the individuals concerned will already know each other, and may have different roles in relation to you and each other at different times.

The benefits of a well-managed relationship

- A sense of ownership by the different groups you need to involve in the project (see above for more on ownership);
- clarity about respective roles and responsibilities, and therefore a greater chance of these being fulfilled properly;
- the continuation, after the project, of productive relationships between organisations which already work well together and the strengthening of new partnerships;
- reduced risk of misunderstanding or damage to relationships, which may be difficult to recover;
- a greater chance of the results of the consultation being taken seriously by those who will be needed to act on them;
- an enhanced reputation for the organisation;
- a widely held view that the exercise was conducted properly and professionally;
- support for any future consultation exercises;
- a 'learning environment' in which all those involved can contribute to the development of good practice;
- a climate of openness which will encourage people to express their reservations or scepticism, rather than you finding these out when they undermine the process.

How to manage the relationship

The case studies provided evidence of the practices and approaches which encourage good relationships in consultation exercises, and which can help to secure the important benefits listed above. The following are all important aspects of managing relationships:

- Clarify your own role and responsibilities and make explicit statements about this. Make clear what you are not responsible for, and what is outside the remit of the project, as well as what is inside.
- Make sure everyone else knows what is expected of them. Different approaches suit different degrees of involvement. Ground rules or terms of reference are needed for partners, specifications and contracts for consultants. Your expectations should be in line with their resources and level of interest in the project.
- Make demands which are realistic within the context of your existing relationship and its history, as this will influence others' reactions to them.
- Make public your plans for the project, including objectives, methods and timetable. Continue the flow of information while the process is going on. Produce progress reports or updates. People who are not immediately involved can easily think that nothing is happening, even though you are fully occupied with a particular stage of the work. Keep up the momentum and the flow of information.

- Make and keep promises. If your plans have to change because, for example, the timetable has slipped, explain this to all involved.
- Consider how best to involve all those who you hope will support and take an interest in the work. Advisory and working groups, and consultations with staff, can be a useful way of disseminating information about the process and securing support for any proposed changes, as well as bringing expertise into the project.
- Pay attention to all points of contact. For example, well organised and chaired meetings, efficient administration, clear and timely information, can all help to show that the process is being managed properly and taken seriously.

The relationship with consultees

A critical factor in successful consultation is the creation of a good relationship with those being consulted. This is not a one-off task at the time of recruiting them or at the time of the actual consultation. Keeping them informed after their formal involvement has finished is important as well.

Types of consultees

When considering how to manage the relationship with consultees, you should consider the characteristics of your particular consultees, as discussed in Stage Two. Important considerations include:

- their amount of understanding of the subject of consultation;
- the reasons for, and level of, their interest in it;
- their willingness to listen and ability to change their views or negotiate (a particular difficulty for those who have been mandated to represent others);
- their time and resources.

Benefits of a good relationship with consultees

- A better response to your requests for input. This might take the form of a larger number responding and/or responding in a more considered, detailed or focused way.
- Saving on the costs of consultation by avoiding the need to, for example, recruit new consultees, chase responses or repeat exercises.
- Maintaining interest and involvement throughout the longer consultation processes.
- Minimising disruption to the process by any elements who oppose it or its objectives.
- An enhanced reputation for the organisation, especially if it is seen to act on the results.
- Positive reactions to the consultation amongst consultees, and positive messages being given by them to others.
- Support for future processes and respect for the outputs.
- An improved relationship with consultees, once the exercise has been completed.

How to manage the relationship with consultees

These are generally applicable principles. Different types of consultee and different methods of consultation will require them to be applied in different ways, as we illustrate below.

Clarify and explain your role and responsibilities

In Stage Five, we explained the difficulties in making the purpose and process of your consultation clear. The importance of doing so is emphasised by evidence from the case studies. This includes making clear:

- what is inside and outside the remit of the consultation;
- what will be done with people's contributions (including any commitments on confidentiality and anonymity);
- the timetable for the process;
- methods of providing feedback to consultees;
- the extent to which the organisation and others are committed to consider, act on or be bound by results.

Those organising the consultation about the new art gallery in Walsall emphasised that the public were not being invited to comment on the overall design of the gallery, which was the subject of an architectural competition. But they were being asked for their ideas about the facilities and services it should provide.

In the Eastern Health and Social Services Board and Council consultation about the future provision of learning disability services, some of the families/carers were uncertain about the purpose of those meetings. The nine service options which the Board put to each meeting were not well-known to the participants before the meetings.

Members of the Bradford research panel had expectations of involvement in meetings and discussions. Their understanding of this was based on the common sense meaning of the word 'panel'.

Explain consultees' roles and responsibilities

Consultees will want to know the extent of their commitment – how much time consultation will involve, over what period, and the form the process will take. Of course, it is not possible to be precise about this with methods of consultation which rely on developing a process in response to events (such as the A259 planning conference) or on handing control of the process to the consultees (such as the Science Museum's consensus conference or the Housing Action Trust). But this should also be made clear. Any ground rules or codes of conduct will also need to be explained and understood.

The organisers of the consensus conference were careful to explain to members of the lay panel exactly what they thought would be involved. Nevertheless, at least one member reported being dismayed at the demands placed upon the panel and at the 'seriousness' of the process, which added to the weight of responsibility. S/he considered withdrawing, but did not do so.

We referred above (Stage Five) to the registration of those attending the A259 planning conference as delegates. This status brought certain responsibilities. There was also a pre-conference meeting, some weeks before the conference opened, which explained the purpose and format, and gave people the opportunity to ask questions about any matter of procedure.

The Arts Council of Wales invited representatives of organisations to attend meetings of the working group to discuss the policy drivers under consideration. Because their role was not precisely specified, those invited arrived with a range of expectations, including that they would be joining the group and that they would be attending with or without others. Most were surprised by the formality of the meeting.

Understand consultees' motivations and expectations

Despite your efforts to make the process and purpose clear, consultees' expectations and understanding may be at odds with your intentions. Misunderstandings can develop during a process, even where there was clarity at the beginning. Many were revealed during our own research with consultees in the case studies, and some of this feedback was, incidentally, of use to the organisers. You can counter such risks by building in some sort of monitoring or feedback during the process, if it is a long one.

It is not surprising that groups will use consultations to press for their own objectives, even if these are not part of the consultation agenda. Organisations will use the consultation as a vehicle for raising their own profile, advocating for their own role or constituency, for example. You need to be aware of this. Similarly, responses may be less than straightforward from organisations or individuals which depend on you financially or in other ways.

If the history of relations between you and the consultees is a tense or unhappy one, and particularly if previous consultations have not been effective, it is important not to ask or promise too much. People will have low expectations in these circumstances, and it is better to exceed them than to disappoint. This is also important if you are inexperienced in consulting.

Sometimes, people's doubts and scepticism about an exercise can only be dealt with by carrying out an exercise which they can see to be genuine and well-organised.

The jurors in Lewisham had doubts at the beginning about how genuine the organisers were in wishing to consult the public and hear their views. These misgivings were removed by their experience of the jury process and its reporting.

Manage the contact with consultees

People who provide time for a consultation exercise appreciate, and deserve, well-run meetings and efficient administration. This creates a sense of confidence in the process, and a sense that their contribution is valued. A comfortable physical environment is also important. We heard a number of complaints about poor audibility, crowded meeting rooms and so on. However, beware of appearing too lavish with hospitality! This may be a small part of the total costs, but many consultees object to what they see as a waste of public resources.

Keep your promises

It is important to fulfil commitments on timetables, communication and so on. If you cannot, explain why.

Provide feedback to consultees during and after the process

Feedback during the longer consultation processes can help to make them transparent and enhance both the quality of further responses and confidence in the process. It is fairly common practice to circulate successive drafts so that consultees can see the influence that has been brought to bear on them, and have further opportunity to comment.

> *The chairman of the A259 planning conference decided to produce a set of draft resolutions before the conference adjourned. This was a response to his concern that the conference was felt to be getting nowhere. He wanted to state where the conference had got to and to show delegates that the output reflected people's contributions, in a balanced way.*

The lack of feedback to consultees after a consultation process is one of the major weaknesses in practice across all methods and organisations. Where results were being used, consultees were largely unaware of this because they are rarely part of the structures or procedures for considering such matters. Lack of communication after the event, and the impression that nothing was happening as a result, was a major source of dissatisfaction amongst the consultees we spoke to during the case studies.

Organisations have a duty, we feel, to show consultees that they have not wasted their time. Communication after the event is also important for the organisation's reputation and for securing commitment to future consultations.

> *Devon and Cornwall police collated the results of the voting on priorities at each of its district-based focus sessions on policing plans, and made these available at the next Liaison Meeting in that district. The annual policing plan was also distributed at the meeting, showing regional priorities and how these had been incorporated into the plan. The cycle was completed by the inclusion of figures showing performance against targets in the plan.*

Walsall Art Gallery held a feedback seminar for those who had taken part in its workshop on the new gallery, at which the organisers of the consultation and the architects discussed what had happened as a result of the consultation.

Providing feedback directly to individuals is more difficult or impractical where there are very many of them, they were anonymous or had only a fleeting contact. But the same purpose may be achieved by keeping the project in the public eye through the use of the media, as we discuss next.

Maintain a high profile for the project

The national and local media can be used where you want to maintain levels of support and interest in a project over a period of time, and/or let consultees know what is happening as a result of their input.

The Inland Revenue's consultees were taxpayers, their agents and employers. It was important for the Revenue to let the wider population of all these groups know how it was preparing for self-assessment and to make them aware of the forthcoming changes. The Revenue placed its consultation process in the public eye by holding press conferences, placing advertisements in the media, issuing public consultation packs and so on.

The Walsall Art Gallery made extensive use of the local media to publicise its work and staged different parts of the project, such as the submission of the lottery application, as public events which were covered by the local press.

From its launch, Edinburgh's 'Call Clarence' scheme was publicised with a specific logo – the lion – and distinctive widespread advertising, including local radio jingles.

Provide ways for consultees to raise their individual concerns

Some consultations will inevitably give rise to concerns about either the subject or the process. People may have individual worries or concerns about their own circumstances which they need or want to discuss. You have an obligation to provide a way in which people can raise these drivers on a one to one level with people who can respond. Also, raising them in consultative forum will disrupt the process.

At the police authority's public meetings in Devon and Cornwall, police officers were available for informal discussions with the public at the end of the meetings. Similar arrangements were made by Eastern Health and Social Service Board and Council for carers and relatives to discuss matters of personal concern with staff of the relevant Health Trusts. The Benefits Agency set up routes for survey interviewees to raise any concerns they had about the interviewers and about any other matters.

Be prepared for a poor response

Even well-planned projects may meet a poor or unexpected response. This is often because the method you have chosen asks too much of consultees in relation to their level of interest, commitment or understanding. You should monitor responses and be ready to change your approach.

Prepaid postcards were used for a trial period in Edinburgh, before 'Call Clarence' was launched. Take-up of these was low, and they were discontinued after the launch of the freefone service.

> *Devon and Cornwall Police Authority initially held meetings which were specifically to discuss the police plan. Attendance was low, but increased enormously when, the following year, they attached these sessions to the regular liaison meetings.*

Consider how to deal with 'heated' consultations

Consultations which involve bringing people together will frequently become heated. This can be useful and productive if it is well managed. Indeed, any consultation which is about a subject on which people have strong views or keen personal interests ought to be lively and involving. However, these discussions should be held within a framework which respects the consultation process and others' points of view

> *The chairman of the A259 planning conference suspended proceedings when a shouting match developed between local people and anti-road groups from outside the area. He told the conference that he would leave the hall for a short period, during which the conference should decide if it wished to continue and to respect the authority of the chair. It is reported that local people made it clear to the 'outsiders' that they were not welcome. They left and the conference continued.*

Where opposing views are already strongly held, particularly by campaigning or lobby groups, consultation is likely to reveal those divisions, and perhaps reinforce them. It is important to recognise that there are times when mediation is needed, not consultation. Consultation is not a way of resolving difficult problems or making controversial decisions easy. The case studies contain a few instances where mediation might have helped to find a way forward, though it was not an option which was used.

Consider how to deal with representatives of groups

Consulting representatives requires a particular approach. Representatives may have been given a mandate which is too narrow for them to be flexible in negotiation with others.

> *Residents' associations in the A259 planning conference held local ballots on options for the route of the bypass. They felt bound to push for the preferred option, and were unable or unwilling to discuss new options which emerged later. The same consultation exercise raised the driver of the status of local authority officers in an*

event which aimed to reach consensus. Their position was that they represented their departments. No view had been taken by elected members and any agreement which was reached would need to be taken to committee.

Be aware of the different types of consultees

Not all your consultees will bring the same sets of skills or levels of experience to the consultation exercise. Attention must be paid to this if they are to have equal voices.

Stage Seven

The Results

Introduction

As we discussed earlier, it is important when choosing the method and planning the process (Stages Four and Five) to consider the abilities and resources that will be needed to deal with the outputs of your consultation. You will need to assess whether you can provide these, and make arrangements for doing so.

Outputs of consultation may take many forms: notes and tape recordings of meetings; written comments; completed questionnaires; records of interviews, and so on. Transforming these into information which can be used for making decisions is a critical stage in the consultation process, and one which is often relatively neglected in the planning and management of projects.

Processing and analysing the results requires time and skill, and continuity of personnel with those planning and running the consultation activity itself. The results should be presented in a form which is accessible and useful for the audience and which is clearly connected to the consultation itself.

Our case studies fall into two groups in terms of requirements for results processing. The largest group contains those which were concerned with short life activities working to a fixed timetable and which were designed to produce outputs at particular stages, to aid particular decisions. Here, we discuss the ways in which their results can be processed most effectively and the sorts of problems that may be encountered.

The second, and smaller, group of case studies is concerned with ongoing participation or responsiveness. These do not produce results for one-off or occasional decision-making. Rather, they are permanent methods of improving the quality of a service. As such they require methods for monitoring and reviewing their effectiveness periodically. The case studies in this group are Edinburgh City Council's 'Call Clarence', Liverpool Young Tate and Waltham Forest Housing Action Trust.

Answering the original objectives

It is surprisingly easy to lose sight of the original objectives of the consultation when analysing the results. Consultations will often raise new or unexpected drivers, and they may not always answer the original questions as directly as you hoped. These new drivers need to be addressed (see below) but the starting point for the analysis is to revisit the stated objectives.

Who should process the results?

It appears to be important that the results are analysed by someone closely involved in the consultation activity itself. Where this did not happen, the break in continuity showed in, for example, reports which were not felt to reflect the original objectives or flavour of discussions and meetings which had taken place.

Where the fully independent views of the consultees are sought, consultees should process and analyse the results themselves, without the intervention of staff from the consulting organisation. This is only possible with methods which are based on intense involvement by a small group.

The panel members at the Science Museum's consensus conference produced their own report, in closed session, with assistance from a word processing clerk and editor only.

A valid and transparent process

It should be possible to see how conclusions and recommendations have been derived from the outputs of the consultation. The relative lack of transparency in the case studies made it difficult for us to assess the impact of consultation on subsequent events. More importantly, transparency is important for your own accountability to consultees and decision-makers and for monitoring and evaluating both the consultation and the effect of subsequent actions.

Transparency is easier to achieve with quantitative data than qualitative. You can present the statistical results, and the conclusions based on them. It is important to use valid statistical techniques. With qualitative data you have to summarise the data and then analyse it, and your summaries may be challenged. Again, accepted research methods should be used.

The processing of qualitative data can be made more transparent by:

- Including summaries of all the comments received during a consultation in an appendix to the final document, as the Housing Corporation did.
- Combining the process and the product. The Arts Council of Wales produced successive drafts of the strategy document which was to be its end product. Each draft was seen to be influenced by the consultees' input. The alternative would have been to carry out the consultation and then produce a strategy, but this would have been a less visible and accountable process.

We referred above to the need, in some methods, for consultees to produce a report independently. Such a process will, by its nature, be less transparent.

The lay panel members at the Science Museum's consensus conference, for example, devised their own process for arriving at the report, behind closed doors. However, the report does, and should, include information about the witnesses heard by the panel and the conference procedures. Some commentators have noted that the report should also include summaries of the evidence given to the panel, so that readers can make their own links between the evidence and the recommendations.

Timescale

This stage of the work should be completed as quickly as possible if momentum is to be maintained.

Using results of different methods

Different consultation methods are often used within one project. This is often found to be a useful approach as the results can reinforce and illuminate one another, especially where quantitative and qualitative methods are used. Both the Inland Revenue and the Walsall Art Gallery found this to be a considerable advantage.

However, if different forms of output point to different conclusions, you need to consider why and not assume that one is more valid than other. It may be that the different methods involved different groups of respondents, with different views, or it may be that questions asked differently elicited different responses.

Presenting results in a form which can be used

Established good practice applies when writing and presenting the information in a form which is suitable for the audience. More than one form may be needed; management committees may require a different format to consultees. Organisational practice will determine whether or not recommendations are included, and in what form.

STAGE EIGHT

Decisions and Outcomes

INTRODUCTION

Most of the case studies show consultation processes which were effectively sustained, often over long periods, and from which results were obtained which broadly met the objectives set at the start of the consultations. Most commissioning organisations displayed a wide range of high level skills in making what are very difficult exercises run to their conclusions with some momentum. Some consultations were, of course, long-term involvements rather than short-term projects, but these too displayed the same high level of commitment and effectiveness in their workings.

The most difficult phase for many of the consultations lay in the processes of decision-making after the consultation and the outcomes from the exercises. The decisions about change, and the implementation of these, was overall the weak point of many case studies. The outcomes of consultations were frequently hard to identify.

At the end of a consultation there is also a point when it may be apparent to the commissioning organisation, or to parts of it, that the results are not necessarily what they might favour (see Stage Seven for more on this). In practice this may mean that organisational politics, both internally and in external relations, will significantly influence the outcomes of the consultation. This should be borne in mind when setting up the process of consultation, in terms of securing ownership at senior levels, both of the process and of the decisions.

The best way to ensure that decision-making is an effective part of the overall process, and that outcomes are therefore achieved, is to specify the total process of the consultation in advance, and to ensure compatibility between the decision-making processes, the possible outcomes, and the matters about which you are consulting. We have explored this in detail earlier in this guide.

That said, there are some key points about the end of the consultation which we want to draw out from the experiences of the 14 case studies:

- end-point or end-points must be clearly identified;
- decision-making, and preparations for it, must involve the right people at the right levels;
- decisions must relate to the purpose of the exercise;
- decisions must produce outcomes which are understandable and usable for the policy, planning or service staff involved.

THE DECISION-MAKING PROCESS

Decisions may be made on the basis of the direct outputs of the consultation. But it is more likely that the commissioning organisation will want or need several stages of elaboration on the basis of the outputs, before its decisions are made. Unless the consultation has involved a pre-given commitment to agree automatically to some specific output result (such as the results of democratic elections), then this elaboration process will always be needed, and a specific decision-making forum, separate from the consultation, will also be necessary.

Who should be involved in making decisions?

The driver of who is involved in this stage has a strong influence on the relevance and effectiveness of the decisions made and therefore of the outcomes. The case studies illustrate a number of drivers of involvement.

Joint commissioners

Some consultations involved more than one commissioning organisation. Lack of clarity about the respective roles of joint or partnership ventures was carried through into the decision-making stages. The 'junior' partners felt excluded from the processes at the end of the consultation, and were more critical of the decisions and outcomes than might otherwise have been the case. Both the Eastern Health and Social Services Board and Council and the Lewisham citizens jury experienced versions of this.

Problem areas

Consultation is not a way of resolving disputes or controversy or of avoiding having to make decisions about difficult or sensitive drivers. The results of consultation may well lead organisations to decisions which will be unpopular with some of those they consulted, and other groups as well.

Contradictions

It is important that the presentation of the results addresses any differences which exist among consultees, saying who holds different views and why. Those charged with making decisions may then have to make managerial or policy decisions, which may take account of wider drivers or which include value judgements. The most difficult situations arise where choices have to be made, and it is impossible to satisfy all the different views.

> *The Chairman's report on the A259 planning conference sets out nine resolutions and says where these were widely supported, presents dissenting views, who holds them and why. The report was unable to achieve its overall aim of finding a consensus on the route for the road, as the objectives of different groups were completely contradictory. It is arguable that this should have been foreseen and that the conference was therefore a waste of resources. The outcome left the Department of Transport with the same intractable problem which it had at the beginning.*

The document produced by the Arts Council of Wales acknowledges the tensions between community and voluntary arts, and shows value and respect for both traditions. It is not a bland report. In practice, the availability of new sources of funding means that both groups can hope to gain. The starkest of choices will not be necessary, unlike in the Northern Ireland case, where resources are not available to provide the range of stated preferences.

Unexpected results

Unexpected results can be a sign of a successful consultation. After all, there is limited value in a consultation which produces only a familiar response.

Some consultation methods, particularly the deliberative methods, encourage new ideas to emerge and allow them to be explored. But unexpected or negative responses can emerge with other methods. An extreme example would be the rejection of all the presented options, and, possibly, the suggestion of new options which the organisation is unable to provide. The case studies do not include any examples of this and it should be rare in well planned exercises. However, if it does occur, it will require a fundamental re-thinking of the consultation exercise and the drivers it seeks to explore.

Disputed results

Well planned and managed exercises, which have included valid and transparent methods of processing the results, stand the greatest chance of finding their conclusions widely accepted. However, the results may still be disputed by different groups for various reasons:

- groups with strong, vested interests or positions which they feel to be threatened may seek to influence decisions by undermining the authority of the process;
- groups or individuals become fully aware of the significance of an exercise too late in the process, and are worried about their failure to participate fully;
- people are concerned about the implications of likely decisions for them individually or their organisations.

The situation will be particularly difficult if those taking any of these positions are those who are charged with making decisions. There were concerns in a number of case studies that elected representatives, for example, found an alternative source of constituents' views to be threatening. In extreme cases, it may not be possible to overcome such hurdles.

Absence of decisions and outcomes

A common weakness is for consultations to end without decisions and therefore without clear outcomes. By far the best way to deal with this is to set targets, tasks and timescales from the start. But it is possible that despite good intentions at the start, the organisation finds it very difficult to make decisions and to pursue outcomes.

External organisations with decision-making powers

This was one particular cause of a lack of outcome which may well be built in to the consultation process itself. This is when the end of the consultation entails sending the results to a different and superior organisation over which there is no control.

If this process is made explicit at the beginning of the consultation, it is wise to reconsider embarking on the consultation in the first place. However well it is carried out, the risk that a silent ending will negate the good process is too great.

> *The report from the A259 planning conference was sent to the Secretary of State for Transport. No direct outcome can been attributed to the report. The Science Museum's consensus conference was not part of any institutional framework which was committed to using its report in policy discussions.*
>
> *The Housing Corporation had already devised its new policy when the consultation took place. As a result, some consultees saw the exercise as having no real outcome.*

Internal divisions of responsibility and power

A second and similar driver is if the end of the consultation involves internal referral of the results within the commissioning organisation. Both specialisations and power levels can cause this. For example, a research team may have the skills to carry out a consultation, and may then feed the results in to a policy team. Or staff may complete a consultation, and pass the results on to the Board or Committee for decision. There are more possibilities of negotiation over these internal difficulties than where the decision-making body is a different organisation.

Relevance of decisions and outcomes

The decisions and the outcomes must be relevant to all target audiences. Broadly this means to the participants, the wider target population of consultees, and to those who are responsible for implementing the policy, plan or service about which the organisation consulted. The most effective way of ensuring this is to continue to involve some of each of these groups in the process of producing decisions and deciding outcomes.

Communication of decisions made to different audiences

Once decisions have been made and the pattern of outcomes therefore prescribed, it is important to include in this communication to all relevant audiences. Within the commissioning organisation there may be varying degrees of knowledge about what has come out of the consultation. But externally there may be none. It is therefore quite possible for an effective decision and outcome process to go hand in hand with a public perception that nothing has resulted from the consultation.

Part Two

Case Studies

CASE STUDY ONE

The Arts Council of Wales: Participation in Arts Activity

ORIGINS AND OBJECTIVES

The subject of this case study is a consultation exercise by the Arts Council of Wales (ACW) to establish a policy for increasing the number of people taking part in the arts. The ACW set up a working group to develop the policy. The group did this using a series of meetings to consult arts organisations.

The group began its work in July 1995 and published its consultative paper *Taking Part: developing participation in arts activity in Wales* in June 1996. The document was widely circulated and responses invited.

Origins of the consultation

Arts Council of Wales

The Arts Council of Wales was formed in April 1994, when it took over the responsibilities previously held by the Welsh Arts Council and the regional arts associations in Wales. It became a separate and autonomous organisation from the old Arts Council of Great Britain, and is a non-departmental public body (NDPB) reporting to the Welsh Office. This reorganisation gave ACW the opportunity, and necessity, to review its roles and operation.

One of ACW's four aims is 'to develop and improve the accessibility of the arts to the public'. This includes 'promoting practical participation in the arts through local, amateur and community arts activity'.

The new ACW had no corporate policy for the fulfilment of these objectives. 'Policies relating to practical participation in the arts, including amateur and community arts' are identified as an area for review in the Council's Corporate Plan for 1996–1999. One of the goals of the Council during this period is to raise 'a national debate about achieving a significant increase in access and participation'.

The new organisation consciously set out to adopt a different way of working from its predecessor, and to have rather different relationships with the organisations with whom it works. Partnership has become more important as changes in remit and funding mean ACW has less potential for achieving its aims solely through its own efforts. At the same time, however, ACW officers perceive an increase in the time they spend monitoring and appraising arts organisations funded by the Council, and they fear that this gives them less time for keeping in touch with others or for development work.

This is the background against which the Council published its Code of Best Practice in May 1995. This document stresses openness and accountability. The Corporate Plan also emphasises the importance of relationships with partner arts organisations, other funders and the public, and hence the importance of ACW's accountability and role as advocate. It makes specific commitments to involve others in the corporate planning process, to hold discussions with local authorities and others and generally to create opportunities for debate and involvement in planning.

Funding for the arts

The availability and allocation of funding for the arts forms an important part of the background to this consultation. Potential changes in funding arrangements, which became known to arts organisations as the consultation progressed, were also important in shaping the consultation and people's reactions to it.

ACW is in receipt of standstill funding from the Welsh Office. The corporate plan makes plain the detrimental impact this must have on the organisations funded by ACW, and on the Council itself. It includes commitments to maintain the overall budget for recurrent grants at the 1995/6 cash level (although not grants to individual organisations) and to increase expenditure on some strategic initiatives and schemes, while reducing expenditure on other schemes.

Thus the prospects for increasing financial support for activities which encourage participation, which had always received a very small part of the budget, did not look promising. At the same time there was concern about the impact of local government reorganisation in Wales on financial support for arts organisations.

The National Lottery had already become a significant source of new funding for capital projects. The result of this was likely to be an increase in demand for revenue funding (for running costs and activities) to enable the potential to be realised. The experience of running the lottery capital funding scheme had led ACW to appreciate more fully the volume of voluntary and community arts activity taking place and made the need for a policy more pressing. A policy should both encourage support for participation by other organisations and funders, and guide ACW in its own funding decisions.

It became clear as the consultation progressed that forthcoming changes in the rules governing the spending of lottery funds would have a direct bearing on the ability to resource the implementation of a policy on participation. Directions issued by the Secretary of State for National Heritage on 1 April 1996 encouraged the Arts Councils to use lottery funds for revenue-only grants for the purpose of facilitating access to and participation in the arts.

There followed a consultation on how these directions should be implemented. Responses to this were due by July 30, so ACW extended the deadline for responses to its published policy on participation by three weeks to have the same closing date. The two policies came, by this stage, to be closely associated.

Different traditions in the arts

From the beginning, ACW and others were acutely aware of the need to manage the long established tensions between the advocates of voluntary arts and community arts respectively. There is competition between these two approaches, neither of which have traditionally received much recognition or resources from Arts Councils, and dealing with this was a challenge for all involved in the consultation process.

The published consultation paper addresses the issue early on when it gives the following definitions:

- 'Voluntary arts' means amateur arts, youth arts, traditional arts, the arts activity of cultural, religious and community groups. Voluntary arts organisations sometimes call on professional resources to augment their activity.
- 'Community arts' means arts professionals creating opportunities for people to develop skills, and to explore and communicate ideas through active participation in the arts.

Objectives

The objective of the exercise was to establish a national policy framework for increasing the number of people taking part in the arts in Wales. The working group was to produce a consultation paper on the options for ACW to realise the objective of increasing practical participation.

In doing this work, ACW wanted to draw on as wide a base of knowledge and experience as possible. This would produce a document which would be more appropriate and of better quality than something they would produce on their own. Such an approach would also secure the understanding, support and sympathy of those whose involvement would be essential to make a policy successful in action.

The consultation process

The methods

The decision to set up a working group of ACW officers and to use this as a vehicle for consultation with others was an obvious choice to ACW. The project was led by the Director of Policy and Planning at ACW, who also chaired the group and played a major part in drafting the paper. He was also responsible for an important decision to involve one person from outside the ACW staff in the group.

Little consideration was given to the possibility of using other methods, apart from thinking briefly about carrying out a survey of people's patterns and levels of participation. They decided this was not necessary at this stage. They did not need a map of activity, which a survey could produce, but access to the knowledge, views and support of arts organisations, in order to create a policy framework.

Apart from the broad approach described, the working group had no detailed plan or fixed timetable as it began its work. The main methods were:

- Inviting representatives of different arts organisations to meetings of the group to discuss the subject.
- Bringing all these representatives together for a further meeting to discuss an early draft.

- Agreeing to a proposal from the Voluntary Arts Network that the Network should convene a seminar for organisations in the voluntary arts to discuss the draft.
- Discussing the issues with chief officers of Welsh local authorities at a meeting with them.
- In between these activities, early meetings of the group discussed issues, concepts and definitions. They went on to produce drafts of sections of the paper for further discussion.
- The publication of the document for wider consultation with arts organisations, local authorities and other national and local bodies in June 1996.

The activities

The working group

Membership

Membership of the group was made up of six officers of ACW and one other, the director of Voluntary Arts Network (VAN), a UK-wide organisation with its office in Cardiff. The ACW officers included the Lottery Director, several arts form officers, one with a responsibility for equal opportunities and the Director of Policy and Planning who chaired the group.

The Director of VAN was invited to make up for the ACW staff's relative lack of knowledge about the voluntary or amateur arts. Staff were aware of gaps in their own knowledge as well as the need to canvass a wide range of views. VAN was expected to make up this deficit, particularly as its director was known to have a considerable knowledge not only of his organisation's membership, but of the policy issues affecting them across the UK.

The VAN presence caused some disquiet among some representatives of the community arts, who felt that VAN, as an organisation funded by ACW, should be in the same position as them – representing interests to the panel – and not being a member of it. However, there is no single national body which represents all community arts organisations which could have been invited to balance VAN's presence. Further, for ACW to invite more than one outsider to join the group might have been too big a step for it to take at this early stage in its development of consultation processes.

Meetings

The group's first meeting was in July 1995. There were a further seven meetings before the draft for consultation was launched in June 1996. At the first meeting it was thought that 'subject to progress with discussions' they would issue a public consultation paper in the Autumn. In fact, it took longer than this, both to clarify the group's own thinking about participation and to consult others. For example, early meetings considered the scope of the document and the extent to which it should extend beyond action for ACW itself. The January meeting considered the pre-draft outline of the document, which defined the issues to be covered, and set the programme for production.

The meetings were chaired and minuted by the Director, who also produced position papers for discussion and, as things progressed, the drafts of what would become the policy document. It was pointed out by one or two members of the group that having the same person chair and minute the meetings inevitably slowed them down. But they also recognised that the relatively slow pace helped to keep everyone on board. There was wide appreciation of the skill of the chair and the care that he took to discuss and explore all the issues, to make sure all views were aired and that compromises, where necessary, were made openly. The process could have been quicker, but at the cost of losing some involvement and support.

Invitations to attend the group's meetings

Most of the 12 or so organisations who were invited were umbrella groups, who presented ACW with a ready-made framework of representatives to consult. There were a few outside this framework, including Arts Care, which works with disabled people, and the National Eisteddfod. The aim was to hear a wide range of views, while recognising that they could not hope to get a comprehensive picture.

The knowledge of officers was very important in deciding who to invite. They knew most of the individuals and the sort of perspective they would bring. They were conscious of who would be most useful, and also of who needed to be heard in order to give the group as representative a picture as possible.

The procedure was to invite two or three people to a part of each meeting. There was general agreement amongst both members of the group and those who were invited that this process was not well handled. The working group was keen to hear the perspectives of those who came and therefore did not set an agenda or define the issues for discussion. Because their role was not precisely specified, the visitors arrived with a range of expectations, including that they would be joining the working group, and that they would be attending with or without others. Most were surprised by the formality of the encounter, and by the expectation that they would make a presentation of their organisation's views.

Further, their status as a representative was not clear to all those being consulted. While some felt comfortable in representing their organisation's views on this issue, others thought they should have had the opportunity to carry out their own internal consultation, on pre-defined questions, if their views were to be claimed as representative.

Invitations were generally perceived as a recognition of importance and expertise, and were taken as a sign of approval by some smaller organisations. Others guessed that they were invited because ACW knew they would not be 'difficult'.

Encouraging participation in the arts is central to the work of these organisations. Not surprisingly, those who went to the meetings sought to do more than contribute to the overall policy development and set out to advocate for particular interests. These included: the support of community or voluntary arts perspectives and/or their own art form; raising the profile of their own organisation and establishing its credibility; and advocating the role of umbrella organisations in the administration of lottery funds.

While there was general agreement that the contribution expected from those being consulted was unclear, the reactions to the actual experience varied. Some felt it was the approach least likely to get anything useful out of them, and came away feeling demoralised. The experience was likened to 'being interviewed', 'confronting head table', 'naughty schoolchildren being called to the headmaster's study' and 'making statements from the dock'.

Despite this, others felt able to deal with the situation, thought they had acquitted themselves well and been able to convey their views. One factor in this appears to be the individual's experience and previous contact with ACW. It was easier where the relationship was established and positive. But all those who came were more conscious than ACW was of its role as a key funder of their work, and this made them feel rather more vulnerable than ACW may have realised.

It was also clear that those who attended would have been considerably more negative about the experience if they had not later seen that their contribution had made a difference to the product. They also noted that the actual encounter was handled with care and courtesy by the chair and the members of the group. There were many tributes to this.

Members of the group came to recognise the faults in the process and regretted the difficult situation they had created, but most felt that they had received a great deal of useful information from the meetings. Indeed, this was generally thought to be the most useful element of the whole consultation process, as it was possible to explore issues in greater depth in such meetings than is possible in a larger group.

Meeting of all those invited to the working group

All those who had been invited to meetings of the working group were brought together to comment on a draft of the consultation document. For ACW, this was a useful meeting. The organisers made efforts to allow everyone the opportunity to speak and to make sure the meeting was not dominated by a few.

On the whole, the participants recognised this and found the meeting was a positive experience. The number of people there meant it felt more comfortable than attending a working group meeting alone or with one or two others. This occasion was described as 'more of a consultation, less of an interview', although differing levels of vulnerability and adversarial behaviour were still described.

The nature of the document being discussed at this meeting clearly contributed to people's positive reactions to the process. They could see that they had already had an impact on it. While it was helpful to have a fairly complete draft to discuss, and to receive this well in advance, there was a sense that it was still open to change.

Consultative seminar for voluntary arts umbrella organisations

This was suggested and organised by VAN, who felt that such a meeting would be the only way to elicit the views of their diffuse and mixed sector. Those who attended this Saturday meeting were sent briefings in advance by VAN, and on the day they were given the opportunity to comment in detail as they were taken through the draft consultation document page by page.

The draft they were considering opened new opportunities for the sort of organisations present, so they were likely to be well disposed to it. But other factors also contributed to the success of the meeting: the clarity and honesty of the draft were appreciated, and the presence of the Chair of the working group and of ACW's Lottery Director indicated that ACW was taking the consultation process seriously.

This meeting was the only part of the whole consultation process to be formally evaluated. Fifteen of the 19 delegates completed the evaluation forms and all reported the meeting as useful or very worthwhile.

Meeting with local authority officers

Local authority officers were asked for comments on the draft as part of a larger meeting to discuss the relationship between ACW and local authorities. This was not satisfactory and produced nothing useful, probably because it was a relatively small part of a large agenda. The reorganisation of local government going through at the time made it more difficult for officers to focus on what was, at that time, a fairly remote policy issue for the future.

Publication of the consultative document

Taking Part was published as a consultative document in June 1996. ACW received about 90 responses. The responses were generally supportive, with some helpful comments and suggestions, most of them of fairly minor importance. ACW recognised that it is usual in such situations for many respondents to use the opportunity to promote the interests of their own organisation. Such an exercise tends to produce comments on practical issues, and not to point the way forward on policy development. No substantial changes were made to the document at this stage.

Managing the consultation process

The management structure was simple. The key role was that of the director who led and managed the project. He was the direct link into the senior management of ACW.

The decision to carry out the consultation had come from a Council decision and was tied into the corporate plan. Thus, the Council's continuing interest and support is expected, especially because of the implications for lottery funding. The Council was consulted on the draft in March 1996 before its publication and approved the final version of the policy and the first actions to implement it in October 1996.

Resources

No new or specific resources were made available for the consultation exercise. The major demand on resources was the considerable commitment of staff time on top of their existing workload.

Meetings of the working group, of which there were about ten in total, lasted about two hours. The Chair estimated that he spent about four hours per meeting in preparation. Once they moved into the drafting phase, between January and March, this rose to about one day a week. Other members of the group were also expected to do certain preparatory tasks outside the meetings and this may have amounted to about six or seven hours for each person. The Chair's administrative assistant was responsible for the administrative work involved.

VAN was paid for the costs incurred in organising the seminar (around £500), but not for the time spent doing this or taking part in the working group. VAN saw the subject of the consultation as central to its role and objectives and so was prepared to contribute time free of charge. The director felt that the nature of the process meant his time was not being wasted.

Most of those who were consulted shared this view. The amount of time they spent depended on their expectations and thus on the amount of preparation and consultation they did beforehand. There was some, but only a little, discontent that their time and contribution were not recognised in financial terms. However, others appreciated the fact that the process required only a small amount of time from them, and made no demands in terms of papers or the preparation of written information. Again, people could see that their involvement had an impact, and this contributed significantly to their conclusion that the time had been well spent.

The impact of the process on its output

There was unanimous agreement that the consultation document was significantly different from, and much better than, the version that would have been produced if there had been no consultation. All those involved could see evidence of their contributions.

The document is based on a wider view of arts activity than those traditionally known to or funded by ACW. It is wider in scope and more radical. People recognise that some issues, such as the importance of training and the role of the networks, would have been misunderstood or understated without the consultation process.

For the time being, at least, the tension between the voluntary and community arts has been well handled. The document acknowledges the tensions and shows value and respect for both traditions. It favours neither but is not bland; it is something which elicits support. Avoiding blandness is important, but difficult, for the outputs of consultation. This one was variously described as 'touching chords', 'telling it how it is' and managing to make people feel 'optimistic if not inspired'.

There is a sense of involvement with the document amongst those who were consulted. It has been taken as evidence of a change in ACW. ACW had used its status as a new organisation to stress that it wished to move ahead and make changes. Although there is, naturally enough, still cynicism or scepticism about how real such change is and the extent of its impact, the document is also a source of positive attitudes.

Members of the working group themselves developed their understanding and changed their views as the work progressed. The fact that participation was being discussed and consulted upon was felt to be a radical departure for ACW. Some members admitted that they found themselves resisting too much change, and were surprised at this reaction, but that their opinions changed as time went on.

All aspects of the consultation process contributed to this development of ideas: the discussions in the working group; the presence of VAN; the two larger consultative meetings. Of undoubted importance was the skill and commitment of those involved. The skill of the Chair has already been mentioned. It was widely recognised that his approach convinced participants, as far as it is ever possible to do so, that this was a genuine consultation exercise.

The presence of an outsider in the group, especially an individual who was able to cope with that potentially difficult role, and to challenge ideas, present new information and arguments and negotiate, was an important catalyst. The group as a whole was able to produce the document it did because it took the time and patience to listen.

IMPACT

Acting on the output of the exercise

The final version of the policy document was decided and adopted by the Council in October 1996. The initiative to develop a policy on participation in the arts was part of the policy-making framework of ACW from its inception. It was designated as a priority in the corporate plan. The responsibility for it was taken by an assistant director. All of these structural factors made it more likely that the policy would be followed by action.

Direct impact

As we have seen above, the draft consultation document was generally well received. It has raised hopes and expectations, but the actual impact of the policy will take some years to be felt. It is hoped that a concern with participation in the arts will be woven into the work of the ACW for the next few years, stimulated both by the consultation process and resulting policy, and by the availability of lottery funding.

During 1996 the Council discussed a wide-ranging restructuring of its operations, affecting both staffing and its committee and advisory structures. One of its objectives was to establish a structure which would help to deliver access policies such as *Taking Part* more effectively. One outcome has been the decision to create a new senior post of Director of Access and Participation, heading a new department.

ACW went out to consultation in January 1997 on proposals for major changes to its committee and advisory system. The restructuring process has not been a direct result of the *Taking Part* process, but has been informed by it.

It is the nature of the participation policy that it involves working with other organisations. The longer term impact will therefore depend in part on the success of ACW in forming relationships with local authorities, for example, and influencing them to develop strategies for the arts which include significant elements of participation. Much will also depend on the availability of lottery funding for encouraging such policy development at local level, and for making it more feasible to implement them. All concerned recognise the need for significant resources if significant change is to take place.

The policy would certainly have a less visible impact without lottery funding. Over the next few years it may appear that the lottery is solely responsible for changes in funding and therefore for new activities and approaches. However, many of those involved believe that the policy will provide a vital and strategic basis for the distribution of lottery funds. It is intended that the new lottery guidelines, when published, will cross-refer to the policy on participation. It is expected that ACW will be better prepared than other arts councils to administer any new sources of revenue funding, and to maximise their impact.

The long-term, and overall, hope is for more opportunity and choice for all those wishing to take part in the arts in Wales. The representatives of the organisations involved in the consultation express a hope for changed attitudes and for a greater status for such activities. There is a sense of anticipation and optimism while, at the same time and understandably, they are reserving judgement to see if the resources, and the will, to make changes are forthcoming.

Indirect and unintended impact

Within the Arts Council of Wales

Those involved in the process at ACW have greater confidence in the document because of the consultation. This was the first major consultation on this issue and the fact that it worked well has had a wider impact on the organisation. It helped to pave the way for the extensive consultation which ACW subsequently undertook on the new lottery 'Arts for All' guidelines and contributed to the thinking that went into it.

Awareness of participation in the arts has developed beyond those directly involved in the consultation exercise. Some of those in closest contact with the process became informal advocates for a radical departure in policy and this has started to influence their colleagues. The project also provided an important context for discussions about the lottery and helped to develop thinking in that area.

Further, the experience of carrying out this consultation enabled ACW to learn more about this way of working. Although a low key exercise, it was described by one as 'ground breaking' and is more widely recognised as likely to influence the way ACW approaches future issues. Those involved felt that the process had helped ACW to form some new or stronger partnerships which would contribute to a greater trust and continuing dialogue on this and other issues. Not least, they realised that they could be surprised and influenced by what they heard.

On a more cautious note, it was also recognised that care will be needed in making decisions about which issues will and will not involve consultation. Both ACW and those who observe it are pleased with the indications that the organisation is becoming more open and accountable. However, while expectations are inevitably raised amongst those with a keen interest in the organisation and its work, managers have become aware of the dangers of falling into the time-consuming consultative mode on a wide range of issues at all levels.

Outside the Arts Council of Wales

There are indications that the consultation process has made a contribution to a shift in attitudes towards ACW. Amongst arts organisations in Wales, it was pleasing to see ACW move ahead of the other arts councils by taking this initiative on participation. It is expected that this document will enable positive change to happen, and that these things would not happen without ACW. ACW has been seen to be open and responsive and, as a result, appears rather less remote.

Enthusiasm and some new skills have been developed amongst those new to the consultation process, especially those who organised the consultative seminar for voluntary arts groups. Some have subsequently joined other committees or working groups. It was pointed out that, in this way, the quality of debate and process of consultation slowly improves.

For some of the smaller and less visible organisations, taking part in the process was experienced as a recognition of their contribution and value. They felt their relationship with other groups to change, and more networking has followed.

Future work

ACW is aware that its consultation has not been successful in gathering the views of local authorities or building relationships with them. A further meeting with local authority officers is planned, in the hope of strengthening the relationship.

Assessment

The success of the project

This was a successful consultation process. Although the impact cannot be known as yet, the process itself has produced a policy which appears to have support across a wide range of interest groups. Substantial restructuring of ACW in order (partly) to implement the policy was being discussed. New funding is becoming available. All of this suggests that the policy has a good chance of producing increased and improved opportunities to participate in the arts.

This was a fairly modest and low key consultation exercise, and this is a partial explanation for its success. Resources were not available for anything on a larger scale, but, in fact, the exercise developed by ACW was appropriate for an organisation newly created from an old structure which had seemed remote and secretive to many. The process gave a clear signal that this was a different way of working, but did not create any more potential pitfalls for itself than were necessary. Those outside ACW who observed and took part in the process recognised the new approach. Their scepticism was not lost, but they were also constructive and receptive to signs of change.

As the consultation proceeded, it became clear that there were to be changes in the rules governing lottery funding, and that these would create new opportunities. This was a very important development as it made all those being consulted feel there was a much greater possibility of the sort of real change which they would welcome. They became more keen to take part and the whole exercise became inextricably associated in many minds with the possibility of new funding for arts organisations.

The management of the process was linked to the policy-making and management structures of ACW at the highest level. The seniority of the staff involved meant that ACW was seen to be taking the exercise seriously. The working group, despite the problems in the consultation process with representatives, generally impressed people with its willingness to listen. The group produced drafts which had clearly been influenced by what they heard, key evidence that the process was a genuine one.

Research methods

We interviewed all members of the working group and four of those who were consulted, as representatives of their organisations, by the group and who attended one or both of the subsequent consultative events. All interviews were one-to-one, and face-to-face. We also studied documents associated with the project.

The fieldwork took place in the summer of 1996, before the closing date for responses to the consultative document. Information about the outcome of the exercise has been obtained through telephone conversations and correspondence with the Chair of the group.

Commentary

Overview

The Arts Council of Wales (ACW) consultation was concerned with developing a policy for increasing the number of people taking part in the arts.

The key points on which we comment are:

- Consultees could see the prospect of beneficial outcomes to the process and this helped to avoid some of the tension that might have made it less constructive.
- The consultation was carried out on a modest scale, which was appropriate for the organisation's traditions and resources.
- ACW adopted an approach which showed consultees that their influence was being felt, while the process was still going on.
- The different consultative methods complemented one another.
- The consultation was led by a senior officer and was linked directly to the corporate planning and policy-making process. This helped to ensure its impact.

Positive outcomes

The possibility of increased funding for the organisations who were asked to take part undoubtedly increased their willingness to contribute constructively to the process. It also meant that organisations with different priorities and philosophies were more able to concentrate on the overall aim of the consultation and less likely to focus only on asserting their own claims to funding over those of others.

The prospect of additional funding (rather than a redistribution of existing resources) reduced the vulnerability experienced by organisations being asked to give their views to a major funder of their work.

A modest exercise

It would have been possible for ACW to take a more ambitious approach to this issue, had resources been available. However, the chosen approach was appropriate for an organisation which had only recently been established in its current form and which was developing a more open and participative style of working. To do more would have exposed ACW to greater risk of failure and disillusionment amongst the keenly interested observers. An unsuccessful project at this stage and on this issue might have inflicted considerable damage on relationships and ACW's credibility.

Choice of methods

While the exercise was modest in scale, it allowed consultees to see that their influence was being felt. Successive drafts showed evidence that new ideas and suggestions were being heeded. The circulation of a consultation document came after more detailed discussions, not before or instead of, as is often the case. These discussions were held with one organisation at a time, or with small groups. Efforts were made to allow people with different levels of experience of such processes to make equal contributions.

Leadership and decision-making

The exercise was led by a director of ACW, who was very actively and visibly involved. This emphasised that it was being taken seriously by the organisation. It was established from the beginning that it would feed in directly to the Council's planning and decision-making, and this was an important factor in making sure that the results would be considered and decisions would be made.

CASE STUDY TWO

The Benefits Agency 1995 National Customer Survey

INTRODUCTION

The Benefits Agency (BA) was established in 1991 as a Next Steps Agency in the Department of Social Security, with responsibility for a wide range of social security benefits. The Agency's structure includes four Benefit Directorates, which deal with centrally administered benefits, including Child Benefit, Disability Benefits, Family Credit and Retirement Pension, and 13 Area Directorates who manage a nationwide network of district and local offices which deal with locally administered benefits such as Income Support and the Social Fund.

From its inception the Agency instituted a programme of activity aimed at improving customer service, one element of which was a national survey of benefit claimants using a broad range of Agency services. The National Customer Survey (NCS) began in 1991, and the latest survey was published in 1996.

The survey has contributed to a number of specific developments/improvements in customer service at different times, and it has also informed the selection of Agency commitments in the BA Customer Charter.

The methodology involved in large-scale customer satisfaction survey was reviewed by the Agency at the end of 1996, and NCS is currently suspended whilst its role is under review.

ORIGINS AND OBJECTIVES

Origins

The Benefits Agency's focus on improvement of its services was an integral part of the launch of the Agency itself in 1991. Customer service was actively promoted within the Agency by its first Chief Executive, and was closely associated with the Citizen's Charter initiative, also launched in 1991. Although there had been work done to improve customer service prior to the establishment of the Agency, customer service development was afforded a much higher profile in the newly-formed Agency. NCS was an important element in this enhanced approach to customer service.

Objectives

The main objective of NCS is to provide information on the views of Agency clients about the services provided by both the Benefit Directorates and the district and local offices, in order to enable BA central management to take these into account in its decisions on service development and improvement.

Because establishment of a national survey was one element in the development of customer service throughout the Agency, NCS is not presented by the Agency as a discrete initiative with a separate aim. At the same time as producing NCS, the central Agency also provided guidance to district and local offices on the conduct of customer surveys and on good practice in research. This parallel provision of enabling materials had the aim of supporting the customer service development on a local basis.

The consultation process

Methods

NCS was only one of the methods selected by the Agency to help develop and improve customer service. Other methods which the Agency has developed include a variety of meetings with interest groups and voluntary organisations at both national and local levels, and a National Conference held annually. These consultation methods are mostly participative.

NCS itself is a large-scale questionnaire survey, involving interviews with a sample of around 3,500 Agency clients on a wide range of aspects of the services they receive. The interviews are analysed to produce indications of customer views on services which are statistically reliable.

An annual satisfaction survey as a method brings certain specific benefits which other methods may not – in particular statistical reliability, and year-on-year comparisons capable of revealing trends and changes. NCS also provided the Agency with measures of customer satisfaction which could be published as indicators of overall patterns in service improvement. Qualitative studies of customer views and priorities were used before the first survey, to help shape the questions to be asked.

NCS activities

The survey discussed in this case study was carried out in 1995, and published in 1996. In the past the survey was the responsibility within the Agency of a staff member attached to the Customer Relations Team (CRT) within the (former) Customer Services Branch (CSB). Since this staff member left the Agency, the survey has been allocated as a project.

The survey was commissioned annually by the Agency, until 1995, from the Department of Social Security's Social Research Branch (SRB), Analytical Service Division (ASD). ASD's general role was to ensure that the Agency's information needs were met, and to ensure that the methods were reliable. Specifically, ASD was responsible for the preparation of the draft specification and timetable, selection of the contractors, and quality control of the survey. CRT's responsibilities were to ensure that the survey was published to schedule and distributed.

Work on the 1995 survey began in February 1995, with meetings between ASD and CRT. ASD prepared a draft tender specification and timetable, and after discussions with CRT put it out to tender. From issue of the tender to selection of a research organisation to carry out the survey took about four weeks. The contract was awarded to a market research company who have won it for every survey since 1992. The contractors drafted the questionnaire, and sent it to ASD, who circulated it more widely within the central organisation to ensure that information needs would be met. ASD also ensured that the survey was methodologically sound.

Although the core of the survey needs to remain the same to enable year-on-year comparisons, one of ASD's tasks was to ensure that additional questions and other information required by the survey's other internal policy customers were included. ASD therefore consulted with BA Central Services and the Branches at this stage. These parts of the Agency are themselves in touch with lobbying groups, have their own consultation mechanisms, and are able to input to the survey in part on the basis of these contacts.

By 1995 the contractors' involvement had become a repeat process which was described by Agency staff as routine. The survey began in April, and the final report was submitted in December/January 1996. ASD was responsible for dealing with problems arising in the fieldwork – in particular any complaints from respondents, which tend to go in the first instance to local offices. However, in practice there are only ever one or two complaints.

Publication took a few weeks, in part because it was a repeat process. Once the survey had been produced, CRT took responsibility for dissemination. 200 copies of the full report, and 400 of the Executive Summary were produced. The Executive Summary was distributed free of charge, and the full survey, also free, was sent to a small number of outlets only, although it was made available on request. At this stage, ASD's role was to respond to requests from policy customers for more detailed information on specific aspects of the survey.

Managing the process

The management of the process was shared between CRT and ASD – each having a different role. The coordination of their responsibilities took place through meetings and circulation of drafts.

A CRT team member responsible for liaison with the representatives of national customer organisations project-managed the process overall, and the addition of an Executive Summary was the CRT project manager's suggestion. ASD managed the survey contract – its design, time and costs. ASD also organised a presentation by the contractors to Agency staff to provide early feedback on the findings. The timescale was described by CRT as tight towards the end.

Resources

The total cost of the 1995 NCS was approximately £200,000, excluding staff resources from the Agency and from ASD.

Local office surveys

Local offices were actively encouraged to develop their own customer surveys, and in October 1992 the Agency produced a guidance package consisting of a disc and questionnaires, *A Guide to Customer Opinion Sampling*, and *Research, A Good Practice Guide*, together with sample questionnaires and other materials, and sample letters in a range of languages.

The Leeds office

This local office has a broad approach to customer service which includes a proactive aspect, defining the service as both that which clients receive when they call at or telephone the office, and as the active taking of information out to the customers. Complaints monitoring is therefore an aspect of customer service at the local level, and in the past included local surgeries, advice points, and talks to groups of users.

At the local level, NCS was an important part of customer service when the Agency was first set up. It was one of the key activities, and with the Agency's one shop initiatives it assumed even greater importance. The Secretary of State's targets for performance, which are in part derived from NCS, are displayed in the waiting room alongside the local office's performance achievements. The early surveys after the creation of the Agency had some influence – for example showing that customers were concerned about privacy.

Local surveys were described as less important in the Agency's broad approach to service improvement, tending to focus on the details of premises and specific aspects of services. There were in fact local customer surveys before the creation of the Agency – for example, measuring caller waiting times.

Resources are a persistent difficulty for local survey work, which is time-consuming. Staff felt that it was difficult and time-consuming to achieve an acceptable rate of return, at around 60 per cent, after two reminders. The last survey, scheduled for the end of 1995, was not undertaken until February 1996.

Recently, a period of substantial organisational change has meant that there have necessarily been a number of customer service managers, and staffing resources have made it difficult to undertake survey work.

The Winchester office

The organisation of the Winchester office and the other local offices within the district is focused on areas of work – for example Income Support, Retirement Pension, and so on – and customer work is additional – described as 'peripheral' – to these 'core' activities in the district structure. However, in Winchester itself, the customer service manager is also the benefits manager, and this helps to ensure that customer service is not sidelined.

Each local office gets a copy of the Executive Summary, and one full copy goes to the District. By the time NCS appeared, the content of the results was already known, and the problems which NCS highlighted described as obvious – waiting times, accuracy, getting through on the telephone.

NCS is further described as very general. It has been used locally, for example, when the Citizens Advice Bureau or the Social Services Department have made critical comments or confronted the Agency locally, to answer challenging questions with statistically reliable responses to complaints based on anecdotes. The Chief Executive of the Agency also meets these organisations at a national level and the survey is also useful for this. There is however no real sustained local use for it, although it can confirm generalisations, and can also provide a benchmark for local surveys.

With an area of control covering one office only, local information about the customers of that office is the most important need, and NCS cannot meet this. The needs of local customers may well overlap with NCS, but these will also be different in some ways. Its limitations for customer work in the Winchester office also arise from the office's having a different customer base from the national average. These differences involve different customer needs: for example, there are very few pensioner claims for income support, because of high rates of good occupational pensions locally; there are only small numbers of ethnic minority claimants; and variations in unemployment rates as short-term contracts end means that Job Seeker's Allowance has taken off more quickly than average, despite very low, short-lived unemployment.

Staff felt that a better approach would have been a national survey compiled from local surveys – ie a composite.

There has been considerable customer survey activity done within the (now abolished) Wessex area in the past. Resources for surveys were allocated at the area level, over a long period of time. Research contractors were commissioned to carry out area-wide studies including for benchmarking; customer views by District; and a Winchester local customer services survey.

In the past few years, the local office has also carried out its own surveys – on service quality, on complaints procedures, and on voluntary sector liaison arrangements. Some surveys have revealed other issues, such as the mutual gap of understanding between social workers and Agency staff, arising from the vastly differing caseloads of the two groups. Surveys have therefore proved useful in realising their direct aims, and in enabling other developments to take place.

The Winchester office has also used participative methods – for example, the office involved a local disability group in the various stages of planning access in the new premises, including a site visit, and perusal of plans.

The impact of the process on its output

The annual NCS sought to provide the Agency with statistically reliable information about trends in customer satisfaction over time. The joint approach of CRT and ASD meant that inputs to the process and quality control were both adequate and effective. The care taken over the process of commissioning the work and publishing the results ensured that reliable information was produced on time. Changes required or sought by policy customers have over the years been included. Through these mechanisms the information in the survey report was as relevant to central policy customers as possible, and was at the same time statistically reliable.

The flexibility and variety in local surveys is seen by local Agency staff as a strength, and the capacity to focus on local need and local services is seen as enabling more useful outputs.

The lack of involvement of anyone other than central Agency staff appears to have influenced the degree of confidence and interest in the survey from outside agencies, contributing to a perceived lack of relevance of the survey to customer service.

IMPACT

At the national level

The Agency provided four examples of initiatives which have taken place as a direct result of the findings of NCS since 1991:

1 a lone parents' forum;
2 refurbishment programme to address privacy, access and facilities;
3 a review of complaints procedures;
4 development of a telephone strategy.

In addition, the commitments and service levels specified in the Agency's Customer Charter have been drawn from those aspects of customer service shown by NCS to be important. This included things like a prompt service, helpfulness, privacy, waiting times, and reply times for letters. Finally, NCS is one of the research outputs used in the DSS's research planning round to identify gaps in knowledge and issues which require further study.

Awareness of any impact of the survey was, however, at a low level amongst voluntary organisations. The overall 'customer satisfaction' figure, which is used as a performance indicator and standard in the Agency's Charter, was the only specific impact identified by them.

At the District and local level

Local Agency staff no longer receive a copy of the full survey, and NCS has not played a key role in local customer service work for some years. It has however had a number of practical and general uses – for example to confirm generalisations at a national level, and provide limited benchmarks for local surveys.

Local offices need information on their own clients and not a general national sample. Although they see overlaps with NCS, the differences require local survey work. However, the creation of the Agency, which produced NCS, also produced an impetus to local customer surveys, and local staff see NCS in this sense as one part of a programme of change which had both a local and a national impact.

Local surveys have been influential in shaping local services within the limits permitted by the national nature of the Agency. The Winchester surveys produced specific changes – a new complaints leaflet and procedure, and a guide for voluntary sector agencies on liaison.

Indirect impact

The experience of NCS over the past five years has led the Agency to reflect on the merits of different ways of measuring customer satisfaction. The 1996 survey did not take place, the customer satisfaction survey method has been reviewed, and a commentary by DSS research staff was published in December 1996.

Local use of surveys has prompted considerable reflection on the best approaches to service improvement. The limits to surveys, and to other methods of assessment of customer service, were recognised by local offices interviewed.

Assessment

By the Agency

Customer service work in general has benefited from the information flowing from NCS, but there seems also to be general agreement amongst Agency staff that NCS was of much greater import in its early days than is the case for the 1995 survey. It was a key activity in its early years, providing useful information on aspects of the service nationally which led to specific initiatives, and which guided the Customer Charter.

There is also general agreement in the Agency centrally that NCS is no longer sustainable in its present annual form. CRT staff described NCS as too general, and felt it would be more effective if targeted more on specific client groups. The Agency's other approaches to customer service are described as participative – forums, the annual conference – and are thought likely to be of greater benefit. Although NCS is not seen as expensive in itself, as a year-on-year survey now yielding few new results it is not considered to be a good use of resources.

The main point made by local staff was that the survey's national coverage of a wide range of aspects of its services tends to inhibit its usefulness at a local level, because its results are too general, and do not allow them to focus well enough on specific client groups or issues. One suggestion was that a better approach would be a national survey compiled from local surveys – a composite, rather than a single general survey. However, it was also felt that overall it was better to have carried out NCS than not.

Local staff also commented on the difficulty of effective customer satisfaction measurement, from a practical viewpoint, given the subjective and possibly fluctuating responses likely for service users. But there were also comments that most available methods for developing customer care are problematic, in different ways, and for different reasons. A local office gave mystery shopping as an example of the problems of getting research to serve customer service development. Mystery shopping visits were quarterly by NOP, and the first one showed problems with privacy; the office was modified, and the next one raised the modifications as a problem. The mystery shoppers also criticised the information display and this led to a rolling electronic display being installed, which, because customers only wait a short time, cannot be read in its entirety whilst waiting. This in turn then attracted criticism from mystery shoppers.

Finally, local staff expressed concern about the broader prospects for customer service work within the Agency. In Leeds, the view was that with the change from the Agency's 'core values' to the four 'rights' (see below), there has been a change in emphasis in customer service work. In Winchester, an example was provided of how new claims procedures were preventing specific aspects of good customer service from continuing.

By the voluntary groups

Voluntary groups' views were of two kinds: those specifically about NCS; and those which focused on the problems created for customer service improvement by the structures and situation of the Agency. Most views expressed here were those of the National Association of Citizens Advice Bureaux (NACAB).

Neither voluntary organisation saw NCS as an effective means of improving customer service, and viewed it broadly as a public relations exercise for the Secretary of State's targets for the Agency. The overall satisfaction percentage is thought to be the only figure used by the Agency, which is seen as otherwise not making much of NCS. The Child Poverty Action Group (CPAG) commented that had the satisfaction percentage been small, they might have been more interested. But as the Agency has been improving over the years, the general level of satisfaction has not been of concern to CPAG.

Neither CPAG nor NACAB staff study the survey regularly and in detail, because of its length, because they have difficulty in interpreting the type of information it contains, and because they do not see it as important to either their own work or that of the Agency. The Executive Summary, whilst read, was not seen as informative or useful.

NACAB's view was that at the local level the issues were well-known: access and communication; adequacy of response when things go wrong; and distances to travel. NACAB has provided submissions to the Agency on these issues. NACAB argues for change to the structures of the Agency itself, because it sees one of the key causes of poor quality service as poorly-trained staff, and local 'freedom to manage' as an obstacle to improving this situation. NACAB is also critical of NCS inability to provide comparative data between district offices, which might help identify poor local practice. The remedy NACAB proposes is to combine a measure of local initiative with a coordinated set of national standards, enforced centrally.

Surveys were also thought likely to be more effective if targeted on specific client groups or specific issues, or both, and the 'overall' satisfaction figure was criticised for disguising the differential satisfaction rates for specific groups – for example, in NACAB's view, lone parents have a much lower rate, as do black and minority ethnic clients, and homeless people.

Methods of study of service quality were also an issue. In NACAB's view, the Agency tends to take a quantitative approach, whereas NACAB prefers a mainly qualitative approach. NACAB sees quantitative research as potentially informative if it is well targeted and specific, but sees qualitative study of customer experience as the best way to assess service performance.

NACAB also believes that the Agency's emphasis on what it calls the four 'rights' – 'the right benefit, to the right person, at the right time, every time' – does not favour a continuing priority on customer service. In comparison with these 'hard' rights, other customer service work is likely to prove 'soft'. NACAB sees the ending of specific funding of local surveys, the withdrawal of the benefit buses, the closure of some local offices, and the ending of outreach working with ethnic minority communities as indicators of this.

In NACAB's view, ensuring better and more relevant services requires a body with a large degree of independence, not subject to cost and political pressures, which would carry out such surveys and publish its own results.

Policy and customer service – different positions

There is a clear difference in positions on the relation between government policy and plans, and customer service in the Agency. This is mentioned briefly here to illustrate one source of difficulty public service organisations may experience in their consultation activities.

The voluntary groups argue that NCS and other customer work is ineffectual in the face of political decisions made by government, in particular about resources. A recent example is that the Agency's running costs budgets have been cut as part of the DSS Change Programme, and that this will have a harmful effect on customer service whatever the results of NCS. The Agency is not seen therefore as having the control it needs over its resources, sufficient to ensure continuing improvement in customer service.

Central Agency staff state that the policy environment does not drive NCS, which has been reviewed from a practical standpoint, to ensure that the Agency receives the best information possible to develop its customer work. Moreover, it is not the case that customer care has been damaged by the plans of the last government.

The future

NCS is under review for both the method and the usefulness of satisfaction survey information in guiding customer service development.

Research methods

This study was based on interviews with central and local Agency staff, DSS staff, and staff in two leading voluntary groups. Central Benefits Agency staff interviewed were from the Business Development and Communications and Customer Liaison Branch. DSS staff were from the Social Research Branch, Analytical Services Division. Attempts were made to arrange an interview with a senior staff member in the central Agency but this was not successful. Staff in two local offices – Winchester and Leeds – were interviewed.

Two national voluntary organisations – NACAB and CPAG – were interviewed. A meeting at CPAG of advice workers, with central Agency staff, to discuss the Change Programme, was attended.

Copies of the national survey and of local surveys were provided, as well as other planning documents, and policy documents from the voluntary groups.

Customers completing the satisfaction surveys are not identifiable and there was therefore no attempt to assess their views.

COMMENTARY

Overview

The Benefits Agency National Customer Survey (NCS) was a large-scale annual customer satisfaction survey of the Agency's clients, carried out from 1991 to 1995. The aim of the survey was to provide information on customer views through interviews with a statistically valid sample of clients. NCS began when the Agency was set up, and as an initiative was linked in with the development of the Citizen's Charter, the NCS overall satisfaction target being a performance indicator for the Agency.

The establishment of NCS was accompanied by the central production of materials for district and local offices, to assist them with their own customer work, including surveys. At the time of this study of NCS, the Agency was reviewing its usefulness.

We identify a number of key points which are examined in this commentary:

- large-scale surveys require an appropriate mix of skills and organisation to ensure that they are seen through;
- local surveys are valued;
- national surveys present particular problems of appreciation of their usefulness;
- there are issues of trust and credibility for central government bodies which evaluate their own services.

Skills and organisation

As a product, NCS demanded considerable skills and organisation to ensure its effective completion, and analysis of results on time.

NCS was carried out by a market research company, commissioned by the research branch of the Department of Social Security on the Agency's behalf. The survey was managed within the Agency by the (former) Customer Services Branch. Although the survey was year-on-year, and the questions were therefore for the most part fixed, serious efforts were made to ensure that any particular issues on which the different branches needed information were included if possible. This complex process was steered successfully by the joint efforts of the research and customer sections. The skills deployed were also considerable: research skills, project management, contracting, and networking within the Agency were all essential.

The value of local surveys

Information packages on surveys and research methods produced centrally by the Agency were of great help in developing local skills and activities in customer service improvement. District and local office staff valued their own surveys, and were able to account for their origins and specify a number of outcomes.

Their view was that local customer service requires consultation which is tailored to local circumstances. In particular, the profile of local customer populations is rarely the national average, and local needs may be for study of particular aspects of the service, perhaps not covered by the national service. Local staff saw the ideal national survey as constructed as a composite of local surveys, although we did not pursue in detail how this might be done.

There is here a measure of agreement about the need for a local component, focused on geographical areas small enough to provide results with some usefulness.

Perceptions of the usefulness of national surveys

Staff in the central office of the Agency in Leeds provided examples of specific initiatives which resulted from the findings of NCS since 1991. These included a lone parents' forum, a refurbishment programme to address privacy, access and facilities, a review of complaints procedures, and the impetus to develop a telephone strategy for contact with clients. Additionally, the commitments and service levels specified in the Agency's Customer Charter draw on those aspects of customer service shown by NCS to be important.

Awareness of these specific effects of NCS was notably lacking amongst the voluntary organisations whom we interviewed. The overall customer satisfaction figure in the Agency's Charter was the only specific effect which they could identify. Local office staff interviewed also saw little specific effect, instead acknowledging the general role of NCS as a 'symbol' of the importance of providing a good service.

The contrast between the influences identified by the central office and the absence of awareness of others of these effects is dramatic. Certainly, the voluntary groups paid no attention to NCS, and saw it as of little value, as a public relations exercise.

In our view this contrast has its origins in part in the exclusion of outsiders and District/local office staff from involvement in NCS. Of course, such involvement may not have been possible for organisational reasons when NCS was established, and NCS was, it seems, set up to meet only the information needs of central Agency management. It could therefore be argued that NCS was not the concern of outsiders. But if this were so, then the use of NCS in the public domain would not be appropriate.

We make two suggestions. First, that the precise role of such surveys should be specified – whether they are management tools only, whether they provide public information and so on. Second, that if surveys are to appear in the public domain, then ways of involving key outsiders should be found, if best use is to be made of the results. Indeed, involvement of outsiders in how to approach service quality may lead to the conclusion that a national survey is not the right approach.

District and local office staff valued local services, and the voluntary organisations wanted surveys to be comparative of local or district practices, and to originate in identified service problems, rather than having a general sweep. This preference indicates a further issue – the view that NCS was, in a sense, starting from the wrong point. This too could be best addressed through inclusion.

Credibility and trust

This study reveals how difficult it is for a large Agency to gain the trust and confidence of groups with whom the local offices have routine and close interaction over service provision. The voluntary organisations doubted the motives for the establishment of NCS, and saw it as being of little use. Alternative proposals were for an independent body to carry out such studies of customer service, and for an approach based on identified problems in service delivery. Although real improvements in customer service are freely acknowledged, the role of NCS in this is greeted with scepticism.

The relation of customer service to policy complicates this further. The division of responsibilities between the Department and the Agency places customer service within the Agency's orbit, and not therefore influenced by policy. This position was put emphatically in writing by central Agency staff in Leeds, and is of course inherent in the departmental-agency arrangements which characterise much of practical public service delivery.

However, the reality is thought to be somewhat different by the voluntary organisations and (privately) by some of the Agency staff interviewed. In a sense the details of this, both of the issue and of who will be proved right, is irrelevant. It seems to us that the problem is inherent in the politics of the structures set up in the early 1990s, and is not therefore amenable to remedy within a framework of consultation or involvement. However, improved involvement of outsiders may help bring the two perspectives closer, thereby improving the influence of any future surveys.

Reference

A. Harrop (1996) Measuring customer satisfaction: some methodological issues, *DSS Research Yearbook 1995/6*. The Stationery Office

CASE STUDY THREE

Bradford Metropolitan Council's Speak Out! Research Panel

INTRODUCTION

Speak Out! is a research panel set up jointly by the City of Bradford Metropolitan District Council (CBMDC), Bradford Health Authority, (BHA), Bradford Community Health Trust (BCHT) and Bradford and District Training and Enterprise Council (TEC) in 1994–5. Each participating agency is entitled to one usage of the panel per year, plus participation in one multi-agency use. The research panel consists of 2,500 local residents selected to be a representative sample of the local population.

Since its establishment, there have been seven Speak Out! panel surveys, the first being in October 1995. These have been both surveys by individual organisations and multi-agency surveys.

The panel has been operating for slightly over a year, and is generally regarded as a success. However, Bradford Community Health Trust is reviewing the usefulness of its continued involvement.

The establishment and running of the panel has been written up as an information pack on the different settings for panels and the approach adopted by Bradford Council in setting up its own panel. The pack has been made available to other organisations.

ORIGINS AND OBJECTIVES

Origins

Although CBMDC has had an involvement in consultation in the past, it is only recently that development of consultation with residents has been supported over a sustained period. For example, in 1991–2 CBMDC carried out a large-scale survey of residents' opinions, but did not follow this up, and has not repeated the exercise. When the idea of a research panel was floated soon after the survey, it was not taken up at the political level within the Council.

The successful initiative for the Speak Out! research panel began within the Council in 1994, and grew from a number of specific circumstances and trends. In particular, there was a change of leadership in the Council which brought favourable consideration of the idea of a panel to the fore. Council research staff in the Chief Executive's department became familiar with the potential of research panels, and were specifically interested in finding ways of using research to support the consultation process. Over the same period there had been greater emphasis on consultation for public sector organisations, which gave the issue greater legitimacy, and other local authorities (such as Kirklees locally) were developing panels which provided examples of good practice.

For the Health Authority and the Community Health Trust, consultation has become part of their general approach to service delivery and planning. The NHS and Community Care Act, the Local Voices initiative, and the Patient's Charter have all emphasised the importance of patient, carer, and community involvement in health care locally.

The TEC is required to consult as part of the operating agreement with the Department of Employment. In practice the TEC has been able to carry out only limited consultation in the past, hampered as it was by a lack of resources. The panel offered an opportunity to develop consultation work on a more systematic basis.

Objectives

The participating organisations have in common the aim of obtaining reliable input from the public to their service provision, policy and planning. There are, however, differences between them in the specific outcomes which they were seeking from use of the panel.

The Council's aim was to assess public satisfaction with its services and panel views on the quality of its services were expected to be the Council's main use of the panel.

The Community Health Trust's aim was to inform the development of services and to help set service priorities. The CHT emphasised the panel was a robust research method providing reliable information. In this sense, obtaining reliable information was therefore one of the CHT's objectives in taking part.

The Health Authority's main objective was to obtain the views of a wider section of the public, as a complement to other inputs from voluntary groups, service users groups and Community Health Councils. The achievement of organisational objectives necessarily includes consultation and participation by the local population, and the panel provided a useful element in this.

The TEC set specific detailed objectives for its summer 1995 survey which explain its objectives in some detail:

- to establish the level of awareness/understanding, attitudes and perceptions of the local population towards local TEC initiatives;
- to explore the awareness and image of the TEC;
- to establish the levels of satisfaction with services received;
- to assess the skill levels and qualifications of individuals within Bradford and the surrounding district.

The consultation process

Methods

All of the organisations involved saw the panel as only one method of consultation among a number of other methods, including public meetings, focus groups, smaller-scale surveys, and consultation with voluntary or professional groups representing the interests of service users or other providers.

As with opinion polls, the research panel provides a reliable means of obtaining the views of a representative sample of the population. But it is also seen as having certain advantages over one-off opinion surveys:

- panels could track changes in views over time;
- panels could be used to collect the views of particular groups in the population or particular service users;
- because panel members are recruited on a voluntary basis they are more likely to have a commitment to responding to questionnaires and so increase the response rates;
- the special needs of certain panel members – such as for large type questionnaires or languages other than English – could be catered for with confidence;
- the cost of the panel once established and used several times is less than a large-scale one-off survey;
- the panel also offers the opportunity to consult members of the population whom it has traditionally been difficult to consult, such as members of ethnic minority groups.

As a joint initiative, the panel would facilitate joint working; promote information sharing; and avoid duplication of effort, and therefore cost.

The TEC saw the panel as an opportunity to consult the end users of TEC services, rather than the organisations who provide services to the TEC. This was a particular gap in the way the TEC collected information.

The panel was also viewed as a potential source of focus groups, although this has not happened at the time of writing.

The activities

Making the case within the Council

The initiative to set up a panel began in 1994 in the research section of the Strategic Management Unit in the Chief Executive's department of the Council. In Autumn 1994 the Chief Executive's department prepared a report for the Council's Authority Management Team and for the Leadership Team – which comprised the Leader and Deputy Leader and the Chairs of the Council Committees. At this stage there was some discussion of the potential overlap between a research panel and the role councillors played in discovering the views of local residents. Some councillors expressed concern that the panel might displace this important democratic function.

Much of the groundwork for the report was carried out by a student on placement within the department. Information on the use of research panels by other local authorities and other public and private sector organisations was a key factor in persuading the Council to take the idea forward.

Developing partnerships

In November 1994 initial discussions took place with the potential partners and the Council approached the other organisations to discover their level of interest in becoming involved. These contacts were at a senior level within the organisations. There were various reasons for involving other organisations – in particular the potential for sharing the costs and the workload, and the opportunity to build on existing joint activities. Although the Council would maintain an important role as coordinator, other organisations would be equal partners in the panel.

The decision to limit the number of partners to four was based on two assessments. First, that more than this number would require unacceptable levels of coordination; second, that use of the panel by individual organisations would be too limited with more than four. Some organisations were invited to take part because they were organisations with which the Council already had necessary or close working relations: the TEC and the Health Authority. The Community Health Trust heard about the panel and asked to become a partner. It was recognised that in the future other organisations such as the police might wish to become involved.

Recruiting the panel

Once the decision had been made to set up the panel, a key stage was recruiting the panel members. This was more complicated than anticipated and consequently took longer than was originally envisaged. But despite this it was considered by those involved to have gone well – especially in terms of the level of interest shown by members of the public in being involved.

Bradford has an adult population (16 years or over) of around 368,000. To be representative, the panel was assessed by research staff as needing to consist of 2,500 members, composed of a series of quotas based on the distributions of gender, race, age, employment status in the population, and including a geographical dimension – the five parliamentary constituencies covered by the Bradford metropolitan area.

Two alternative sampling frames for recruitment of the panel were identified: the electoral register and the register of the (now merged) Family Health Services Authority. The decision to use the Family Health Services Authority Register was taken because it included 16–18 year olds and because it was easier to access, given that the Electoral Register had been contracted out to the private sector and use of it for sampling purposes would have meant additional payment.

A screening questionnaire – a method used successfully by another local authority – was used to recruit panel members. This was sent to 25,000 residents, with an assumed response rate of between 10 and 15 per cent, giving a total of around 3,000 potential panel members. In order to encourage responses, a prize draw of £100 was offered to everyone who responded. In fact, the returns were higher than anticipated and 4,000 screening questionnaires were returned. However, almost 10 per cent of these were unusable because they were not complete. An external agency was used to mail out the questionnaire and process the data which were supplied to the Council as a data file. During the initial stages of developing the panel, training in focus groups was arranged for members of the steering group and for other staff with an interest.

Panel members' accounts of the recruitment process were similar. Members speculated about the reasons for which they as individuals received invitations to complete the screening questionnaire, but were generally clear that the panel was designed as a representative sample of the local population. Selection was thought to be from the Electoral Register, we assume because this is the most commonly identifiable sampling frame.

Expectations about what membership would involve varied. Only one or two members were clear that questionnaires would be the sole mode of contact. Most, reflecting on the word 'panel', expected discussions such as the ones held by ourselves, and in general expected a more active involvement.

Two motivations for involvement were expressed: being heard; and serving/representing the community in fora otherwise dominated by politicians and experts. These motives were expressed in terms of service to the locality, of belonging, and of making a contribution. A secondary aspect was that of 'keeping an eye on them'. Mistrust of politicians was much talked about, but given the fashionable nature of such views, it is difficult to assess how real this was as a motivator. On balance, we consider that the value in participation/involvement and the sense of belonging to a community were the key themes.

The panel surveys

To date there have been seven Speak Out! surveys: in October 1995 a TEC survey for 16–65 year olds; in November 1995 a Council survey about Local Agenda 21; in December 1995 a survey for those people living in the Worth Valley/Keighley area; in January 1996 a multi-agency survey; in February 1996 a Health Authority survey which focused on Health of the Nation issues: in March 1996 a Community Health Trust survey; and in May 1996 a survey for the Council's Social Services Department about services for older people.

The latest survey is another multi-agency survey focusing on the theme of access to services and also asking questions to get feedback from panel members about Speak Out! Access can however mean very different things to each of the organisations and there has been some difficulty in identifying a common theme and in framing questions which deal adequately with these differences.

The agencies are also keen to find out more about what people think about Speak Out! in itself and would also like to discover more from non-respondents. The inclusion of questions in the latest multi-agency survey to gather views about the panel itself is aimed at achieving this.

One of the initial difficulties was around the issue of translating the questionnaires. The Steering Group felt that this was the right thing to do to meet the needs of members of the community whose first language was not English. A letter, translated into 12 languages, was sent to panel members to offer the opportunity of telephone or face-to-face interviews if they could not read a postal questionnaire in English. For the future the Steering Group felt they needed to consider other alternatives in the recruitment of members from other communities – for example hiring interviewers with the appropriate languages.

Participating organisations have run their surveys in several ways. The Council and the Health Authority have carried out surveys using their own resources. However, the TEC contracted out its survey to a private company and the Community Health Trust contracted with the Council to analyse the data and prepare a research report. These differences are based on practical availability of in-house skills and resources: the research and teamwork skills needed to run a panel survey are not all available internally to each of the organisations involved.

There have been some problems with delay, especially when the panel was first set up. The initial idea had been to use the panel first in June/July 1995. In fact the first survey was not carried out until October 1995. This was partly due to an underestimation of the time it would take to recruit the panel and partly because of delays by some of the partner organisations in providing questions for a multi-agency survey.

Participants have expressed concern about the response rates, particularly among certain groups. There were expectations that 'volunteer' panel members would produce higher response rates. For the Council survey the overall response rate was 65 per cent – lower than hoped for. But response rates were much lower for some population quotas: ethnic minorities 38 per cent; unemployed 43 per cent; those requesting large print 43 per cent; and 16–24 year olds 45 per cent. These rates are however high in comparison with most postal survey rates of return. There can also be considerable delays in getting the questionnaires back and therefore in analysing the results. A gap of six months had occurred, and was thought to be too long.

Discussions with small groups of panel members revealed dissatisfaction with some surveys, based on doubts about the relevance of the subject. Most panel members in the groups were unable to answer TEC survey questions as they knew little about TECs. Some health survey questions about health structures were the subject of similar comments. A local authority survey about Bradford overall was praised for its relevance to panel members' concerns.

The content of surveys was also criticised, in that members felt that important local decisions were not put to the panel. The absence of redevelopment of the city centre from questionnaires was a recurring theme in the group discussions.

Maintaining the panel

The panel membership requires maintenance to ensure its continuing usefulness. Over time there is a need to replace members of the panel as they lose interest, move house, withdraw, or because as a result of being involved in the panel and their increased knowledge of services they become less representative of the population as a whole. There is therefore an annual recruitment of 800 replacement members of the panel. In addition, each questionnaire gives members the option to drop out if they are no longer interested in membership and members do routinely drop out in response. Recruitment of replacements for these drop-outs is also necessary.

Communication with panel members is through the Panel Newsletter, which provides information on the results of the surveys. There are no user forums or opportunities for the organisations to meet members of the panel, and Council staff feel this may be a factor in the lower than expected response rates.

Panel members were critical of the lack of feedback. Two different points were made: that there was an almost total lack of information about the survey results; that nothing was known about what, if anything, was being done with the results. Suggestions included more newsletter information, but also greater active involvement of panel members in meetings and discussions.

Panel members also had no clear perspective on the continuity or duration of their membership of the panel. They knew of the option to 'resign', but experienced the panel as a series of disjointed questionnaires, between which they did not know whether they had been dropped from the panel, nor were members certain that the panel itself was continuing at any given moment.

Managing the process

Coordination between organisations: the Steering Group

A Steering Group of representatives from each organisation was set up to co-ordinate the different inputs to surveys. The group meets on a regular monthly basis and the venue for the meetings rotates between the different organisations. Whereas originally the Steering Group meetings were chaired by the Council, this now rotates and the meetings are chaired by the member of the team at whose offices the meeting is being held. The Steering Group meetings are minuted and circulated to Steering Group members. The role of the Steering Group was agreed as:

- to establish an annual forward plan of surveys;
- to encourage the use of joint surveys and joint working;
- to provide advice on the suitability of the use of the panel for particular surveys;
- to promote the panel to other agencies;
- to act as a sounding board on the content of questionnaires.

However, the discussions of the Steering Group to date have focused on the practical operation of the panel rather than more strategic issues such as promotion or development.

An early task of the group was to establish ground rules about how the panel would operate. The following rules have been agreed:

- Each organisation is entitled to one full use of the panel each year and in addition one multi-agency survey.
- Each organisation receives a disc in an SPSS file format with the results of the whole panel survey and is responsible for selecting the results for their own survey.
- All the costs of a survey are the responsibility of the organisation carrying it out and include printing, postage, supply of the questionnaires and freepost envelopes.

- The BHA is responsible for the production of a six-monthly newsletter for panel members, paid for jointly by the participating organisations.
- There is an annual multi-agency survey for which there is a prize draw.
- The Steering Group member representing the organisation carrying out the survey is responsible for the quality and content of the questionnaire.
- The maximum questionnaire length is four sides.
- All questionnaires must make use of the Speak Out! logo and be of the same design.

For the multi-agency questionnaires, members of the group draw up questions to discuss in the group in liaison with their own organisations. As a quality control mechanism the group has a final say in the standard of questionnaires both to avoid sending out poor quality surveys and to make any small amendments which might provide additional useful information for another of the group's members.

Membership of the Steering Group has been reasonably consistent since it was set up. Members are drawn from marketing, quality management and research, within the participating organisations and also have a range of arrangements for liaison within their own organisations. This variety brings breadth to the work of the group by bringing together different perspectives and experiences, and is seen as a strength. To function effectively as a group, members must have the ability to plan and manage the work for the research panel alongside their other job responsibilities. The ease with which members have been able to work together is considered a key strength of the panel.

Management within the individual organisations

Each of the four participating organisations has its own ways of managing its involvement with the research itself.

Within the Council, there is an inter-departmental working team which consists of representatives of the major service departments – housing and environmental protection, and community and environmental services, social services, and education. The Chief Executive's department emphasises the value of this central coordination for the management of the survey. The working team members are drawn from a range of disciplines, including research, information, policy, and marketing. The team meets on an occasional basis to coordinate the Council's input to the research panel, gather ideas for questions the Council should ask, and act as a sounding board for proposed questions.

The Health Authority has a central research section as well as individual specialists within each department. The representative on the Steering Group has the responsibility for coordination between these parts of the Authority, and a range of staff from within the Authority have been involved in compiling their survey.

In the Community Health Trust a business planning group meets on a monthly basis. Discussions include the results of the current survey and questions for the next one.

In the TEC two members of staff had the main responsibility for managing the involvement with the panel: the research manager and the marketing manager.

Only two of the agencies have the resources and skills to manage the process in-house. As a result the TEC contracts out their own questionnaire to an external research organisation, and the Community Health Trust contracts with the Council to analyse the results of one of its surveys and prepare a report. By contrast, the Health Authority and the Council both design, administer and analyse their questionnaires in-house.

Policy customers within the participating organisations

In the local authority individual Departments tend to use the research panel in different ways and for different purposes. For example the Social Services Department used the panel to ask questions of a specific group of users and potential users of services – the elderly. In the Community and Environmental Services Department the panel was used to find out views about crime and crime prevention, in order to inform service priorities. In Housing the panel was used to ask specific question about housing need that it was not possible to collect in other ways.

Resources

The initial set-up costs, which were shared between the four organisations, were estimated at £25,000:

Postage	£7,000
Printing and translation	£4,000
Survey administration	£9,000
Interviewer costs (for the market research company)	£5,000

Each organisation is responsible for the costs of its own surveys, while the costs of the multi-agency survey are shared. The different arrangements for carrying out the survey work within the organisations mean there are different costs and staff time involved.

The annual cost of replacing panel members is about £8,000 – which is shared between the organisations. The cost of the newsletter is around £1,200.

The Council estimates that the cost of using the panel is around £6,000, including costs for printing, postage and data processing. In the first year of the panel the Council was involved with three surveys. Its own full use of the panel cost £6,000, the contribution to the multi-agency survey was £1,500 and the survey by social services of the elderly cost £1,500. The Council estimates that the staff time spent on the research panel costs £5,000 per year.

The Community Health Trust has spent around £19,000, including its survey, and £8,000 towards shared costs for initial set up, multi-agency surveys and replacing the panel each year.

The Health Authority's survey cost around £2,000 for printing, with additional costs for postage. In addition, temporary staff equivalent to four person-days were recruited to send out the questionnaires. The Health Authority have to date analysed the results in-house, but are considering contracting out the coding and data entry, because of delays in getting the results caused by pressures on staff time. The TEC and the Council pay outside contractors for their data entry.

All of the agencies consider the sharing of some of the costs to be an essential factor in the decision to be involved with the panel. None would be able to afford the costs of this method of consultation without sharing the costs.

Staff time for members of the Steering Group, and other staff within each organisation, is a key cost which is not calculated in any systematic way. Central coordination work on surveys can involve two-thirds of staff time at times of despatching questionnaires, but at other times this falls to one day a week. Agencies also report that in both elapsed time and in numbers of days spent, it takes longer to set up and run a panel than they had envisaged. In part this is the result of joint working, which they recognise as involving longer timescales to make decisions and to carry out plans.

IMPACT

Communicating the results

To the panel members

Steering Group members emphasise the need to feed back the results of the surveys to the panel members and, importantly, to give a detailed account of what will happen in consequence. To date there is just one method of communicating the results with the panel members and this is through the newsletter. The original intention was for the newsletter to be produced on a six-monthly basis. So far, only one has been produced. There is some concern that the newsletter only gives a very general idea of how the results will be used and that this should be provided for in more detail.

To the public

There has been little communication generally to members of the public about the panel and its surveys and results are not always press-released. In the local authority there is some sensitivity about publicising the results, which are not always welcome to locally elected members.

Within the participating organisations

The other main audience for the results is the organisations themselves which have carried out the surveys. There are different internal arrangements for promoting the results both between and within organisations.

In the Council a report is prepared for the Authority Management Team, unless the results are specific to one department with no authority-wide implications – in which case individual departments are responsible for making use of the results. After consideration by the management team, the report may or may not be put before councillors. Surveys are routinely reported to councillors on the Education, and Community and Environmental Services Committees, and the Social Services survey was reported to the Elderly and Community Development sub-committee of the Social Services Committee. In addition, surveys are reported to the five area sub-committees. The working team would however like this issue to be given further consideration as it would be a way of promoting the results more widely across the council.

In the TEC the results from the survey are presented by the external research contractors to the TEC's management team and departmental teams.

Direct impact of the panel surveys

On policy and practice

There has been a specific impact on the strategies adopted by participating organisations towards the provision of information. Several comment that they are reviewing where they place information about their organisations and the services they offer as a result of the survey. Survey information will feed into the Council's review of how best to publicise information about the performance indicators required by the Audit Commission.

The first panel survey carried out by the Council included questions about environmental issues, shopping centres and so on, and the results have fed into discussions about the nature and future polices towards town centres within the area. Survey information will also feed into the Community and Environmental Department's consideration of ways of reducing crime and targeting resources for crime prevention initiatives.

In the TEC the outcome of the panel survey was particularly useful to the marketing team, who were already in the process of considering how to put across the message about the TEC and the services it provides.

Not surprisingly, smaller changes take less time than larger ones. Much of the information that comes from the panel does not need specific resources to bring about change – it is more a way of reallocating resources. There is some concern that the panel must be effective as a producer of change. The Health Authority in particular has said that there is little point in taking steps to get the views of members of the public if the results are not used to change policies, and question the point of asking people questions about things that it is known it is not possible to change. The Health Authority's view is that this simply creates unrealistic expectations.

On relations between organisations

Another theme to emerge in assessing the organisation of the research panel is the relationships between the participating organisations. Inevitably, there are more areas of common interest between some of the organisations than others. So, for example, for one of the partners there is less in common with the TEC. For another the extent of common interest between itself and the TEC has come as a welcome surprise and one to be explored further. This raises questions about the longer-term sustainability of the partnership between these four particular organisations and the scope for involving others in some way. There is also an issue about the extent to which there are shared areas of interest between the organisations which can form the basis of the multi-agency questionnaire.

Influence on views on consultation

The research panel has had an impact in raising the level of awareness within the individual organisations of ways of being more customer-focused and of using research methods as a means of consultation. Within the Health Authority it has encouraged departments to take more research initiatives in the form of smaller-scale surveys.

There have been general changes in perception about the value of consultation and the panel has increased awareness of different methods of consultation and how they can be used.

Internal impact on the participating organisations

The research panel has also had an impact in terms of feeding in to other aspects of the organisations' work. For example, the TEC has decided to apply for a Charter Mark and how the TEC consults will be one factor in the overall assessment of whether to award a Charter Mark or not. Without their involvement with the research panel they would have found it difficult to submit the Charter Mark application.

The future

The Council plans to continue with Speak Out! and resources are being set aside to do this. One organisation – the Community Health Trust – is committed to the panel, but is obliged to bear in mind the resources involved and to consider their involvement in this light.

The participants are seeking to develop the panel as a commercial venture, allowing other organisations to make use of it.

Assessment

The success of the project

A general view: early days

The participating organisations share a view of the research panel at this stage as still being in its infancy. It has been running, at the time of writing, for about 18 months. Their general assessment so far is that the panel has been a success. There is a common feeling that there is still much more creative use to be made of the panel, especially in terms of what were seen originally as the benefits of a research panel over large scale surveys. This includes making use of opportunities for using the panel to recruit focus groups with whom issues can be discussed in more detail.

The Community Health Trust's view

The Community Health Trust has doubts about the value of the panel in developing its own services. Obtaining the public's views about services which are to a large extent invisible or, at best, not well known, is not possible using the panel. Combined with the Trust's lack of in-house skills to deal with the questionnaire design and data analysis, this issue is leading the Trust to reconsider whether they are getting value for money from the research panel.

The Council: two different views – panel organisers and policy customers

There are some differences of view between those with responsibility for organising the panel and those making use of the results in service departments. Those using the results place more emphasis on the importance of promoting the panel, communicating results to the members of the panel and to service departments and politicians.

There is an extent to which some of the users of the information feel that it is locked up within individual departments or organisations and there are not enough systematic ways of sharing the results. They consider that there would be benefit for them of finding out more about the results of the surveys carried out by the other organisations in the consortium.

The panel is also felt by the organisers, but less so by the policy customers, to have enhanced joint working between the organisations. Some of those responsible for policy implementation describe the panel as being invisible to most people, and this reflects their concerns about the need to promote the use of the panel and the results of surveys more effectively within and between organisations. The policy customers would also like to see the panel being used more proactively as a way of informing future policy development.

Steering Group views

There is a feeling among Steering Group members that there is a need to find ways to engage their own organisations in the potential of the panel and to encourage service departments to make use of it.

One of the advantages seen by some members of the Steering Group is the ability to use the panel to gain the views not just of existing users of services, but also of potential or non-users or particular groups of the population (such as members of the ethnic minority communities with whom they find it generally more difficult to consult). On the other hand there is also a concern that for some types of service, such as those offered by the Community Health Trust, it is very difficult to get views from the general population, who have little awareness of even the existence of some types of service.

Panel members' views from discussion groups

The members who took part in the discussion groups expressed similar views regardless of age. The small numbers interviewed are not representative of the panel, and in reporting their views we reflect on how their views compare with those of the panel organisers.

There was a general feeling of dissatisfaction with the level of involvement, lack of information and absence of feedback. Panel members clearly expected a much greater interactive process when they agreed to take part, and disappointment was strongly expressed. In this, the views of these members coincide with the organisers' assessment that not enough feedback has been done, and not enough has been made of the results.

The idea that the results of the panel were unlikely to be used was raised by all groups. The general lack of feedback and knowledge about what is done with results led to speculation by most panel members that little or nothing is done with the results. One discussion group had doubts about the sincerity of the Council's intentions, although this was a theme which did not develop in the discussion into a coherent account of why a panel would be mounted if the Council did not intend to use it.

The content and form of the questionnaires also raised issues for most members. The purpose of questionnaires on subjects about which members knew little was not known, and there was some resentment at questions which they could not answer. Some members experienced such questions as a test. Views on the value of spaces to write text versus tick boxes were mixed, with preferences both ways, but a general agreement that a mix was needed.

The most striking general difference from the organisers' perception is the slightness of the panel as an experience for its members. Where the organisers perceive a project, with continuity and real substance, the members see a few questionnaires punctuating long periods of inactivity and complete silence. The panel is not prominent in local affairs – it is not reported, and there is no knowledge of its effects or role. Indeed, there is no knowledge of anything beyond the single newsletter. This general perception is partly a description, and partly prompts the expression of a desire to be more involved.

Note: Selection of the panel

The intention as explained above was to select the panel members to be representative of Bradford residents. Quota groups were used made up of: age (16–24, 25–64 and 65+); gender; ethnicity (white and non-white); employment status (unemployed, employed and inactive); and geography according to the five parliamentary constituencies.

108 quotas were devised, although a number of them were empty. Within each quota respondents were selected at random. In a few categories a market research company recruited additional members.

Research methods

We interviewed members of the Steering Group and policy staff from the participating organisations. We studied documents including minutes of the Steering Group, several questionnaires and summaries of their results, the Newsletter, and a Research Panel 'how to' guide.

Bradford Council kindly invited a random selection of panel members, stratified into three age groups, to meet us for a discussion. Attendance was voluntary, and an expenses fee of £10 was paid. Four group discussions took place: two older age groups, one working age group, and one younger age group. In total, 22 individuals took part in the group discussions. One group was facilitated by a staff member from the health authority.

The fieldwork took place from Summer to Winter 1996.

COMMENTARY

Overview

Bradford Metropolitan District Council, together with the local Health Authority, TEC, and Community Health Trust, set up a research panel of the local population, to conduct surveys of residents' views on issues relevant to local services and policies. The Speak Out! panel consists of 2,500 local residents selected to be a representative sample of the local population. The panel is used once a year by each participating agency, and once a year for a joint survey. Unlike the Benefits Agency customer survey, there is no year-on-year uniformity in the surveys sent out.

We identified a number of key points which are examined in this commentary:

- The panel requires a mix of skills, and considerable resources. This makes a partnership approach useful.
- The types of survey the panel is useful for requires careful thought.
- Understanding of the panel, and its value, must be fostered with panel members.
- Care must be taken to make the uses of the results of panel surveys explicit and public.

Partnership, resources and skills

Both the recruitment of the panel and the surveys within it require research skills. Maintaining the panel requires organisational skills, and conducting surveys requires both. Analysis of survey results required skills not available in all of the organisations involved in the Speak Out! panel. Some participants resolved these skills shortages by buying them from the private sector. One organisation contracted with the local authority. The sharing of costs was identified as a major benefit by the participants.

The joint work which characterised the Bradford panel was led by the Council. The complexity brought by such joint work was not a difficulty for the participating organisations. However, a difficulty lay in the different patterns of management of panel activities within each organisation. In particular, relations with policy customers within each organisations differed in their patterns, and there were some discrepancies between the views of the different sections within the Council, with, unsurprisingly, the panel organisers seeing its benefits more clearly.

Whilst joint work was a clear strength, it does not bring with it an automatic single perspective, or a short route to joint service ventures or other forms of cooperation. The different roles and expectations of the participants were understandably largely unaffected.

Types of survey

The participating organisations' individual surveys had different purposes, including assessment of satisfaction with and preferences for local services and facilities, obtaining suggestions for change, and assessing levels of awareness of a participating organisation and its activities. Survey results to date have been used in an advisory capacity, to inform and add to developments in policy and services, and as a consequence we could not assess any differences in impact of the different purposes.

Certainly some panel members were bemused by some questions, because they knew little of the organisations or the topics of the questions. By contrast, some surveys – notably about the local environment – were praised for their relevance. The differing experience of different panel members – whether they had used health services, or the services of the TEC – seemed to condition strongly the degree of approval of any particular survey. Indeed, the Community Health Trust acknowledged its own difficulties in asking the public questions which seek to inform developments, when the public is unlikely to know what the Trust consists of, and what it does.

What then is the right kind of survey, and is there one kind only? Regrettably, we are able to give only some general indicators. Survey questions are more likely to reveal the views/preferences/ideas of the panel members where they are about something the members know about and care about. 'Why not ask us about the development of the town centre?' said the panel members whom we interviewed. Perceived relevance is important. A note of caution must be sounded here, because options and preferences when sought can provide unreliable information if the choices are abstract and/or offered as wish-lists.

Surveys have been targeted on sub-groups of the panel – for example older people – and such targeting can help to increase the usefulness of the responses. Targeting will improve relevance. Questions which seek information about specific experiences of panel members – Have you used this service? What was it like to use? – are more likely to provide solid responses.

Care of the panel

We found a discrepancy between the understandings of what Speak Out! was about, which is a good lesson for all attempts at involvement of the public. It would not be a parody to say that, for the Council, the panel makes a key contribution to its overall long-term programmes of citizen involvement and enhancement of democracy. For the panel members whom we interviewed, Speak Out! was the odd questionnaire through the post.

The detail of this difference of perceptions lies firstly in the commitment of the Council to its programme, and secondly in the very different experiences of those who have developed and run the panel, and those who fill in the questionnaires. Both views are, of course, valid – the panel is both of these, at the same time. Developing the panel may be a full-time occupation, but filling in the questionnaires is not.

Where such research panels risk falling flat is therefore in losing sight of this discrepancy and not caring for and nurturing the membership. Members interviewed by us were uniformly disappointed at the lack of feedback, and uncertain about whether they were still members. Their commitments to speaking up for their communities, 'being heard' and so on, through the questionnaires, was not being enabled by the panel, because results were unknown and apparently had no influence.

Use of the results

As we say above, panel members were unaware of any uses of the survey results. Indeed, at the time of our interviews, they had received only one feedback bulletin from the Council. Accounts of the uses made of results were on the whole non-specific, advisory, making contributions and so on. We find this unsatisfactory. Uses to be made must be spelled out, if the credibility of the panel, and its long-term health, are to be maintained.

CASE STUDY FOUR

Devon and Cornwall Police Authority: Annual Policing Plan

ORIGINS AND OBJECTIVES

This case study concerns the public consultation about priorities for the next annual policing plan for Devon and Cornwall. Consultation took place during summer 1996 to inform the 1997/8 plan, which was published in March 1997. The consultation was organised and carried out by the police authority, in cooperation with the police force.

Origins

Police authorities were reconstituted under the Police and Magistrates Court Act 1994. The new authorities, which took office in April 1995, have fewer members than their predecessor bodies. Previously, all members were either councillors, representing local authorities, or magistrates. Now some members are appointed, having been selected from those members of the public who have expressed a particular interest in serving on the police authority. The new police authorities are required both to consult the public and to publish an annual policing plan. The draft policing plan is prepared by the Chief Constable and sets out priorities and budgets. It is intended to establish the policing issues which will receive the greatest attention, and to assist the police in planning the use of resources. The plan contains targets, and performance is to be measured against these targets.

In Devon and Cornwall the authority opted to carry out a consultation exercise concerned specifically with people's priorities for the policing plan. In most constabularies there is no specific consultation about the policing plan and input for the plan is drawn from public consultation on policing generally. Although the consultation exercise built on developments over a long period, it was the establishment of the new authority, with some new members and new staff, which led directly to this initiative. The police force was content that the authority should lead the process. The methods are thought to be unique to Devon and Cornwall.

Objectives

The overall aim was to identify the issues of greatest concern to the public, to inform the policing plan for the following year. The handbill distributed at the consultation meetings asked 'What are the issues that you feel the police service should address next year?' and went on to explain that 'Your valued contribution to this process is to share with us your thoughts on the policing issues of most concern'.

For both police and authority there was a dual purpose to the exercise: to both receive and give information. As well as hearing about public concerns, they set out to improve the public understanding of police responsibilities and operations, and to educate the public about policing matters. Specifically, they wished to make clear that there is a finite budget for policing, within which priorities have to be set. It follows that the police force cannot meet all the demands upon it.

The intention to use the information gathered from the public is described in rather general terms. This reflects the view that the consultation exercise was an addition to, and reinforcement for, other informal methods of gauging public opinion and attitudes to the police. Further, public opinion is but one of several inputs to the policing plan. Other key inputs are the assessments by the police force itself, and the National Key Objectives for policing set by the Home Secretary.

Underlying the formal purpose of the consultation is the belief in the importance of being seen to consult, and of giving the public an opportunity to express views direct to the police and the authority.

The process

Methods

The process by which the police consult the public has its origins in the Scarman enquiry into the Brixton riots of 1981. Before this, under the leadership of John Alderson, Devon and Cornwall police was widely thought to be at the forefront of developing community policing and an ethos of communication and liaison with the public. Following the Scarman report, police forces were required to set up consultation arrangements with a view to encouraging cooperation between police and community. The Devon and Cornwall police, which had established a network of local liaison groups in the mid 1970s, then set up a series of consultative committees, each of which covered a specific geographical area and had about 15 core members, drawn from local organisations.

The new authority, when it began work in April 1995, continued with a process of reform of the consultative committees, which had begun a few years before. The committees had been replaced with open public meetings. These meetings were initially called 'Liaison Groups'; in early 1997 it was decided to change the name to Liaison Meetings, to reflect the fact that they were open public meetings and not restricted to a particular membership.

The purpose of the meetings is to develop a dialogue between police and public. There are 16 groups, one for each district council area. Each meets four times a year, at different locations within its area. Meetings are chaired by members of the police authority.

The consultation about policing priorities was an addition to this established structure. In the summer of 1995, in its first year, the new authority organised a series of self-contained meetings to which the public were invited to come and express their priorities. Attendance was described as disappointing, with a total of 200 people coming to nine meetings. Publicity for the meetings included 2,500 letters and posters to parish councils, neighbourhood watch groups and other local organisations. For 1996, it was decided to include a discussion of the policing plan and priorities as a 'Focus Session' at the regular Liaison Group meetings. As a result, a programme of 16 meetings has involved 670 people.

Both the authority and the police intend to continue refining their approach to public consultation, but this broad method is described as the best they can devise to meet their needs. There was brief consideration of a postal survey, but they were aware of a very low response rate (5 per cent) achieved by another force. Further, a survey would not achieve their objectives of informing and educating the public, or of generating dialogue as well as response.

While the focus sessions have the specific purpose of consulting the public about policing priorities, the police force also gathers more general information about public attitudes in a number of ways. The police stress that a range of sources of public feedback contribute to their understanding of public opinion and thus to the policing plan.

Contact with the public at the Devon and Cornwall annual county shows complements the focus sessions. At the shows, the public's view of the force is explored through questionnaires distributed to visitors to the public display stands. The questionnaires used in summer 1996 had a particular focus on styles of policing and attitudes to police patrol, issues which are prominent in the discussions at focus sessions.

Other means of dialogue include attendance by a police officer at parish and district council meetings. The police also contact members of the public who have been involved in domestic burglaries, road traffic accidents or crimes of violence, to assess their level of satisfaction with police action, and reasons for any dissatisfaction.

Activities

The focus session on the policing plan is held at the beginning of the summer meeting of each Liaison Group. The Groups are open public meetings, held in the evenings, in venues such as village halls and schools. Police and the authority take responsibility for different parts of the meeting. The whole meeting is chaired by a member of the authority, but the focus session is led by the clerk to the police authority and a police officer with special responsibility for this consultation process, working together.

After a brief introduction, members of the public are invited to voice their concerns and priorities. Topics mentioned are summarised and listed on a flip chart. When the ideas from the floor come to an end, the public are asked to vote for the three issues on the flip chart which they consider to be most important to include in next year's plan, in order of priority. Voting slips are then collected. The whole process takes a maximum of one hour, usually less. The collated results are fed back to the next meeting of that Liaison Group. During the session, the police officer and clerk to the authority respond to points raised by the public by giving information about issues such as limits to police responsibility, budgets, the need to balance priorities and so on.

The results of the consultation

The vote by 671 people, at 16 meetings, identified a total of 60 issues which individuals thought should be in the top three priorities for policing in 1997/8. First choices scored three points, third choices scored one. Thus, a total of 4,026 points were awarded. Almost a quarter of these went to the top priority, high visibility policing. The top ten of the 60 priorities received a total of 3,095 points, more than three-quarters of the total.

Assessment of the process

Both the authority and the police consider that the process has been more effective this year than it was using last year's format, when meetings on the policing plan were held separately. The main reason for this conclusion is the more than threefold increase in the number of people involved, which resulted from attaching the Focus Session to the regular public meetings.

There is also some suggestion that the quality of input has improved. Now that they are on the second year of the process, the annual cycle of consultation, plan production and reporting on performance against its targets, has been completed. Those who attend meetings are made aware of this cycle, as they receive feedback from the previous vote, see the annual plan and then the annual report, which reports on performance.

A further reason for the improvement is that both police and authority have been getting used to a new working relationship, and to the concept of a policing plan. Both feel that the process is being handled better as they become more practised.

Those who attend the meetings show a high level of satisfaction with them: more than half had been to two or more meetings. Over two-thirds said the meeting was interesting, three-quarters thought it had been worthwhile coming, and almost 60 per cent thought the meetings were well organised.

In assessing the process, a number of issues were raised by the different parties involved – the police force, the authority (members and staff) and members of the public who participated. These are discussed below.

Who should do the consulting?

The respective roles of the police and the authority are not made very explicit at the Liaison Groups. It is likely that the majority of the public are not fully aware of the distinction between them. Those who carry out the joint police/authority presentation of the focus sessions deliberately do not emphasise their different roles, as they are concerned to demonstrate the partnership which exists between force and authority, and to show that they are working together on the consultation process.

However, it seems to be important that the authority should let it be seen that it is in overall control of the process. Senior police report that they feel under rather more pressure to respond to public consultation carried out by the authority, with its remit to represent the public, than they would be with consultation carried out in-house. This is seen by the police as a positive advantage.

Meetings are chaired by police authority members. Some long standing attenders of the public meetings, who are elected members of local district and parish councils, feel that the meetings should be run by someone further removed from the police than they perceive even the authority to be. For them, an independent local chair would be preferable to a police authority member. They suspect that authority members are reluctant to challenge police officers, because of what they see as too close a relationship between force and authority. Some of the elected members of local authorities feel this to be more likely in the case of police authority members who were appointed rather than being local council representatives.

Who attends the meetings?

A major concern, reported by all involved, is the failure of the meetings to attract an audience which they would deem to comprise a reasonable cross-section of the Devon and Cornwall public. The summer 1996 meetings attracted an average attendance of 42 people. Both the authority and the police worry less about numbers than they do about the age and class range at the meetings. Meetings contain a preponderance of retired and middle-age people, probably from the higher socio-economic classes. The absence of young people (teenagers and above) gives particular concern.

Police and authority express concern that they are 'preaching to the converted' – that they are talking almost exclusively to those who are likely to be generally supportive of the police. Of course, it is not known how representative those attending the meetings actually are of the population of Devon and Cornwall. Our own investigations for this case study showed that more than half those attending the two meetings we observed were there to represent their Neighbourhood Watch groups. This suggests that the organisers' perceptions are probably well founded – they are talking to a group who are, first, able and willing to commit time to voluntary activities in the community and, secondly, who are likely to be particularly supportive of moves to strengthen law and order.

Reasons for attending the meetings

Almost two-thirds of attenders said they came to the meeting because they wanted to support the police, almost half because they feel strongly about policing matters, and almost two-thirds because they feel it is important to take part in public consultation. Fewer than 15 per cent wanted to ask questions or make comments. Thus, attendance seems to be largely motivated by a sense of community spirit, support for the police and a strength of feeling about police matters.

It is accepted by the organisers that the opportunity to contribute specifically to the policing plan is not the main reason for coming to a Liaison Group. Communication about policing generally is the primary motivation. Representatives of local councils, who have attended meetings over a long period, consider the plan for the whole police authority region to be a rather remote concept for the public at large. It is not perceived to make any real difference to their day-to-day experience of policing and crime, which is what they want to talk about most.

Encouraging a useful input to the plan

The organisers see advantages in the immediate reactions their process elicits, a process which does not allow time for debate. It is felt that debates, if they develop, tend to become concerned with local issues rather than those which apply to the whole of the authority's region. (Purely local issues can be referred to the main session of the Liaison Group meeting, and may inform the Divisional Policing Plan.) Debates also make issues, and the relationships between them, appear more complex. By contrast, the chosen method and the vote quickly produce a list of concerns, in order of priority.

At the same time, the organisers would prefer the votes to be cast by a better-informed public. Authority members vary in their views on this: some accept that people will put forward ideas which are entirely the result of local and personal experience and/or ask for services which cannot be delivered for financial or operational reasons. This view holds that it is then for the police to interpret and use the information as they see fit. It was also suggested that it would be inappropriate to expose too many of the inherently political questions, such as those to do with resources, to public comment.

Other members feel that more should be done to inform people before they suggest priorities. This could be done by providing background information about, for example, the budget, the role of the authority, and national and local needs.

In contrast to the concerns about the level of public understanding, the choice of voting as a method is accepted uncritically. The only criticism, raised by one informant, was that the process tends to lose the subtleties of some of the points which are raised. As points are made in the meeting, related topics tend to be grouped together as one subject.

An opportunity for dialogue

The overall view of the different groups involved in the process is that the meetings provide a real opportunity for dialogue between the police and the authority, on one hand, and the public, on the other.

About three-quarters of those attending the two meetings we observed felt that it was easy for people to say what they wanted to say, and only slightly fewer than this thought the police were listening to what people had to say. For those attending the meetings, receiving information was clearly more important than giving it: almost all of them said they came to hear what the police had to say, and about 40 per cent of them volunteered the opinion that this was the most important aspect of the meeting.

Long-standing attenders of the meetings, the local council members, have a rather different perspective of the dialogue from the participants as a whole. The former group has seen the format of the meetings change to enable more dialogue to take place. An intimidating array of 'top brass' had been replaced by a rather more open and approachable style. However, some defensiveness on the part of the police was still observed.

All were agreed that the chairing of the meeting was the key to facilitating dialogue. A readiness to control the vocal and to limit repetition was essential, as well as a willingness to press the police when necessary.

Geography and timing

The Devon and Cornwall police force covers a large geographical area. Each group meets in four different locations each year, but travel times and distances can still be considerable in this largely rural area. There is a limited choice of venues, and complaints about audibility were fairly frequent. The timing of the meetings determines the groups who are most likely to be able to attend. Daytime meetings used to exclude the working population and meetings are now held in the evenings.

Managing the process

The consultation process, which is the statutory responsibility of the authority, is under continuous review through discussions between the clerk to the authority and the police officer who jointly conduct the sessions. As the only people with an overview of the process throughout the region, they are in a position to identify best practice amongst the members and police officers involved, and to suggest and implement changes to the overall approach.

Resources

The police estimate that £1,828 of officer time is spent conducting the focus sessions each year, supported by £304 of administrative staff time. Authority estimates of staff costs, which are based on the same hourly rates, give the same figures. Approximately £1,000 is spent on publicity and postage and £2,000 on hiring meeting rooms, giving an overall total of £7,250 approximately, for the year.

This figure excludes the time spent on planning and reviewing the sessions, and collating the results. It also excludes the very considerable travelling time involved in attending many of the meetings.

The impact of the consultation process on its output

The public consultation is one input to the policing plan for the following financial year. Others are the force's own assessment of priorities and the National Key Objectives for policing, issued by the Home Secretary. The draft plan is prepared by the Chief Constable and adopted and published by the authority.

In producing the plans for 1995/6 and 1996/7, the three sets of objectives were found largely to coincide. This is taken as an encouraging indicator of consensus and of the effectiveness of communication and consultation. This overlap between the three sets of input means it is not possible to observe the extent to which the public consultation influences the plan's content. Senior police recognise that, because the priorities in the plan largely match the public's priorities, they could claim that public consultation has enormous influence on the plan's content. But they also note that, because of the other factors which also influence the plan, it would be misleading to claim such a direct relationship.

The 1996/7 plan includes a list of the ten broad issues identified in the consultation as the main priorities, and the public can see these concerns reflected in the objectives for the forthcoming year. For example, a demand for high visibility policing appears as a priority under a heading of 'public reassurance', with targets of increasing by 2.5 per cent the amount of time spent out of the police station by uniformed constables, and increasing by 3 per cent the satisfaction of the public with perceived levels of foot/mobile patrols.

The process of informing policing priorities is a subtle one, mediated by police knowledge and professionalism. To continue the example of high visibility policing mentioned above: the police and the authority know that this is not an effective method of countering crime, but that it is something favoured by the public. The task is then to reconcile what the public 'think they want with what they need'. This is dealt with by discussing, in the plan, the need to use resources effectively and by including the relatively modest targets for increasing visibility mentioned above. Such targets can be approached by strategies other than simply diverting resources. For example, through making more use of special constables and less of plain-clothes police cars.

The plan also explains where public priorities fall outside the remit of the police, such as the concern with sentencing, the courts and the prison system.

Thus, the public consultation is seen to influence the content of the plan. It adds to other sources of feedback to the police and the authority about public concerns, and enables these to be reflected in the presentation of the plan. But the plan is based on three sets of demands, and the question of how much weight to be given to each, were they to come into conflict, has yet to be posed.

Some members of the authority voice some disquiet about the amount of notice which is taken, by the force, of public opinion. This is a general concern and one which is related specifically to the plan itself. They mention having overheard comments about 'window dressing' at public meetings, and, as the new authority gains in confidence, express the view that the police should act more readily on concerns raised by its members on behalf of the public.

Impact

Acting on the output of the exercise

The results of the vote taken at the Focus Sessions are collated to provide authority-wide figures. These form one input, along with the National Key Objectives and the results of the police's own internal staff consultation, to a two-day seminar in the Autumn for senior police officers to discuss a plan for the next financial year. At the seminar, the results of the public consultation are presented and interpreted by the police officer who ran the Focus Sessions with the Clerk of the Authority. Once the draft plan is prepared by police officers, the Divisional Commanders begin work on divisional plans, to reflect the authority-wide objectives and local needs. A number of drafts of the plan are submitted to the authority for their consideration before the final draft is adopted. The 1997/8 plan was first considered at the authority's December meeting, and was adopted at the February meeting.

For this annual cycle, a new stage in the process was introduced. A seminar was held in January 1997 at which the authority could discuss the plan and other strategic issues with the Chief Constable and the Deputy Chief Constable. It was decided to hold such an event as a formal part of the plan development process every year. Some members had previously expressed concern about what they saw as their limited influence on the plan, and this event marks a new stage in the involvement of the authority in its preparation.

Direct impact

As we noted above, this public consultation is concerned with the exchange of information between the public, on one hand, and the police and Authority on the other hand. Observation suggests that the consultation process is contributing to the aims of educating and informing the public, and improving their understanding of police matters. Importantly for the police and authority, it also means that they are being seen to consult the public.

To assess the impact of information received by the police, we need to examine the influence of the consultation on the plan. As we have seen, because of the consensus between the different inputs, it is not possible to do that with any precision. Beyond that, the impact of the plan on police activity would be the ultimate criterion for assessing the impact of the consultation.

Annual plans have been produced since 1995–6. The cycle of accountability – consultation, plan with targets, report on performance – has now been established. However, police officers, members of the authority and the long-standing members of the Liaison Groups have a range of views about the impact of this process. Related to this, they also have different beliefs about the need for and value of a plan at all. It is widely felt that the annual regional plan would be regarded as something rather remote by the public, particularly as the role of the police, as seen by the public, changes little from year to year. Indeed, it is hard to imagine that the major demands on police resources, at a regional level, are likely to change much from year to year.

Its greater impact is likely to be as a tool for managing the service, and views differ on its impact here. The force has a number of mechanisms and structures to assess proposed activities against the plan, and to measure performance against it. Some members are quite satisfied with the way the plan is used and feel that the need for a plan as a management resource is minimal in a well-run police force (as they feel this to be). But they recognise that the plan might have a public relations value.

Other members feel that the plan should have a greater significance than it appears to them to have at the moment. It is intended to be a tool for managing a finite budget, setting targets and monitoring performance. For these members, there is a concern that the plan and its targets are not yet fully embedded in the running of the service. For this reason, it seems likely that some members will continue to press for the plan to be seen to have a greater influence.

Indirect impact

The overall process of public consultation has had a gradual influence in changing attitudes. It is not possible here to disentangle the specific impact of the Focus Sessions as they are part of the wider process of public consultation.

For the police, it has brought a new understanding of the ways to introduce change, based on greater communication with the community. By providing another source of feedback on public views, the consultation has enabled them to further their understanding of barriers to overcome in changing public perceptions of the police. It has helped them to identify the need for educating and training their staff to deal with the public in a more open and communicative way. The police feel that they are now more open with the public, because they have a vehicle for explaining why they take certain actions. The consultation meetings provide an opportunity to correct any misguided or ill-informed public views in a general setting and therefore in a non-defensive way. Consultation mechanisms provide an important safety valve, an opportunity to raise issues if and when hostile reactions occur or are threatened.

The future

Those responsible for the process have developed it over a two-year period, and expect it to continue to change and improve. Reaching the current position has not been easy; problems have been overcome and lessons learned along the way, and the approach has changed as a result.

The main preoccupation is how to consult a wider range of people and, in particular, how to involve young people. It has been accepted that consulting young people requires a different approach as they are unlikely to come in any numbers to the Liaison Meetings. A programme of visits to schools and other settings where young people gather began in late 1996. The possibility of discussing policing matters with other community organisations (not only those involving young people) is also being discussed.

The consultation process seems likely to develop along these lines in the future. The overall method used in the Focus Sessions, including the voting on priorities, is generally accepted as the most suitable for the circumstances.

Assessment

This case study is concerned with an unusual, perhaps unique, initiative. No other police force and authority is known to consult the public specifically on the policing plan, using a method which involves so much direct contact with the public. It is still in the relatively early stages of its development and is expected, by those responsible, to be further developed and improved. One informant described the consultation process as 'guided choice' which will develop further; although the mechanism exists for people to raise new issues and for new groups of people to become involved, it is necessary for the process to mature further before this can be expected to happen.

The process which has been developed has tackled some formidable constraints of geography, particularly when it is noted that the whole exercise has to take place during a relatively short summer period in order to feed into the planning process. The number of people involved has increased considerably since the beginning, and the approach produces a clear set of priorities to guide the planning process.

It provides local opportunities to the whole population of Devon and Cornwall to comment on matters which affect them all, directly or indirectly. It also offers a convenient and transparent way to demonstrate to the public the link between their votes and the plan's content. For both police and authority it has the added benefits of providing a forum for informing the public, and a way of being seen to consult. In its own terms, then, this can clearly be seen to be a successful initiative. Moreover, it is relatively cheap to run.

As the relatively new authority continues to develop, members are likely to search for ways of further improving the process and for using feedback from the public. The commitment of staff will also ensure that the approach continues to develop. This will involve a search for ways of broadening the range of people taking part in the consultation programme.

Research methods

We interviewed: the clerk of the police authority and the police officer responsible for the liaison meetings on two occasions; a senior police officer; members of the police authority; and four members of local organisations who had been attending consultative meetings over a long period. We also attended two liaison group meetings at which we distributed questionnaires to the public.

We also studied documents associated with the consultation process and the policing plan. Fieldwork took place between the Spring and Autumn of 1996.

Commentary

Overview

The Devon and Cornwall Police Authority, in cooperation with the police force, holds a programme of regular public meetings around the region. During the summer round of meetings, a separate 'focus session' asks for the public's views on priorities for the forthcoming annual policing plan.

The key points identified by the researchers were:

- Concurrent objectives have influenced the form of the consultation and may produce more apparent tension in the future.
- Skill and commitment, facilitated by legislation which created a new police authority with new responsibilities, have enabled the development of new approaches to consultation, building on a long tradition.
- The method is not ideally suited to the purpose because it does not involve a representative group of people who are equipped to contribute to strategic discussion. Supplementing this approach with a more deliberative method would probably be worthwhile.

Multiple objectives

The existence of several objectives for the consultation exercise are a source of inherent tension. The concerns to educate the public and to present a partnership of police force and authority as well as to elicit the views of the public mean that the purpose and process lose clarity. This tension may become more apparent as the process matures.

To give a considered view about policing priorities, the public does need to both receive information and to engage in dialogue about the issues (see below for the suitability of the method). While the consultation exercise, for these reasons, attempts to 'educate' the public, the police and the authority are the only sources of this information. Thus, the public is not assisted to come to an independent view.

Evolving an approach

This case study clearly demonstrates how an organisation can learn from experience in developing its approach to consultation. The transition from the old style consultation has been successful, despite the objections of some who had been involved. The organisers have also used their evaluation of the first year of consultation on the policing plan to make significant and successful changes to the approach for the second year. We attribute these developments to the skills and commitment of those involved in managing change in both the authority and the force. We expect the process will continue to evolve and the impact of the consultation to increase, for the same reasons.

Suitability of the method for the purpose

The method is not ideally suited for the purpose, for two main reasons. First, the public who attend are demonstrably not representative of the Devon and Cornwall public. Secondly, their ability to contribute to a discussion about authority-wide, strategic priorities is limited by lack of knowledge and possibly lack of interest. The contributions are mainly about local, topical or personal concerns.

Quantifying the views of such a group, by counting votes, runs the risk of endowing the results with a statistical validity they do not have. In fact, the scores are not directly influential on policy, but are instead a general source of information and indication of public views. Thus, the results are not actually used in a way which is inappropriate to their origins. But the counting of votes and allocation of points are nevertheless misleading as they suggest a validity and an intention which do not exist.

We consider that more interactive and deliberative methods would be suitable for consulting the public about authority-wide, strategic priorities. These could be complementary to the existing method, which is undeniably valuable in allowing all who want to to have a say, and in enabling dialogue between them and the police.

Discussion groups, for example, would allow the authority to consult a wider cross-section of the public about priorities, and to give them the necessary background information to make a more informed contribution than is possible in the current format. Before embarking on such an exercise, the police force and the authority would have to develop clear procedures for considering and acting on the conclusions of the groups.

The role of the Police Authority

The developing relationship between the police force and the new authority (established in 1995) forms the background to this consultation. The lead taken by the authority, with the full support of the police, in organising and carrying out the consultation has contributed to its effectiveness to date.

The involvement of authority members in the meetings is important, and their growing involvement in the planning process may be an indication of a trend towards greater assertiveness by members. If so, this is likely to influence the conduct and impact of the consultation in future years.

Transparency and accountability

The consultation process has established a cycle of accountability in that the consultation process contributes to the policing plan, and performance against the targets in that plan are made public. However, accountability to the public through direct consultation is not a requirement. The methods of using the consultation results and the fact that there are several inputs to the plan also mean that it is not possible to distinguish the impact of the consultation. In such circumstances, it is quite possible to live with the lack of clarity of purpose and process referred to above.

CASE STUDY FIVE

Eastern Health and Social Services Board and Council: Specialist Services for People with Learning Disabilities

INTRODUCTION

The Eastern Health and Social Services Board (the Board) is the purchaser of health care and social services in its area of Northern Ireland. The Eastern Health and Social Services Council (the Council) represents the public interest in a context where both purchasing and service provision are not the responsibility of democratically elected bodies. The Board and Council have a statutory obligation to meet together once a year, and in addition, Council members and staff attend Board meetings, and Council staff take various active roles in working and development groups. Relations between the two underwent changes in 1995, and are still evolving.

The Board is obliged by statute to consult, although only explicitly in relation to closures or substantial changes to services. The Council has carried out a variety of consultation exercises on its own initiative.

In 1994 the Board began a process of review of the future of specialist care for people with learning disabilities. A paper which offered options for the development of a strategy for the treatment and care of people with learning disabilities was discussed at a series of public meetings around the area, chaired by the Council's Chief Officer, in Summer 1995. The results of these meetings were presented in a paper to a Board meeting in September 1995, where no clear strategy was agreed. A second phase for furtherance of the strategy was set in motion at this meeting, and a group convened which produced a second paper, based on limited consultation with selected individuals and groups. This second paper was adopted by the Board in September 1996.

This case study is of both the learning disability consultation exercise, and the relations between the Board and the Council in the course of that exercise, and more widely.

ORIGINS AND OBJECTIVES

Origins

Involvement of the Council in Board activities

The Board and Council have formal relations which involve a meeting once a year. The Council also takes part in Board meetings, and has a range of other relations which are evolving.

From 1992 to 1995 the Board met every two months in public, and in closed session in each month between. The Council Chair and Chief Executive (CE) met the Chair and CE of the Board monthly. The Chairman and four members of the Council had speaking rights at Board meetings – attendance at meetings of the Board was very popular with the Council and there was competition for the speaking rights. Council members, including alternates, had speaking rights. The Council's general view, however, is that Board decisions were actually made at private meetings.

In 1995 a new Chair and Chief Executive of the Board took office, and sought to reform the pattern of relations between the Board and the Council. The new Chair sought to create a situation which would allow the Council to contribute a strategic, rather than a local viewpoint. To help achieve this he reduced the number of people from the Council who had speaking rights in Board meetings from five, to the Chair and CE of the Council only. In addition, the Council no longer received copies of confidential papers or attended the confidential section of meetings. Council members were not very happy about this reduction.

A number of practical arrangements also characterise relations between the two bodies. The Board sees a draft of the Council's work programme in order to avoid overlap, and there are monthly meetings with the senior management team of the Board. In the recent past there was a joint working group on complaints, at officer level, which involved a joint seminar for health providers, training sessions and a leaflet.

Recently Council members have been invited onto a range of working and planning groups, including around the Locality Sensitive Purchasing initiative.

The learning disability consultation

There are both national and regional strands to the origins of the consultation. At the national level, changes in government policy for learning disability services had to include reduction of the number of hospital places used to provide long-stay care. In addition, the (nationally-driven) Locality Sensitive Purchasing initiative, which emphasises consultation, had been adopted by the Board. Finally, consultation in the field of learning disabilities was increasingly common throughout the health service.

Alongside the national impetus, by 1994 the Board itself reached the point of wanting to review the future of specialist care for people with learning disabilities. Services within the Board's area are run by four Community Trusts, one of which – the North and West Belfast Trust – is responsible for services at the large local hospital for people with learning disabilities. In the region, people with learning disabilities number around 3,300, of whom 300 are resident in this large hospital.

Concerns about this hospital had arisen in a number of ways:

- an inspection by the Northern Ireland Hospital Advisory Service (NIHAS) had led NIHAS to approach the Board with some concerns;
- concerns were expressed by the Council as the statutory consumer body;
- a visit to the hospital by Board members had taken place as a result of learning of the NIHAS report.

The Board established a working group in 1994 to review the future provision of specialist treatment and care for people with learning disabilities. The report of this group was produced in Spring 1995, and offered nine options. The report was inherently controversial in that some of the options examined could have involved the closure of the large hospital.

A seminar for the professionals involved in the services (the Eastern and Northern Boards, the Trusts, the Eastern Council, the Mental Health Commission and Mencap) at which the report was discussed showed that for the most part they wanted community-based services, but did not want to close the hospital until new services had been developed. At this seminar different viewpoints were expressed. The North and West Belfast Trust argued for a 'campus' model, retaining the hospital in a revised form. The Board itself leaned towards one of the community options. The Board was further concerned that without changes it would soon be the site of one of the largest 'traditional' institutions for people with learning disabilities in Europe. The potential for change was however inhibited by a shortage of resources, a large amount of which were used to maintain the hospital, which, despite this, was underfunded.

Without the resources to develop alternatives, the Board could not plan a phased closure. But as long as resources were going into inadequate maintenance of the hospital, the money was not available to develop new services in the community. Development of a community approach would therefore involve reduction of expenditure on the hospital.

This is the context in which the decision to consult widely with the public, and with the families and other informal carers of the users of the services, was made. Although the Board is obliged by statute to consult, this is only explicit in relation to closures or substantial changes to services. The Council's view is that there are grey areas where consultation may or may not be required. The Board's previous approach to consultation has been to invite comments on draft documents. The Board's involvement in this exercise was therefore a new departure.

The consultation was shaped by changes in the Board's approach to its work. A new drive towards openness was part of an effort to ensure that the Board was not seen as secretive (a criticism made at times in the past). Under the revised arrangements, all Board meetings were opened to the public, with debates taking place and decisions made at these open meetings, based on options presented by officers, without prior recommendation. Board staff report that these changes greatly influenced the conduct of Board business, and the options paper on the future provision of specialist treatment and care for people with learning disabilities was produced by Board staff under the new arrangements.

The Council itself has carried out a variety of consultation exercises on its own initiative – for example focus groups to look at provision by a Trust for carers. The involvement of the Council in a Board learning disability services consultation exercise was also a new development in the relationship between the two organisations.

Objectives

The consultation had a number of objectives. The primary aim in consulting was to obtain the views of interest groups, the public, and the carers/families of users of learning disability services on the future shape of specialist treatment and care for people with learning disabilities. Specifically, Board staff wanted views on nine possible options for change before deciding its new strategy.

In addition, the Board was concerned to ensure that it met its obligations to consult in as fair and appropriate a way as possible. Here the Board had two things in mind. First, the Board was aware of strong feelings about the location and organisation of services, and needed to ensure that the consultation was inclusive. Second, the experience of being judicially reviewed over the closure of residential homes was something the Board did not want repeated.

Method

The consultation involved the Board's customary method of inviting comments from organisations on the options paper, and an innovative method of open public meetings aimed at individuals rather than groups.

The proposal for public meetings, in a variety of locations, at a variety of times, was influenced by the Council's experience of different methods – surveys, meetings, focus groups, and interviews. The Council felt that a postal survey was not a useful method for the issue, and whilst focus groups were feasible, they would limit the numbers of participants, and would require a very strong information input. Open meetings would ensure that the anticipated strong interest in the issues from families of people with learning disabilities could be expressed, and that the likelihood of judicial review would be diminished.

The consultation activities

Setting up the meetings

The options paper was presented to the Board in March 1995, after which a multi-disciplinary planning team was established, consisting of Board staff involved in the purchasing of learning disability services, the local Trusts, and the Eastern Social Services Council. Board staff, specifically, were from planning, nursing, and social services backgrounds.

The Board Chair had asked the Council to assist in the process, and the Council agreed to this in order to help the public and carers by being an independent broker – helping and facilitating. Meetings had to take place by the end of June, because of the extended July holiday in Northern Ireland. The team's brief was to consult and report to the Board by September 1995.

The structure and format of the public meetings was discussed at length. The task was to achieve a balance between detail and clarity of options, without presenting a preference, to emphasise that the Board was there to listen. A number of steps were taken to assist in the presentation of what was seen as a complex issue in a simple format. The presentation was divided into an introduction by the chair, a video, and a presentation with transparencies on an overhead projector (OHP), the presentation script was circulated to Executive Directors on the Board, to ensure that it represented the Board's views, and Board staff revised it to remove some of the jargon.

The meetings were to be attended by the Board staff responsible for the purchase of learning disability services, who stressed the importance of 'ownership' of the consultation. The team agreed that the CE of the Council should chair the public meetings, and the Council also took an advisory role for any matters arising in the meetings. The Council suggested notes of all of the meetings, to be typed and sent to the Council's CE for approval as Chair, and this was agreed.

Board staff took different roles: preparing a publicity leaflet, the video, and the presentation. In consultation with the team, the social services research and information section devised a structured approach to the records of the meetings, and agreed to analyse them. The Trusts' role was to provide venues and to be available if a participant raised a specific issue relating to the provision of local services or to individual cases.

Invitations were sent out by the Trusts to all carers from their records. Public advertisements were placed in the *Belfast Telegraph*, which has a regional spread, and is read by both 'communities'. Press releases were issued, and BBC Radio Ulster interviewed the Chair of the planning team.

The four Community Trusts set up the venues and sent out the invitations. Carer support was offered if needed, plus help with transport. Accessibility for carers was a key factor, both physically and in relation to times of meetings. These were at different times of the day, to meet the needs of different groups – for example for mothers with children, some meetings were in the morning from 10–12, and for employed people, in the evening. There was a geographical spread, with meetings which were close to each other scheduled for different times, to maximise choice. The pattern for this was based on local knowledge. The invitations listed all the meetings, and individuals could decide which to attend.

The opportunity to talk one-to-one was offered at each meeting, and an induction loop and signers (the latter not used) were available at each meeting. Forms with addressed envelopes were available at the meetings for comments to be sent in later.

The targets of the meetings were primarily carers and relatives, not people with learning disabilities. Board staff regretted not finding a better means of including significant contributions from people with learning disabilities.

The meetings

Seventeen meetings were held in all, titled 'Your services – your say'. The aim was to accommodate 60 to 70 at each meeting. Board staff in the planning team made the presentations at each meeting, using the prepared OHPs. Board Executive

Directors attended at least one meeting each, and several went to the hospital meeting. Each meeting had one or two Trust staff there – usually known to the other people who attended the meeting.

Meetings lasted one to one and a half hours, followed by tea, and the chance to chat generally in small groups or twos. There was a note taker at each meeting and a summary of the reports was produced after the round of meetings had finished.

The presentation was followed by questions addressed to the Board staff. Some questions were very general, but many were about specific circumstances. Anger was frequently expressed but people were also generally appreciative of the effort the Board was making. Most contributions were from individuals, as organisations had already had the chance to make written comments on the document. Some provider voluntary organisations attended but only as observers. There were contributions from a small number of people with learning disabilities. There were both question and answer sessions and some debates between participants. Many participants knew each other personally.

Attendance was typically between 10 and 30, with several meetings having more than 90 participants, two with only three people, and the hospital meeting with more than 400. The poorest attendance was in leisure centres – which are not associated with the service – one of which had access problems. After the hospital meeting, evening meetings in day centres and adult training centres (which have parent/adult groups) were the best attended. The small meetings were considered useful, as the participants could discuss in-depth informally, often around their own experiences, after the formal presentation.

A consistent theme in most meetings was concern about what services would be provided in the future, and Board staff used this to get participants to think about what they themselves wanted. This had some success – for example innovative proposals about respite care were made.

The hospital meeting was organised along the same lines as the others, but was larger, went on longer, and was treated by the hospital 'parents and friends' as a 'save our hospital' campaign, with demonstrations, placards, a parade, and speeches. Several Executive Directors of the Board attended this meeting. Television cameras and the press attended. The parents and friends were angry and hostile, speeches in favour of the hospital were applauded, and the friends had prepared questions for people to ask, including some patients brought to the meeting by staff, who made very emotional contributions. The parents and friends of the hospital had also held a dry-run meeting one week before the actual meeting and invited the press to this meeting as well.

Around 40 comments sheets were given back after the meetings.

The Council's view of the meetings

The Council found participants pleasantly surprised to be consulted, as they had not had the experience before. Useful discussions took place in the small groups, and individuals were able to raise issues with Trust staff. The general view of carers that more specialist services in the community were needed came to the fore over the course of the meetings.

The Council identified a number of difficulties with the meetings. Lack of expertise in dealing with people with learning disabilities was a problem, and ideally more effort should have been made to include service users in the consultation. The Council also felt that the information and presentations were not well understood and contained too much jargon, despite the efforts of Board staff to remove it. A summary of the report, which was made available at the meetings, was also jargon.

The Council felt that participants, especially from the community, who were not using specialist services, were unsure of the purpose of the meeting. Had the Board sent out better information in advance this might have been avoided. There were also problems about the room layouts and the CE dealt with this by rearranging rooms to informal patterns.

The view of voluntary groups

A number of voluntary groups attended meetings, including Disability Action, LEAD (the Northern Ireland coalition on learning disability) and Mencap. The Board also asked some of these to attend the hospital meeting. LEAD members met and had informal consultations on the issues as well as attending meetings, and produced a combined response with Disability Action. Mencap also responded formally to the report. Voluntary groups praised the Board's thoroughness and attention to detail in taking all possible practical steps to ensure effective participation.

Mencap was critical of the effectiveness of the publicity and suggested that the Board should have used the mailing list networks of the voluntary groups as well as the press advertisements to reach a wider audience. Mencap itself sought to encourage learning disabled people to attend, by writing to Adult Training Centres, Gateway clubs etc. and was critical of both the Board and the Council's lack of effort to reach learning disabled people.

Mencap had taken the view at an early stage that the report itself lacked detail, that the options were not worked out well enough, and that their presentation in such a form was likely to cause disputes. The voluntary groups generally felt that at some meetings the presentation of the options proved counter-productive, as it encouraged a polarisation of views.

They also found that many participants were unfamiliar with the report and used the meetings to tell the Board what they wanted. In the tea and chat sessions at the end, people who had expressed similar opinions exchanged views, as did Board and Trust staff.

The voluntary groups found that the perception of many participants initially was that hospital provision was what was being reviewed, but what came across in most of the meetings were issues about provision for the whole population. The earlier meetings were attended in the main by users of community provision, and the hospital was not discussed in these. Nor did the community problems discussed and identified involve the hospital as a suitable site of specialist provision. Overall, voluntary groups felt that the process centred eventually too much on the hospital and the broader needs of all people with learning disabilities were lost.

There was some feeling amongst voluntary sector participants that the Board should have provided leadership. Given that the Board favoured community provision, they should have argued for it and at the same time explained why they have not developed it.

Other responses

The Board received 75 written responses to its options paper, from the range of health organisations, from voluntary groups, housing providers, local authorities, trade unions, other Boards, the public, and relatives/carers.

The September 1995 Board Meeting

The Board held its September 1995 meeting in public following the consultation. This was a formal meeting at which a paper was presented, by an Executive Board member, the Director of Public Health, which sought to address the concerns of both the community and of those with relatives in hospital, and tried to satisfy both ends of a polarised debate.

Speaking rights were granted to an MP who spoke for the parents and friends of the hospital, to representatives of the Community Trust, to the trade union UNISON, to a carer, to a Royal College of Nursing steward at the hospital, to Mencap, and to the Chair of LEAD. A practical difficulty was that the room was not big enough, with not enough chairs provided by the Trust which hosted it at Lagan Valley Hospital. This made a heated meeting into an overcrowded heated meeting.

In the discussion, Board members made proposals which had not been the subject of consultation. For example, the Board gave a commitment to investigate a 'village community' model – which was not one of the options – and a statement was inserted that no-one should be moved without the agreement of relatives, as a result of which some resettlements were immediately cancelled. Both points were the result of the pressure exerted at the meeting, not of the consultation.

Mencap took the view that the Board's decisions at the meeting were strongly influenced by an earlier visit by non-executive directors of the Board to the hospital, which was guided by hospital managers, and which conveyed the impression that 'people like this' could not live in the community.

There was a general view from those involved in the consultation that as the Director of Public Health had had no involvement in the consultation, it was unsurprising that the priority given earlier by the Board to the consultation exercise was lost in the paper, which focused in the main on the problems of the hospital.

The Board's mixed conclusions enabled different parties to believe that their favoured option had been adopted, and others wondering what had been decided. This left a situation in which further work was needed to develop a policy.

The development group and the 'Select Committee' event

At the September 1995 Board meeting, the Director of Social Services was asked to carry through the recommendations. He established a 'core development group' to assist him in taking the recommendations forward and in devising a model of community services. Membership was drawn from the Board (including the staff who had run the consultation meetings), the Community Trusts, the hospital and the voluntary sector. The parents and friends of the hospital were not invited to take part, on the grounds that their interest was solely in hospital-based services.

The Council was not invited to be a member of this group, and the Council's contribution to the group was arm's length only – by raising questions at Board meetings after the September agreement. The Board's view was that the Council has a distinct and separate role, and that drafting policy/strategy documents is not part of that role. The Board also expressed concern that the Council was overstretched, although the Council points out that this concern has not been discussed with them.

It was not until January 1996 that the group met for the first time, mainly because of the Trusts' problems with time. The group held a two-day event in June 1996 when the members, plus invited others (including the Council and the parents and friends), heard 'evidence' for a day from professionals, users, and carers, including about a 'village community' model. The core group then deliberated for a further day. The Board describes this as a 'Select Committee' model. The Director wrote up the results as a paper to the Board.

The Council is critical of both its exclusion from the group and the short notice of the event, which prevented the CE from attending. The Council's Chair went to the first day, but was not invited to the second. The parents and friends of the hospital were likewise unhappy about their exclusion from part of this process.

The final paper – September 1996

The Board Chair's restriction on recommendations from staff had been relaxed somewhat by the time the paper was discussed, allowing the report to make proposals. The report sought to avoid the polarisation which characterised the original consultation, and took its lead from the general viewpoint expressed in the consultation, that the need was for development of services in the community. The report was not about the future of the hospital, and it rejected the idea of a village community on the hospital site, proposed further development of community services, and that money should 'follow the patient'. The Board also established workshops to discuss issues, with staff presenting ideas. This has enabled discussion of views to take place again outside of the public forum.

This report was accepted quietly, although the Board believes that reaction is likely to develop as time goes on. The Board's view is that the report is in accord with the results of the consultation. Whilst the consultation was focused mainly on the future of specialist treatment and care services, those consulted were concerned that there was a low level of services in the community. However, voluntary groups consider that the families in the community are happier with the result than are those with relatives in the hospital.

Resources

Board staff time spent on the consultation exercise was substantial, although a breakdown of this has not been provided. Here we indicate the tasks performed, and estimated time where possible.

Time at meetings may be assessed as one half day per meeting, of which there were 17. A minimum of two Board staff attended each meeting. Other Board staff time includes the following activities:

- meetings of the group established to mount the consultation;
- social services research staff time;
- the preparation time for the video, publicity etc;
- writing up the results of the consultation;
- preparation of two reports;
- the 'Select Committee' event.

Direct costs to the Board have included the video, leaflets and advertisements – estimated at £4,000.

The Council CE attended all meetings, reviewed the notes, and received copies of the reports. The Council itself had no direct expenditures.

Other costs incurred are those of the Trusts – at least two Trust staff attended each meeting, numerous hospital staff attended (although their role seems to have been mostly as participants rather than as facilitators). The costs of setting up the meetings was borne by the Trusts – premises hire etc. The amount of this is not known.

Management

The consultation was run by a project team, which included the Chief Officer of the Council, and Trust staff, and which also brought in staff from the Board's media section and social services research. The Board has stressed the need for a mix of skills to ensure the success of the meetings – chairing, publicity, administration, research, presentation. Cooperation with the Trusts is described as good.

Some aspects of organisation were less than ideal – for example the short timescale for the public meeting consultation was tiring and too intensive, more time was needed for the analysis of results – six to eight weeks would have been better, decision-making procedures did not have adequate time to operate afterwards.

Practical problems included invitations which arrived late from the publisher in inadequate numbers and which ran short and had to be photocopied. The lateness of invitations required that two extra meetings be held in September as they were not sent out in time. But overall, the team reported no unresolvable difficulties with the process.

There were difficulties in carrying forward the results of the public meetings phase of the consultation which arose in part from problems about ownership of the results. This is explored below.

The impact of the consultation process on its output

The consultation method used allowed participants who were caring for relatives in the community, rather than in the hospital, to express their views and wishes for the first time, including in ways not anticipated by the project team. This unexpected aspect of the output was a key influence in the eventual strategy decisions of the Board, made in September 1996. The method also allowed the

Board to collect all of the views of carers and family members in one report, providing a useful source document of benchmarks for future work.

However, two aspects of the original consultation process contributed to the problematic character of its direct output, the first report. Both raise useful issues for the conduct of consultations and the suitability of different methods for different circumstances. First, the method involved the presentation of options to open meetings, and this brought out strongly the pre-existing opposing views about the future strategy for special services to people with learning disabilities. Although the Board took action to ensure that the necessary decisions were eventually taken, by initiating a second phase of consultation, the original public meetings phase did not contribute greatly to the resolution of the Board's problems about strategic deployment of scarce resources.

In addition, the parents and friends of the hospital introduced forceful campaign methods into the process, and presented the consultation as an attempt to close the hospital. This group was supported by the professional groups and trade unions in the hospital. They used the press and political support to put their view across and influenced the Board's responses with these methods. The contending view, which was held by relatively unorganised carers not involved with the hospital, had no parallel campaign, and was unable to present a viewpoint in public with equal force. This imbalance created difficulties for the even-handedness of the Board's decision-making.

Finally, a key link between the stages of the process was weak, and unable to carry it through. Board staff on the team which led the consultation were second-level officers, and this seems to have contributed to a problem of ownership of the consultation by the Board itself, when the first report was produced and debated. The Executive Director who presented the report had not been directly involved in the consultation, and some of the Board members who made the decisions in September had not attended consultation meetings.

The report itself was as a consequence less well-related to the consultation than might have been the case, and proposals agreed by the Board at the September meeting included ideas which had not been the subject of consultation, and which had not previously been considered. As a result, a further group and paper, which operated without public consultation, were required to take the strategy forward. This second process involved what were described by one of the voluntary groups as 'informed insiders', and was led from start to finish by a Board Executive Director.

IMPACT

Acting on the output of the exercise

The direct output of the consultation – the first report – was eventually superseded by a second report, adopted one year after the first report. The Council is critical of the delay in reaching a new strategy, pointing to the period of more than one year after the consultation when no action was taken to address the main message of the public consultation – that services in the community were inadequate. The

Council's own consultations had revealed the same views, and the Council found carers frustrated at the lack of progress.

Direct impact

Strategic development of services is by nature long-term, and at the time of writing there has been no specific impact on services.

Indirect or unintended impact

Board staff take the view that networks between themselves, the Council, and the voluntary groups, although already good, were much improved by the frequent contacts and joint work over the consultation. Being seen to consult may in itself be valuable in policy development, in the view of some Board staff.

Mencap's view of the Council's involvement in the process is that in acting as the 'honest broker' the Council may have changed its 'voice'. Prior to the consultation, the Council would have advocated community care, and expressed concern at standards within the hospital, but the powerful expression from the hospital lobby made the Council less vocal. However, the Council comments that it did indeed debate the issue and that its recommendation for the community option was forwarded to the Board. Mencap is somewhat doubtful about the wisdom of the Council's taking on this broker role for this exercise.

THE FUTURE

The Board sees a future of exploration of different methods of consultation. Ideas such as the nature of 'representation' of the 'community' are under consideration. The voluntary groups have noted the anxiety caused amongst Board staff by this consultation, with all of its problems, but agree that the Board is clearly looking for other, more successful ways of consulting. Despite concerns, Board staff are keen to work with new models for consulting.

The new framework for consultation is Locality Sensitive Commissioning (LSC), and the LSC teams overlap with the Board's strategic planning teams. These teams have already been meeting the Trusts to explore possible structures for consultation, in which voluntary groups might be involved, and how to discover users' priorities. LSC teams will develop their own networks, and are only just beginning.

In addition, in the mental health field, there are new regulations which require that strategic targets must be settled by 1998. The Board carried out a first stage consultation on this in autumn 1996 – an internal consultation with Trusts and voluntary organisations. They intended to approach carers, users and staff later, and were considering focus groups. The Board has also held meetings with day centre users and carers on the future and views have been recorded and analysed.

Assessment

Success of the method

The Board's view

Overall, the Board believe that despite the difficulties, the consultation did produce better decisions. The 'community' case was strengthened, and the previously unvoiced views of carers in the community were heard.

The Board describes the consultation as an experimental process for a 'difficult' client group. Board staff recognised that consultation can produce dissatisfaction, if people do not get what they want out of it. Although the debate around the consultation was polarised, creating difficulties for the Board, this was caused not by the consultation, but was endemic.

The strength of the public meeting method is said to be that it elicited the views of the community, and not just of the interest groups. However, there was some feeling from Board staff that the public meeting method was not the best way to consult with the hospital's supporters. However, the view was also expressed that it is only to be expected that consultation may galvanise individuals, producing the expression of strong views.

The Board accepts that in adopting the second paper in 1996 it did not adopt one of the options from the original paper, which were about structure, but instead turned the outcome into a person-led service. However, they do see the final paper as fitting one of the original (community) options. They also see the two-day 'Select Committee' event as a success: by bringing people together to 'share' a problem they engaged with it and a way forward was found.

Some Board staff felt that the Board should have stated its intention to eventually run the hospital down, and that this difficult decision could not in the end be avoided. This was succinctly expressed as 'money only follows firm decision-making'.

Voluntary groups' views

The voluntary groups expressed satisfaction with the way in which the board conducted the consultation, noting in particular the attention to detail in the preparation and carrying out of the public meetings, and the willingness of the Board to meet the needs of participants.

Three criticisms of the overall process were made. First, the Board might have made more effort to talk to users – very few were involved. Second, the consultation was essentially flawed, in that the Board's response, as expressed in the first paper, was completely inadequate. Third, the long delay in finally reaching an effective strategy was undesirable – promoting a lack of confidence in the process for participants, who see that nothing is changing.

The voluntary groups also pointed out that the final result – the second paper and the decision to adopt the 'patient-led' strategy – was produced by 'informed insiders', without consultation.

The Council's view

The Council recognises a general difficulty in the field of health, because the resources involved and the size of changes are factors which slow down potential change. The delay between consultation and results can therefore be considerable.

The Council was pleased that the consultation was more than an exercise in circulation of a draft document. The Council sees one of its roles as to encourage consultation in the commissioning of services, and was pleased that the Board planning team were out in the community and had the chance to see things at first hand. This had an immediacy which cannot be conveyed by written responses and complaints.

But the Council was critical of the lack of involvement of Board members – three Executive Directors went to one meeting each, and non-Executive Directors did not go at all. By contrast, a member of Council (a different person in most cases) attended most of the meetings. If Board members had attended more of the consultation meetings they would have understood the strength of community feelings about not using the hospital, and would not have been swayed by the hospital's campaign style.

The Council also felt that the feedback from the public meetings was poor, and that a summary of each meeting, with the Board's decisions, should have been communicated. The Council made three requests for this to be done. There were no discussions, evaluation, or other learning from the experience or information on how it was taken forward by the Board. Finally, the delay in making decisions about the strategy was unacceptably long.

Relations between the Board and the Council

The views of the Council and the Board on their mutual relations revolve around the same facts, but reveal very different perspectives.

The Board's view

The Board expressed a commitment at Board senior management level to make the Council's role work, including the Council's role in commissioning. Whilst the Board discusses the appropriate 'level' of involvement of the Council regularly, it finds their role problematic. The Board does not want the Council to effectively become Board officers. Although the Board discussed Council membership of the strategic policy group, there is a risk of conflict with their role as representative of the community interest if they do become policy-makers.

In practice the Council is not always able to attend meetings which they are involved in, and cannot therefore keep abreast of all the papers and issues. Council attendance at policy team meetings was quoted as an example. Moreover, the Council did not respond to the second paper produced in the consultation exercise. Note that the Council's view of this is very different (see below).

The Board considered having the Council on the group which produced the second paper, and realises that the Council was not pleased to be excluded. The Board's view is that if the Council is included in a process then it cannot stand back from it and would 'own' it. This would inhibit the Council's ability to represent the interests of the different groups. The Council's role as the independent chair of the consultation meetings was to 'hold the line'.

The Council's view

The Council's view of relations with the Board is broadly that these were unsatisfactory in important ways before the consultation, and remain so. Although staff to staff relations with the Board are good, the Council expected involvement in the whole consultation exercise, and was surprised when this did not take place. If the Council were invited to play a similar role in the future, they would need to be persuaded, and would want to negotiate the terms and conditions in detail. The Council's much greater experience of research with users is not drawn on by the Board, which knows little of how to consult. By contrast, the Council's relations with the Trusts over consultation exercises and research are much more satisfactory.

The Council does not have a clear picture of how the Board carries out needs assessment, sets priorities, thinks about how to place contracts, develops quality standards, or decides on services to commission. The Council sees copies of Board papers, but remains unclear about the processes, and would like to bring the Board's work more into the public domain. Given that there is no equivalent in Northern Ireland of community care plans, Trust responses to the purchasing prospectus are not in the public domain. The Council would like to influence commissioning at Board level, but has not been able to do so since being set up.

Practical and procedural problems exist both over attendance at meetings, and over commentary on Board papers. The Council has difficulties in attending meetings only because of insufficient notice, a lack of regularity and so on. The Council has 30 members who are able to attend planning meetings. The Council was unable to comment on the Board's second paper for two reasons. First, the Council received the paper with a deadline which it could not meet, as it had no intervening meeting scheduled. Second, there is an endemic procedural problem, in that because the Council meets in public, it cannot discuss draft Board papers before they have been agreed in a form to go to the Board for discussion. Consequently, at the Board meeting when the paper was discussed, the Council could not have had a considered view.

There have been some signs of improvements, with meetings with the four heads of the LSC teams, and discussions about ways to engage with the community.

Research methods

We interviewed members of the Board at senior (executive) level and the officers who ran the consultation and took part in the groups which drafted both reports and the original options paper, and the Council Chief Officer. More than one interview was carried out in several cases. Members of two leading voluntary groups were interviewed, who were also members of the Council. One of these was a carer. We also studied copies of all reports, the summary of the consultation meetings, and a number of background documents relating to government requirements for service development.

A Note on the Eastern Health and Social Services Board and the Eastern Health and Social Services Council

The Eastern Health and Social Services Board

The Board is a special health authority which purchases health care and social services in its area of Northern Ireland. It was established in 1973. The Board has executive and non-executive directors. The latter are a barrister, two solicitors, a professor of social policy, an accountant, and the Dean of Medicine at the university, all paid. There are also five executive directors who are senior officers employed by the Board. There are ten Trusts in the Board's Area – four are Community Trusts, five are Acute General Hospital Trusts and one is an Ambulance Service Trust. Recently the Board has been reduced in size, and staff have moved to the Trusts.

Both the Board and the Health Trusts have a statutory obligation to consult with the Council on changes in service provision.

The Eastern Health and Social Services Council

The Council was established in 1991, with a statutory responsibility to represent the interests of the public in both the purchaser and provider aspects of health and social services. The Council is funded by the Northern Ireland Health and Social Services Executive, with eight staff. The Council was established in circumstances of general change, when, for example, the purchaser/provider model of health provision and GP fundholding were starting. Relations with the Board are evolving.

The Council has a statutory obligation to meet four times a year, and currently meets every two months. In addition, there are ad hoc committees. Council membership is required to reflect the geographical spread of the Region. 40 per cent of members are District Councillors, others are individuals from voluntary groups – Age Concern, the Multiple Sclerosis Society, Crossroads, the Northern Ireland Council on Disability (NICOD) – plus individuals from professions – a retired school principal, a minister of religion, a barrister, lecturers, consultants. Members are not paid. All are appointed by the Health and Social Services Minister.

There was a Council representative on each of the Board's planning teams: physical disability; learning disability; mental health; maternity and child care; older people; dental; and health promotion.

Commentary

Overview

The Eastern Health and Social Services Board (the Board) is the purchaser of health care and social services in its Area of Northern Ireland. The Eastern Health and Social Services Council (the Council) is a consumer body representing the public interest. In Summer 1995 a paper with options for the development of a strategy for the treatment and care of people with learning disabilities was discussed at a series of public meetings around the area, organised by the Board and the Trusts, and chaired by the Council's Chief Officer. Some of the options were strongly opposed by a public 'save our hospital' campaign, and different and opposing views emerged from the meetings.

Following the meetings a paper was presented to a Board meeting in September 1995, at which no clear strategy was agreed. A second group was convened and produced a second paper, based on a more limited consultation, using an investigative method. This was adopted by the Board in September 1996.

This case study was both of the consultation exercise itself, and of the relationship between the Board and the Council, as evidenced by the exercise. We identify a number of key points which are examined in this commentary:

- Allowing consultees to make decisions about a service development strategy is an ambitious approach, which is difficult to see through.
- Making strategy decisions in the context of strong views and campaign approaches requires a mix of methods.
- Shared understandings between a purchasing organisation and its watchdog are difficult to achieve.
- A commitment to openness can cause difficulties for decision-making and this must be thought through.

Decision-making by consultees

The paper produced by the Board as the basis of the consultation offered a series of options, listed without an indication of the Board's preferences. These options were presented by Board staff to a series of public meetings for discussion. The intention was for the Board to settle on an option on the basis of the results of the consultation. This ambitious approach was unsuccessful in its goal, but not inevitably so. The Board was not seeking to avoid decision-making, or to ask service users to arbitrate internal disputes. Board staff interviewed had fairly definite views about the options, but the offer of options was a genuine attempt at openness. Other drivers were important – requirements to consult, avoidance of the risk of judicial review. But the explicit driver – offering choices to users and their carers – was the primary element.

In retrospect Board staff could see why the approach did not work. Whilst some concern and vocal protest was expected from some consultees, the heated campaign which developed was not anticipated. Without the campaign it would have been more likely that the consultation would have produced the necessary decisions.

A mix of methods

Public meetings method cannot cope with campaign tactics. The campaign swamped one large meeting, as well as the Board's decision-making meeting. It also prevented different views, expressed more quietly, from having the same force. Second, a development strategy is a difficult subject for a consultation, and consideration of the issues requires a framework which permits information exchanges of some intensity.

One criticism of the public meetings made by the Council was that since attenders were not briefed in advance, those not involved in the campaign had little idea what they were about. A single meeting is a difficult forum in which to remedy this for an entire strategy. But many meetings were attended by carers whose family member was living at home, who did not see themselves particularly as service users, but who came to the meetings and explained what they wanted from the service-providers. These contributions fell in part outside of the options on offer, and are seen as the most important product of the consultation by board staff, who discovered needs about which they knew little. Had these meetings been more investigative, they might have been more useful.

After the consultation had ended, the Board set up a new procedure, ostensibly to take forward the results. This took the form of an invited working group, plus some inquisitorial sessions described as the 'Select Committee' method, after which a senior manager wrote a new paper, adopted quietly around one year later. This second paper shifted the focus away from the nine options, reaching conclusions which in effect favoured one option, but which was not expressed in this way. Two factors made this successful in terms of decision-making. First, unlike the public meetings consultation, this was led from start to end by the same senior manager. Second, participation was limited, and in particular the campaign group was not fully included. As consultation, this was slight in comparison with the earlier phase, but in our view the inquisitorial approach was better suited to the situation.

The working group took evidence, a method which would have allowed the campaign to put its view across. Campaign members could then have organised their own meetings to further the campaign. But an investigative approach cannot reveal needs which are unexpressed and unorganised. You cannot invite people you do not know about to give evidence, and unorganised individuals are unlikely to respond to a public call for evidence or a written paper.

It seems likely that a deliberative approach would meet both objectives, but it would be costly.

A lack of shared understandings

Relations between Board and Council can be described as good at a practical and personal level, but muddled at the organisational level. The accounts offered to us by Board and Council staff differ in almost every respect about their relationship. The Council wants improved and better organised access to the Board's processes. The Board wants the Council to remain at arm's length to sustain its independent role. Some improvement was hoped for by both sides with new central government requirements for approaches to local purchasing.

The consultation exercise revealed these differences clearly. The Council saw itself as a key player, and was concerned that it was not included in the process once the public meetings had ended. The Board was grateful for the Council's independent role as chair of the meetings, but did not want the Council to be involved in taking Board decisions, as this would prevent the Council from adopting a critical independent stance.

Openness and decision-making

Specific aspects of the Board's commitment to openness contributed to the difficulties in decision-making around the new strategy. Board meetings were all held in public, and officers were encouraged to present options without recommendations. The Board could then deliberate and reach decisions in public. This approach led directly to the presentation to the public of nine options for change, and to the failure of the Board to reach a satisfactory conclusion after the consultation had ended.

We have already commented on the suitability of public meetings for strategic decision-making, but there is a further issue which is highlighted by the Board's public decision-making. At the Board meeting which considered a paper written after the public meetings, non-executive members of the Board made suggestions which were included in the Board's decisions but which had not been raised in the consultation. In this they may have been influenced by both the presence of large numbers of vocal people, but also by lobbying.

The problem here is that of 'the public' or 'service users' versus 'interest groups' – an issue addressed in the citizens jury and the consensus conference. To mount a large-scale public consultation is expensive, but to add new items to its outcomes, for whatever reason, proved even more costly. In the Council's view there were two causes of this. One was that non-executive members were not involved in the consultation, and did not attend the meetings. The other was that a tour of the hospital, organised for Board members by hospital staff, succeeded in presenting a strong case for hospital care.

CASE STUDY SIX

Edinburgh City Council: 'Call Clarence'

INTRODUCTION

In the late 1980s Lothian Regional Council (now abolished and replaced by four unitary authorities) began a shift towards a customer focus for its services. As part of this shift, the Council began to examine how to improve its road and pavements repairs programmes. A new scheme, aimed at replacing an internally-directed service with a customer-focused service, and at the same time increasing the efficiency and effectiveness of repairs as a result, was established in stages from 1990 to 1992. This new scheme was a one-stop-shop freefone service for all road, pavement and street lighting repairs, and was launched with a specific publicity strategy and logo of a lion named Clarence, and the slogan 'Call Clarence'. The Council's repairs strategy and priorities for repairs were subsequently revised through an analysis of customer priorities and types of defects reported, producing a major shift in the Council's approach to road maintenance.

Clarence is now run jointly by the four unitary authorities, and is franchised as a package to other authorities in Scotland. Plans to expand the sale of Clarence are now in hand.

This case study is therefore of the use of a telephone-based complaints system and its potential for providing information of benefit in the provision of services. It is not strictly about a consultation exercise, but is rather a study of an approach to service provision which is, potentially, inherently consultative.

ORIGINS AND OBJECTIVES

Origins

There were two aspects to the Council's perception of the need for change. Firstly, in the late 1980s there was no consistency between the ways complaints were dealt with between the four sub-regions. This brought out issues of equity of service for residents of the different districts, and of efficiency, in that different methods were being used. Second, because the Highways Department exercised its own professional judgement in deciding priorities for repairs, there was no effective public say either in how repairs were done or in what was done, and priority was typically given to whoever made the most fuss. The Council held the view that footpaths and pot holes were minor repair issues, but this was not shared by the public, which gave these a high priority.

In practice the Department was not good at locating and repairing pot holes, and in itself this increased accident insurance claims. A considerable amount of staff time was devoted to attending to enquiries and complaints on an ad hoc basis, leaving work unplanned and therefore inefficient, and disrupting the overall work programme of the Department.

The Department further believed that it was seen by the public as remote and monolithic, and that there was general public dissatisfaction with highways maintenance. Finally, road repair was not an 'interesting' issue in the region, unlike, for example, education and social services, and an element of the new approach therefore involved seeking to effect a change in the level of 'interest', in order to raise its profile within the Council itself and thereby make improvements more possible. The Regional Council business plan proposed a customer focus for all services, and within this the Highways Department sought to reposition itself in the eyes of the public, and to encourage the public to see themselves as the Department's customers.

Although this was in the main an internal development, Council staff knew of experiments by other local authorities with helplines – for example Exeter had a service called Lucius, and a postcard system. These examples did therefore play a small part in encouraging the development of Clarence.

Objectives

There were two main objectives in revising the approach to road repairs:

1 to enable a customer-focused and customer-led service;
2 to enable more efficient and effective management of enquiries and complaints about highways from the public.

The overall aim was an improved, customer-led service with the potential to revise the approach to defect remedy in the light of evidence of customer preferences and demand. Because of the perceived inefficiencies in the approach to repairs, it was assumed that a customer focus would bring increased efficiency.

The consultation process

Methods

In the past, residents of Lothian with complaints about services were able to telephone the Council, or complain to members at their surgeries. Councillors' surgeries did receive a lot of complaints, but this is described as a tortuous route for complainants seeking remedies. A telephone call to the Council was dealt with through a central switchboard, and callers would typically be passed from one extension to another: again, a tortuous route.

The choice of Clarence as a method was based on the Council's experience of these traditional methods, and of a reply-paid postcard scheme for notification of road repair problems introduced throughout the region in April 1988. Postcards were distributed through Regional and District Councillors and Community Councils, initially in one division of one of the four districts (Edinburgh), for a trial period of six months. The scheme was extended to the remainder of the region for a further six months in November 1988. Either a member of the public or a councillor could send a completed card to the Department if there was a road maintenance problem. At the same time a local cycling pressure group – Spokes – issued its own cards for their own members.

A review in 1990 identified low take-up of the postcards as an issue, and a Linkline 0800 telephone line to report defects was introduced in November 1990, as an addition to the postcards. The original number was 0800 622235 – but the Council wanted a more memorable number – and it was later changed to 0800 23 23 23.

Three advantages of the use of a freefone telephone number were identified. First, instant access – picking up a phone is easier than collecting and completing a postcard, and telephones are widely installed in homes. Thus information on defects would increase. Second, a 'one-stop-shop' approach would overcome the previous problem of telephone callers being passed around to different extensions. Third, the use of clerical staff to receive complaints would free technical staff to concentrate on repairs. The system adopted was also capable of recording the total number of calls, how many did not get through, and how many were made when the service was not staffed.

Because the postcard was free it was decided that the phone would be freefone, avoiding potential problems of cost being a deterrent. To meet the Council's priorities, the new service was also required to provide an information base for decision-making about priorities for repairs.

Activities

Setting up and developing Call Clarence

Call Clarence was established by the Highways Department on a trial basis in November 1990, and the proposal for a new system enjoyed broad support from all political parties. Initially staff were seconded on and trained in telephone work. Telephone calls were logged on-screen into a database both to ensure ease of recording and passing on of details of repairs needed. Staff were expected to have customer service skills, enthusiasm, commitment, and were required to record each enquiry without passing it on. Keen individuals were recruited from general clerical backgrounds over a period of six months.

Call Clarence was given a distinct identity through the design of a logo which depicted a lion named Clarence. The name was invented first as an acronym, and the lion was subsequently chosen for two reasons: first, there is a lion on the Lothian Region crest; and second, a lion named Clarence featured in a 1960s television programme, Daktari. The original lion was drawn in-house by the region's centralised marketing staff.

Clarence was piloted region-wide, although not extensively advertised until March 1991. A report to the Transportation Committee in March 1991 declared Clarence a success, and in March 1991 the Committee approved a region-wide launch, including the erection of specific road signs to advertise the scheme, a press campaign, a tear-off reply slip with a leaflet, and a plastic card with the phone number, which went to every house in the region.

A market survey of Clarence customers in 1992 showed a number of problems: callers were not given a reference number; the service was getting through to motorists rather than to pedestrians, because signs were put alongside the roads. The study also showed that usage was higher amongst higher social class groups, and older age groups.

Following this report, Clarence was relaunched with some modifications in 1992, a number of changes being made to increase awareness and use of the service. Changes were made to operations, publicity, and to the logo itself. The physical shape of the lion Clarence was changed after concluding that it looked too cuddly. An external agency designed the new lion, whose head can now be used separately from its body. The original lion was designed not to be gender-specific, but the new lion was more masculine than the earlier one. Sponsorship was sought and in March 1993 agreed with McAlpine. Later a video about Clarence was made.

Running the service

At the start, it was not known how many calls there would be. From full operation in 1991 there were four telephones plus two spill-over extensions which received 12,000 calls in that year. This represented 95 per cent of contacts with the Department. This rose in 1995 to almost 37,000, over half of which were about street lighting and a further 10 per cent about potholes.

The maintenance staff who carry out repair work feed back to the Clarence team, enabling the team to explain outcomes to any callers who do ring back. This is an important part of the service. However, such feedback from maintenance does not always take place. There are well understood types of priorities for different types of repairs, and the Highways Maintenance Code of Practice lays down standards of good practice. There are currently publicised time targets for the street lighting contract.

Franchising Clarence

The technology offered by the 0800 number permits the franchising of Clarence. Each franchise has the same number, but the telephone system detects where the call is made from and routes it through to the correct Clarence base. Stirling, and Tayside, separate unitary authorities which had not been part of the former Lothian Region, are the only current Clarence franchises.

Stirling is adding cleansing complaints to the service, of which there were 78,000 in 1995. There are currently 20,000 calls to Stirling Clarence in a year. In Stirling there is also an education complaints system which uses Clarence software, based on data-ese, but which is not advertised as such.

Managing the process

The development of Clarence took place within the Council's transport section largely without outside inputs – either from other Council departments, or from other organisations. Potentially relevant local user organisations including Spokes – a cyclist campaign – and the Cockburn Association – a civic amenity group – were not involved, nor were motoring organisations.

Clarence was originally established by the region, and Edinburgh City Council now manages the scheme, and the other three former districts use the Edinburgh team for their Clarence service, and pay on a proportional basis. A Clarence user group has been established made up of the Councils who use it. Other local authorities who have a Clarence franchise have their own teams. At the time of this case study (Summer 1996), the Council was not in a position to say whether this approach to the spread of Clarence was working.

Changes to the departmental structure include changing the name of the maintenance section of the Highways Department to that of Local Areas Services. There is a road network manager for a geographical area, with a separate road lighting section. The repair manager arranges inspection and repair and then either urgently repairs or builds repairs into the programme.

Resources

The operatives were trained, along with other customer service staff across the region, using an outside company for a daily fee of £2,000. In 1993 sponsorship of £50,000 was obtained over three years (1993–1995) from McAlpine.

The computer system was set up in-house. Direct costs included telephone equipment, and marketing and staff – both ongoing. Adverts were carried on Radio Forth – with a jingle.

The budget head was that of the overall road maintenance division. Annual running costs approach £200,000, with contributions from the sub-regions. Sponsorship continues to be sought along with additional management fees from franchisees.

User views

Users are the residents of Edinburgh and effective examination of their views was not feasible. Edinburgh Council reports that the public took to Clarence enthusiastically, with many spontaneous calls from the public to say how pleased they are that problems have been dealt with.

Impact

Influence on Policy and Services

A large volume of business is being handled by Clarence. Around half of the calls are about street lighting, which had previously been a low priority for repairs. Clarence effectively revealed the level of public concern about street lighting, as a result of which the contract for lighting maintenance, when drawn up, required that 95 per cent minimum lighting stock be working at any one time.

There has also been an influence on both road repair priorities and on how road repairs are carried out. In the past repairs were done in batches, and faults were held until the slot for their 'batch' came up. Inspections were every six months. Repairs are now done within much shorter timescale – in some cases singly, according to categories of urgency.

Councillors have noticed a decline in complaints at surgeries, and insurance claims have fallen by 25 per cent. There was concern that the improved service might encourage unrealistic expectations, but there appears to be acceptance that some things take longer to repair for various reasons – for example, if they are not actually hazards.

It was recognised that a priority system based on customer preference would skew the budget towards what customers wanted. Edinburgh expressed the view that the objective of efficient internal use of staff has been met. Stirling, however, believes that Clarence has made road repair 'inefficient' in terms of use of resources, with the budget for repairs overspent because of this. In this view, this is a 'cost' of democracy. We are unable to comment on this difference.

Some concern was expressed that residents might only ring Clarence about the types of problems which they know will be dealt with – in this case lighting. If this did occur it would create a loop in the feedback into repair priorities, but there is no evidence for this – it was only a concern expressed to us.

Edinburgh Council have now moved to using Clarence as an information-giving tool, giving advice on road conditions and roadworks.

Internal impact on the participating organisations

The reorganisation into unitary authorities has taken up a lot of time, and Clarence's impact is difficult to gauge because of the other changes taking place.

The Council quality-assured Clarence in 1995 as part of the quality assurance of the Highways Maintenance Section. The City Development Department is concerned that with diminishing resources road maintenance is under-funded, and this may be beginning to devalue Clarence. Roads tend to have a lower priority when resources are tight, and funds have declined by over 10 per cent, and continue to do so.

THE FUTURE

In the future the Council wants Clarence to be about transport as a whole. Other authorities have begun to use it for buildings – for example, schools and playgrounds.

Clarence is operated through Microsoft Access, but staff would like an interactive system capable of carrying a wider information network – with Clarence operating through a geographical information system (GIS) – an on-screen map which identifies the exact position of the repair needed, and which can be marked on the screen. The identified need is then noted centrally by the GIS, which itself generates information for each Inspector. A GIS could be tied in with roadworks, and could be used to identify utilities defects as well. Development of suitable GIS software is still required.

The Council's view is that the former regional authority in principle was not liked by the (former) central government. Now that the region has split into unitary authorities it is possible that central government may be more helpful than in the past.

The Council would like to take further initiatives to enable the local authority to get closer to the customer. The Council has now revamped its former 'Busline' into 'Traveline' (an advice service on public transport), and plans to integrate this with the Clarence phone number. Selling Clarence on franchise more widely has recently begun.

Assessment

Edinburgh Council's view

Clarence reduces customer frustration, greatly improves the interface with the customer, makes better use of limited technical resources, and improves the image of the local authority. Clarence has made a notable contribution to the organisation of defect management.

One consequence of the improved repairs situation is that the Council is increasingly involved in legal actions by the public. As the service gets better, so more demands are made, and the more each single instance of a repair problem is highlighted. Paradoxically, this can mean that better repairs leads to worse publicity.

There are two key points which the Council identified as essential to developing a similar system:

1 a bigger budget is needed for launching – it took two years to get it known;
2 repairs must be resourced to match the Clarence system.

Clarence allows the public access to the Council, and in a sense the public become unpaid inspectors.

Research methods

Interviews were carried out with senior staff from Edinburgh City, Mid-Lothian, and Stirling Councils in summer 1996. In addition, the Clarence office in Edinburgh was visited and the system observed in action. Committee reports on the establishment of Clarence were studied. Two independent market studies of Clarence, in 1992 and 1995, were made available to us. A copy of the Clarence information pack, logos and toy lion were provided.

Commentary

Overview

In 1990 Lothian Regional Council (now abolished and replaced by four unitary authorities) began the development of a scheme aimed at improving its road and pavements repairs programmes. The scheme is a one-stop-shop freefone service for all road, pavement and street lighting repairs, which is publicised using the logo of a lion named Clarence, and the slogan 'Call Clarence'. Repairs are carried out in accordance with the priorities evidenced by the complaints received by Clarence.

The scheme, which is now managed by Edinburgh City Council on behalf of all four unitary authorities, has expanded in the last six years, has been adopted by all four, and has also been franchised to other local authorities, with freefone technology which allows the same number to be used for all schemes.

We identify a number of key points which are examined in this commentary:

- Both customer access to the repair services, and the organisation of services have been improved significantly by Clarence.
- High profile launching of such services is essential.
- Repairs need to be resourced to match the demand generated by customer responsive services if they are to maintain momentum and credibility.
- Enhanced access brings greater demand for repairs, and this may be more costly.

Access and organisation

The evidence for the success of Clarence lies in the large increase in contacts by the public about repair needs, which have trebled in the past five years. Enhanced access has meant a better appreciation by the local authorities of what the public's priorities for repairs are. This has fed into the approach to repairs management, and the batch systems in use previously have been revised in favour of specific response times for different degrees of urgency. The involvement of the public in this way has been described to us as encouraging members of the public to become unpaid inspectors.

High-profile launches

Staff responsible for Clarence were self-critical of the inadequacy of its launch in the early days. In practice it took two years for Clarence to take off, a problem which could have been avoided with an adequately funded launch programme. This touches very directly on one of the most difficult issues for public service organisations. Whilst it is difficult to provide improving services, and to involve the public in the development of these, it is even harder to convince the public that something good is on offer. In this case publicity, followed by experience, got there in the end.

Resourcing repairs

One of the paradoxes of the success of Clarence is the need to increase resources to keep pace with demand. This was at the time of our study a developing problem. Resources allocation is of course in part a political decision, not within the control of the staff running the service. This division between operations and overall resources is a key issue for many public services. Indeed, in this guide the Benefit Agency case study reveals similar issues in the relations between the Agency and government.

Access and costs

Within this resources issue there were two views of efficiency offered by the local authority staff whom we interviewed. One the one hand, the reorganisation of services to meet public priorities was described as more efficient, and on the other as less so. We were unable in the framework of this study to arbitrate these differences. However, both views are potentially correct. The 'less expensive' view looks to the overall approach and asserts that much more is being achieved for the same outlay. The 'more expensive' view asserts that public preferences cannot be made to fit into, for example, batch repair schedules as efficiently as management systems can do this. What this implies therefore is a new definition of efficient, linking perhaps democratic notions with the current notion of 'best value'.

CASE STUDY SEVEN

Highways Agency: Round Table Planning Conference

ORIGINS AND OBJECTIVES

The Highways Agency organised a 'round table conference' to consider needs for improved transport facilities in the Guestling Thorn/Rye area of East Sussex, and possible solutions to transport problems. The conference was held in two sessions in January and April 1995, and the report of the conference was published in September 1995.

Origins

In August 1993 the Department of Transport announced its intention to pilot the use of round table planning conferences. Following trials in Hereford and Cornwall, the Minister for Railways and Roads announced the formal introduction of such conferences in August 1994. The A259 trunk road was to be the subject of the next one.

Round table conferences were presented as part of a package of measures to reduce the time taken to agree on and build new roads, and to improve value for money and efficiency in the roads programme. They were intended to be held in the early stages of planning a scheme, with the aim of shortening the time taken to reach decisions about road building. They were not to replace any statutory procedures or change the rights of objectors.

A round table planning conference is described as an informal forum for groups and individuals to discuss transport needs and problems in a particular area. There is an independent chairperson to facilitate debate and encourage constructive and non-repetitious contributions, to seek consensus on a way forward, and to report to the Secretary of State for Transport. There are no pre-set proposals on the agenda. Non-road options may be discussed. The Highways Agency and their consultants are there to give advice and information.

To consider this innovation, it is necessary to understand the usual approach to consulting the public about road planning. The established pattern is for the Department of Transport/Highways Agency to consult local authorities and other statutory bodies in confidence before presenting a small number of route options for wider public consultation. This public consultation usually takes the form of an exhibition with brochures and a questionnaire to elicit the views of the public. The report on this consultation exercise is one source of information for the Minister's decision on a preferred route for the road.

The announcement on the preferred route is followed by more detailed assessment and design work. Then, if objections are received, there is a public inquiry. It is an inquiry into the choice of the specific preferred route. Anyone may give evidence and voice objections. Following a report from the Planning Inspector, who chairs the inquiry, the Department either confirms its choice of route or announces other work to be done. It is not possible to decide on a different route at that stage.

The August 1994 announcement of planning conferences had said that they would be held 'at an early stage of scheme planning, as part of or as a precursor to formal public consultation'. In fact, the Hereford trial conference had been held after a public inquiry. This inquiry had led to a decision to withdraw the proposed route, because of the level of objections. However, the Cornwall trial had been held before any public consultation at all.

Despite the intentions to hold a conference in the early stages of planning, the A259 conference was called after an earlier public consultation exercise (held in May 1993) on the Guestling Thorn and Icklesham bypass had proved inconclusive. That is, it produced no consensus or overall majority for any one option. No preferred route was announced. The consultation exercise had set out several options. They included one to the north of Icklesham and Winchelsea, across the Brede levels, and several routes which passed to the south of the village of Icklesham and the existing road. The stalemate came about because the people of Icklesham broadly favoured the northern route, but this was objected to by other interests, including environmental groups and residents of another village to the north.

Government was thus faced with an impasse; any choice of route would be deeply unpopular with certain groups. It is thought by many that the conference was called to avoid or delay having to make such a controversial, ministerial-level decision, especially in the prevailing climate of large and well-publicised protests against road building schemes.

Objectives

The pre-conference publicity brochure stated that it was to decide the way forward, following the inconclusive public consultation. It also stated three objectives – the conference was to seek agreement on: the need for an improvement to the transport facilities; the objectives of any solution; an acceptable solution for meeting the need and objectives of any scheme, taking account of all the relevant interests.

The geographical scope of the conference was also stated at this point. Preferred routes for the Winchelsea and Rye bypasses, on the east of the conference area, had been announced in July 1991. However, they were to be included in the conference as well. The western end of the Winchelsea bypass had been included in the public consultation of May 1993, but not the rest of these schemes. Thus, the scope of the conference was considerably wider than that of the previous consultation exercise.

To the west of the conference area, there was already a published route for the Hastings eastern bypass. Road schemes along the whole route of the A259 were presented as part of the Department of Transport's programme for improving the south coast trunk road.

THE PROCESS

Methods

The Highways Agency made the practical arrangements for the conference, but the way it was conducted was essentially a matter for the independent chairman. He was Robin Wilson, a former president of the Institution of Civil Engineers, who has extensive experience of highway planning and public consultation about it. His brief was to arrange and facilitate debate, to encourage constructive and non-repetitious contributions, to report to the Secretary of State on the views expressed at the conference, and to seek consensus on a way forward. Beyond this, he received no formal guidance. He has explained that he took decisions about the methods and approaches to use in the light of the circumstances as the conference proceeded.

Robin Wilson established a number of principles for his own role as Chair and for the conduct of the conference, building on his general experience and what he had learned of the two previous conferences. These included:

- The word 'conference' implies taking part in discussions, reaching a conclusion which all are party to, and a duty to produce an end result.
- A conference has delegates. People wishing to attend had to register, either as individuals or representatives of organisations. They were told they had to attend for the whole time, to enable discussion to develop. People were also encouraged to organise themselves into groups, as contributions made on behalf of groups would carry more influence, and save time and space.
- There would be no voting or majority decisions. The aim was to seek consensus. Minority views must be brought into any recommendations.
- The role of the chair was to facilitate, not to come to a view himself. It was for the group to reach a view, and he would guide the process for them to do so.
- Any written submissions could be placed in the conference library, established for that purpose, but it was not the role of the chairman to read them.
- Speakers were allowed to speak for as long as they held the attention of the conference, but the chairman intervened to stop repetition or seek clarification.

The activities

Publicity

Brochures about the conference and registration forms were sent to all residents of the area covered by the conference, to those who had responded to the previous consultation, and to local, regional and national organisations who were thought likely to have an interest.

Pre-conference meeting

A pre-conference meeting was held in December 1994, for the chairman to outline the objectives, scope and procedure and to answer questions about any of these. At this meeting, the results of the inconclusive public consultation were issued, including the numbers who favoured each route. It is not usual for the Department of Transport or Highways Agency to release such information from public consultation, until a preferred route is announced.

Registration

People and groups were encouraged to register as delegates to the conference. Delegates received an information pack, with background material on the area and its transport patterns. A total of 280 delegates were registered; 144 as representatives of 90 groups, 136 as individuals.

Accommodation

The conference was held in the Icklesham village hall, which accommodates 120 people. Three porta-cabins, linked with video and sound systems to the main hall, provided accommodation for up to 90 more. The main hall was full for most of the time; the cabins were between half and two-thirds full.

The conference table in the main hall sat 42. These seats were initially allocated to those delegates who had expressed a desire to speak on the day's topic. As the conference progressed they were allocated to those representing larger groups, statutory authorities and other major interests. The chairman sat at one end of the long table so that delegates could address each other across it.

Timetable

A draft programme was provided for the pre-conference meeting. This proposed eight sessions of 2 to 3 hours each, over four days. The draft programme directly reflected the objectives of the conference: the first 2 to 3 sessions were to investigate the needs for improvement, sessions 3 to 5 were to consider constraints, and sessions 5 to 8 were to look at options for improvements. In fact, the conference lasted a total of nine days and eighteen sessions. There was a first part of six days (10–17 January) and a second part of three days (3–5 April). Seven days had afternoon and evening sessions, two had morning and afternoon sessions.

The first part of the conference considered needs and constraints and began to look at options. The second part of the conference considered, in turn, the choices for Guestling Thorn and Icklesham, Winchelsea and Rye.

Adjourning the conference

Towards the end of the first part of the conference, two new routes, different from any which had previously been considered, were proposed for the Icklesham bypass. These emerged when the chairman detected an interest in small-scale improvements, and the possibility of an on-line (closely following the existing road) route. He facilitated the development of these ideas by using an overhead projector in the conference, drawing the possible routes on a map projected for all to see, as people in the hall made suggestions. Both new routes passed closer to the village than those put forward at the public consultation. One included a tunnel under Winchelsea and thus proposed changes to the preferred route there.

The chairman adjourned the conference to allow time for consultants to develop a more detailed proposal for these routes, and a rough costing. During the adjournment, exhibitions were held in Icklesham and Rye to give people the opportunity to study the new route options.

Draft resolutions

Before the conference adjourned, the chairman also presented five draft resolutions for the conference to consider. This was a response to his concern that the conference was getting nowhere. The draft resolutions were intended to state where he thought the conference had got to and to allow people to see an output which reflected their contributions and was balanced.

Seeking consensus

The strength of opposing views emerged clearly during the first part of the conference. Those who were present comment, in particular, on the disagreement over the route for an Icklesham bypass. This was essentially the same disagreement that had surfaced at the previous public consultation. Most Icklesham residents favoured the northern route, put forward at public consultation. However, this option was vehemently opposed by the Save the Brede Valley Group, formed after the consultation in 1993, with the purpose of preventing any road building in the valley.

During the first few days of the conference, the chair of the Icklesham Parish Council and individual residents of Icklesham became increasingly concerned that they were being outnumbered at the conference. They were alarmed and surprised to find so many other groups from outside the village at the conference, as they had understood it to be concerned primarily with their own local interests. Having supported the northern route at public consultation, they were further dismayed to find that new proposals, much closer to the village, were being put forward. They had thought that the conference would only consider the 1993 consultation routes, not that new options might be developed.

The Icklesham Residents' Association was therefore formed to represent the views of Icklesham people at the conference. During the adjournment, the association organised a secret ballot of all on the electoral roll, to establish which route had most support. There was a response of almost 90 per cent. 65 per cent of respondents favoured the northern route from the 1993 consultation. This became a mandate for the residents' association.

During the weekend at the end of the first week of the conference, the chairman of the newly formed Icklesham Residents' Association invited those who were seen as key players to lunch and a meeting at his house, to be chaired by the local MP. The aim was to explore the possibility of compromise and common ground, outside the conference hall. It is reported that it became clear during that meeting that no compromise was going to be possible between the Icklesham Parish Council and

Residents' Association on the one hand, and the Save the Brede Valley group on the other. Both continued to argue for their established positions.

The suggested new routes emerging from the conference also caused concern in Winchelsea, where many residents had not understood that the town came within the scope of the conference. They had thought that the 1991 preferred route was set, and not open to change. The possibility of a new option, including a tunnel under the town, prompted the formation of the Winchelsea Residents' Association. They also organised a poll of local residents. The desire to put their case effectively led one group to hold fundraising events so that they could pay experts in the field to represent them at the conference.

The conference was also attended by interests and pressure groups from outside the area. At one point, one local group was accused by another of bringing in people from two London-based groups with a known anti-roads position. The intervention of these groups led to what some describe as 'a shouting match' in the conference hall. The chairman announced that he would leave the hall for a short period, during which the conference should decide if it wished to continue and to respect the authority of the chair. If not, he would leave. It is reported that local people then made it clear to the 'outsiders' that they were not welcome. The conference then resumed.

Conference report

The conference report, including the resolutions, was produced by the chairman after the conference had ended. He had offered the conference the opportunity to meet again to comment on the wording of the draft final resolutions, but it was agreed that this was not necessary. The report contained nine resolutions, based on the five earlier draft resolutions and subsequent discussions. The report noted where the resolutions were generally supported, where there were dissenting views, what these were and who held them.

In brief, the resolutions report a consensus on the need for improvements; agree a bypass route for Guestling Thorn and note that the Hastings eastern bypass should not be built without it; record regret that no consensus was possible on how to improve the Guestling Thorn to Rye section, but put forward two new options, one of which includes the Winchelsea tunnel; and support the current preferred route for the Rye bypass, with minor modifications.

Assessment of the process

As a method of public consultation, the planning conference generated strong and varied views among the participants. These were inevitably influenced by the fact that the conference achieved little or nothing for most of the groups we spoke to. However, there were some very positive reactions to aspects of the method as well as criticisms.

Some of those we spoke to felt that the particular problem this conference had tried to resolve would be impossible to resolve through any consultative method. But they thought there was a potential role for the round table conference in planning road schemes, if it was used and structured differently. This potential is discussed at the end of the case study, under 'Assessment'.

The following aspects of the conference were fundamental to its success or failure as a process, in the views of those involved.

Timing and geographical scope

It was widely thought that the Department of Transport had been naïve if it had expected the conference to resolve questions on which those who took part in the previous public consultation had been clearly divided. In the intervening 18 months, views had, if anything, become more entrenched. Some groups had spent the time preparing their case.

The subject of the previous consultation had been the Icklesham and Guestling Thorn bypass. Residents of these villages felt they had made a clear choice of route then and were taken aback to find the matter open for debate again.

The geographical scope, wider than that of the previous consultation exercise, had been announced but was apparently not understood by people in the eastern part of the conference area. Residents in these areas were surprised to find that the conference affected them, as they thought their bypass routes were settled. Some groups reacted very negatively to new options being proposed.

The different views of the conference's scope are illustrated by attitudes towards Icklesham village hall as a venue. Some thought the conference needed a bigger, more neutral venue and that the choice of Icklesham was misleading, and allowed that part of the scheme to assume too much importance. Representatives of Icklesham, on the other hand, were dismayed to find that the conference was giving what they saw as an unfair amount of attention to the views of others from further away or with 'single issue' interests.

Attendance and representation

There were strong views about who should be entitled to attend, and the basis on which they should speak. The conference was open to all, both groups and individuals, and many felt this was the only possible and fair way to approach it.

One concern was that speakers should be required to declare their interests. Many felt that speakers' points of view simply reflected where they lived or had other interests, and that these interests should be made explicit.

Other arguments concerned the relative weight to be given to the views of those who were not local residents, such as conservation bodies with a national remit to consider wildlife sites, or to take a strategic overview of road planning. When considering local preferences, how local should people be to have a say? And people were suspicious that more attention would be paid to the articulate professional than to the amateur.

The role of representatives of organisations also caused some suspicion. One concern was that speakers might not represent views of their members fully or accurately. One approach was to give representatives a mandate. However, this tended to make them inflexible, as they were unable to negotiate or compromise without referring back to the group. This was not generally practical.

There was some confusion over the role of the county council officers. Their position was that they were there to give their professional advice, which was based on a county-wide perspective and on the extensive study which had been undertaken to respond to the earlier consultation by the Highways Agency. They did not have a mandate for the conference itself and were not there to represent the authority's views, which would be determined by councillors. Any conference outcomes which required a council decision would have to be taken by elected members, at a later date. Meanwhile, two members of the county council who were at the conference were representing particular interests and views, not necessarily the views of the council as a whole.

Facilitating dialogue and consensus

By the end of the conference, all who participated had a clear understanding of the views of the different groups. The strength with which different views were held was also understood. This overall picture is not so easily obtained from a public consultation, or available to so many players.

It was easier for some people to speak than others. Confidence, experience, the ability to think on one's feet and deal quickly with complex points were all important. Some people found the process intimidating. The skill of the chairman was generally agreed to be absolutely fundamental to a successful conference. The chairman here was widely praised for doing a difficult job well, for being fair and for enabling everyone to make a contribution. His engineering expertise was generally thought to be an advantage. One group, however, were critical of the chairman on all these points.

As the conference proceeded, it became clear that there was little or no scope for consensus on some issues. The chairman has since expressed the view that the process could be developed if the chair took on a rather different role. The aim would be to break an apparent deadlock by holding discussions with small groups outside the main conference hall, in the hope that people could retreat from entrenched positions and enter into more of a dialogue. Possibilities might include mediation or conciliation, by means of brokerage or shuttle diplomacy.

Time commitment

Many delegates were at the conference for all or most of the nine days. This was a considerable commitment from those who were unpaid representatives of voluntary groups and/or had jobs and other responsibilities, and was a major drawback to the process for many.

It presented difficulties also for some of the smaller statutory bodies with limited resources and a wide range of responsibilities. Not all of these were able to attend for the whole time, or at all. They were used to one-to-one discussions with the Highways Agency, followed by a public inquiry. The conference was in addition to these processes, not a substitute for them, and the demands it made on their time was a major problem.

Managing the process

As explained above, the chairman had autonomy in deciding how to run the conference. He controlled the timetable, decided how long to allow for each issue and each contribution. He could extend the overall length of the conference as he thought necessary. The decision to adjourn the conference for work to be done on new routes was his. The chairman worked closely with the Highways Agency and their consultants, who supported him and were available to discuss progress.

Resources

The total cost to the Highways Agency was approximately £0.5 million. This included fees for consultants to study the possible new routes and the cost of mounting the conference. The costs of the conference itself include the accommodation, the technology required to link the overflow huts to the main hall, information material and brochures, and technical and secretarial services bought in from East Sussex County Council. The chairman had two staff to assist him.

For delegates, the major cost was their time. This was considerable, as we explained above. A specific example comes from one of the county council officers who attended the whole conference. He reports that he spent the equivalent of four weeks in total working on the conference.

The impact of the process on its output

The conference showed that new options, not previously identified by the authorities, can be developed in such a forum. It also showed that consensus can sometimes be reached on replacing existing plans with new proposals. The conference also confirmed some existing plans.

All of these achievements have tended to be overshadowed by the failure to agree on the central part of the route, and by the upheaval caused by proposing changes to some routes which were thought to have been agreed.

IMPACT

Acting on the output of the conference

The chairman's report of the conference findings went to the Secretary of State for Transport. It was sent to all conference delegates and other interested parties, and was published by the Department of Transport in September 1995. The press release which announced the report's publication also said that the Secretary of State would announce a preferred route in due course.

Impact

The objectives of the conference had been to reach agreement on: need; objectives of a solution; and of an acceptable solution for meeting the need and objectives. The overall aim of planning conferences was to speed up the decision making process on road building.

The conference had agreed a resolution on the need for improvements, and it had agreed solutions for parts but not all of the route. The need for new road building was not, in the end, accepted by government, which changed its mind about building the road at all. One section of the scheme remains in the road building programme, the one on which consensus was reached. Without the conference, this may not have happened. As the conference failed to reach consensus on solutions for the whole route, and as views about this remained strongly opposed, it seems unlikely that it would have speeded up the process of decision-making on road building, had the scheme remained in the programme.

After the conference, government decisions about the A259 were made in two stages. The results of the Review of the Trunk Road Programme, published in November 1995, put all three schemes (Guestling Thorn and Icklesham, Winchelsea, Rye) in the longer term programme, creating the expectation that there was no realistic prospect of work being done on them in the foreseeable future. However, the preferred route protection for the Guestling Thorn bypass was not withdrawn as the scheme may be taken forward in a programme of smaller scale Network Enhancement Projects.

In further changes to the trunk road programme, which were announced after the November 1996 budget, all three bypasses were withdrawn all together. The Hastings eastern bypass remained in the programme. Both announcements refer to overall policy changes on road building, which resulted from financial constraints, the need to make better use of existing roads and to pay more attention to environmental concerns. The number of schemes in the road programme was reduced by more than 60 per cent between March 1994 and November 1996.

It was widely believed by those involved in the conference that the outcomes of the conference had made it convenient for government to withdraw the scheme altogether. This view holds that the conference had originally been called to avoid having to make a controversial decision. When the conference provided further evidence of the strength of the different views discovered by the previous public consultation, then the obvious decision was to take the opportunities to defer and then withdraw the scheme. Financial constraints are not accepted by those who participated in the conference as the real reason for these decisions.

The impact of these decisions has been felt differently by the communities of the area. For the Save the Brede Valley group, the result was all they hoped for. Winchelsea lost the bypass it thought had been agreed. Icklesham felt it had lost its opportunity to get a bypass, and that this happened because of the unreasonable influence of those from outside the immediate vicinity. The view of some of the statutory bodies is that the unwillingness of Icklesham to compromise cost the village its bypass. Underlying all this are a range of views about the importance of the A259 as a strategic route.

Assessment

As we have seen, the conference achieved its objectives to a limited extent. But for almost all concerned it was seen as a waste of resources because of the subsequent decisions to cancel the scheme. There was also a view that the conference could have a useful role to play in different circumstances. We therefore conclude with a summary of people's views of the potential for this sort of exercise in the planning of road schemes.

For some participants, the conference is not an idea worth pursuing. They argue that consensus, where it exists, will emerge with or without a conference. They believe that the conference is not a cost-effective method and there is a preference for going straight to the usual, statutory public inquiry, which would take place anyway. The inquiry's formal process of evidence and rebuttal is preferred to the dialogue aimed for by the conference.

Many participants felt one of the main values of the conference to be the exchange of information it created. This was done much more effectively, and included many more groups and organisations, than the usual consultation process. Much more information was in the public domain as a result. The conference was much preferred, by many, to the adversarial format of a public inquiry.

The benefit of this could be properly realised if it happened at an early stage in the planning process, before any other public consultation or announcements of preferred routes. The conference could then be used to explore public opinion and perhaps to develop ideas. If a conference takes place early on, before people feel their personal interests are directly threatened and before positions become so entrenched, then some of the process problems identified above would be less of an obstruction. In this way, the conference has the potential to subsume the usual public consultation, though it might be necessary to carry out the usual form of consultation once route options were defined.

There is a debate about whether conferences could achieve anything in the most controversial or sensitive areas. This is related to whether they are to be used to explore opinion and ideas or move as far as seeking consensus. However, the important point is made that any process would not remove the need for difficult and probably unpopular decisions at government level. Moreover, government must be prepared to act quickly on the conference report, which quickly loses value and credibility.

Research methods

We interviewed: staff of the Highways Agency; the Chairman of the conference; representatives of statutory organisations who took part; and representatives of local groups and residents' associations. Background documents, the conference report and Highways Agency/Department of Transport papers were also studied. Fieldwork took place in the latter half of 1996.

Commentary

Overview

The planning conference was organised by the Highways Agency to consider the need for improved transport facilities in this area of East Sussex. The conference was open to all and was intended to seek consensus on solutions to transport problems.

We identified the following key points about this consultation exercise:

- Planning conferences are an addition to the normal consultation and decision making process, not a substitute for any part of this. Despite earlier trial conferences, there are unresolved questions about the timing, scope and role of the conference.
- The conduct of the process of a conference is a major factor in its success or otherwise. If conferences are to be used in the future, we consider that ground rules and principles developed for this conference would be a sound basis for guidance on procedure.
- The investment of time and energy by those participating in the conference should be met by an equal commitment to a prompt and open decision making process by the Department of Transport.
- It may not be possible to avoid difficult and controversial decisions, which involve value judgements. Road building is a prime example of this and it would be naive of any organisation to think consultation could do more than delay and, possibly, inform that decision.

Role of the conference

Seeking consensus on an issue which will have a direct impact on people's day-to-day lives is inherently very difficult. It is made more so if the conference takes place, as this one did, after an earlier consultation which had helped people to establish firm views and expectations.

The conference did not remove the need for controversial decisions. In our view it would be unrealistic to have expected it to do so. It is also unsurprising that, given the timing of the conference, many participants suspected that this was not the real purpose and were sceptical before it began.

The conference process

The planning conference demonstrates that where strongly held views are in contention then absolute fairness in the processes is particularly important. We consider that the chairing and conduct of this conference provide many pointers to good practice, and demonstrate what can be achieved even in heated circumstances.

Decision-making

The commitment of time and other resources by delegates reflected the strong interest they had in the outcome. This investment was not met by a responsive decision-making process – there was no commitment to a decision-making timetable and decisions were influenced by wider national and political considerations, without the reasons for the decisions being made explicit.

It is proper, we believe, that the conference resolutions should not be in any way binding on decision-makers. It would be hard to justify such a rule unless the consensus had been reached by a group which was accepted as representative – and there would have to be consensus also on which interests had a right to be represented. However, the decision-making after the A259 conference appeared, and was, remote from the intense experience of participating in the conference. The disaffection which followed was not the result only of disappointment with the outcome.

Future conferences

Given this mismatch, we consider that there is a case to be made for either limiting the conference to the exchange of information and development of ideas only, or for increasing the potential for the conference to reach consensus. The first option would take some of the heat out of the process and lead to a much better understanding of public views than is possible in the usual approach to public consultation. The second option might involve allowing the chair the opportunity, for example, to hold separate meetings between opposing groups in order to reach a consensus through mediation.

CASE STUDY EIGHT

The Housing Corporation: Meeting Black and Minority Ethnic Housing Needs

INTRODUCTION

The Housing Corporation (the Corporation) is a non-departmental public body, funded by the Department of the Environment (DoE), responsible for the registration and supervision of registered social landlords, and the provision of funds to them.

From March 1995 to January 1996 the Corporation carried out a consultation with a range of organisations on its proposals for a new approach to meeting the housing needs of black and minority ethnic communities. The consultation was in two stages. A series of meetings with different organisations were followed by drafting of a new policy document which was circulated for written comment to the same organs.

The Corporation consulted with black housing organisations and networks, local authority associations, other housing bodies, and with its own regions. The initial meetings, described by the Corporation as 'listening meetings', were held in London and in most of the regions. The draft policy document was circulated in November 1995, and a large number of responses were received. The revised policy was published in its final form in Spring 1996.

ORIGINS AND OBJECTIVES

Origins

The Corporation has a duty under Section 71 of the Race Relations Act, and Section 56 of the Housing Act 1988, to prevent unlawful discrimination and promote racial equality in housing. To help to meet this obligation, the Corporation had two consecutive five year strategies, the second of which – *An Independent Future* – was due to end in March 1996. Both strategies had a 'positive action' approach based on promoting and supporting housing associations for black and minority ethnic tenants.

The context for the consultation had both a routine, general aspect and a specific aspect. The Corporation is generally required to consult when reviewing strategies and the 1991–96 black and minority ethnic housing associations strategy required a final review in its last year of operation, in order to move to a third strategy. The Corporation describes consultation as one of its traditions, although there are different views about the genuineness and effectiveness of its consultations. The strategy was subject to annual reviews within the Corporation, and the final review was therefore planned as part of the routine work of the Corporation.

The specific context was government concern that the two strategies had involved an approach to meeting black housing need which involved the establishment of organisations which required funding for their maintenance and development. The Corporation was under pressure from the DoE for an earlier review – pressure which the Corporation resisted, in order to ensure that a thorough and proper review was carried out at the right time.

As a non-departmental public body, the Corporation was subject in 1995 to a 'prior options' review, which entailed a review of all of its primary purposes and activities. There was also a White Paper in June 1995, *Our Future Homes,* which provided the focus and which led to the 1996 Housing Act, which removed the Corporation's role in the promotion of individual or particular types of organisations which deliver housing.

The Corporation knew therefore that the DoE would not agree to a repeat of the previous strategy based on funding specific housing associations and would need instead to focus its funding on meeting housing need.

Objectives

The general aim in consulting was to ensure that the revised strategy was understood by all of the stakeholders, and to give all parties the chance to comment and make proposals about the detail of it. The consultation did not offer options for the central approach. The consultation was not therefore about the nature of the new strategy, but about its detail, and about encouraging support for it through an open and inclusive approach.

THE PROCESS

Methods

Two methods were used – one the 'traditional' method of circulation of a draft document, the other a series of meetings: with key organisations at both regional and national levels; with regional staff; and what were called 'listening fora' – meetings for black associations, local authorities and others, held on a Corporation regional basis.

The circulation of the document is described as the 'formal' consultation. This was sent to all local authorities, all black housing associations and all relevant associations such as those of local authorities, of housing interest groups, and of black groups. The 'listening meetings' informed the drafting of the document.

The activities

The then Deputy Chief Executive of the Corporation had responsibility for the strategy for black housing need, and was involved in the process at arm's length. The consultation was run by a core team and a working group, set up by the Director of Housing Management and Research (the Director). The Director established a core team to steer the review and the writing of the new strategy document. This team was made up of the Director, the Head of Promotion and Advice, and the Initiatives Manager (who was the Corporation's Race and Housing Adviser until mid-1994 and whose previous responsibility was to implement the second strategy).

In April/May 1995 the Director also established and chaired a working group, consisting of the core team, four senior staff from the Corporation's regions, and staff from the Investment Division and the Regulation Division. The Corporation employed a consultant specialising in race issues and housing to work with the Initiatives Manager.

There were four activities: meetings with and presentations to specific groups, a presentation at a meeting of Regional Directors, meetings in all but one of the regions for black associations, local authorities etc, and circulation of a draft consultation document. The work began with an evaluation of the previous strategy, undertaken by independent researchers at Leeds University and steered by a sub-group of the core team with minuted meetings. This evaluation concluded that the strategy had reached and exceeded its targets.

Regional Directors' Meeting

A presentation of the issues by the Initiatives Manager was made at a meeting of the Regional Directors, chaired by the Deputy Chief Executive of the Corporation, who also had responsibility for regional affairs.

The regions have a key role in discussing and implementing any strategy for black and minority ethnic housing and follow-up for the next strategy would be through the regions. This meeting sought therefore to ensure that internally Corporation staff were involved in and committed to the process. In particular, the Corporation's regions vary in their character and approaches to housing provision – for example, the North East Region decided to develop one large black association in each of its areas, whereas in London there is a proliferation of small associations, as well as some large ones. Enthusiasm in the regions was perceived as variable and internal promotion was thought useful.

Meetings with key groups

Meetings with the Federation of Black Housing Organisations (FBHO), the Chartered Institute of Housing (CIH), the Housing Associations Charitable Trust (HACT), the National Housing Federation (NHF), the Commission for Racial Equality (CRE), and local authority associations were held in Autumn 1995 at the Corporation, to discuss the issues around the end of the strategy and future options. The Director spoke at an FBHO conference, and the Initiatives Manager made a number of presentations to organisations.

FBHO had a further meeting with the Corporation and Cambridge University researchers commissioned by FBHO 12 months before the end of the strategy, to evaluate it and make recommendations. They presented their findings to the Corporation.

The listening meetings

The listening meetings began in September 1995. There were six of these, all held in regional offices. Most meetings had around 20 to 30 participants. The Initiatives Manager and the consultant prepared a briefing for the Housing Corporation staff presentations, with the core team sharing the presentations. Core team staff took notes of the issues raised, and fed these to the working group, structured under headings which reflected the types of issues raised – for example, regulation issues or financial issues. The Corporation reports that it did not send copies to all participants. We found only one participant who reported receiving a copy of the notes.

Decisions about which organisations to invite were made in consultation with the Corporation's Regional Directors. The meetings were attended by black associations, local authorities and others with an interest within each region. The situation in London is however seen as particular, with a larger number of housing associations, and attendance for the London meeting was largely restricted to black and minority ethnic groups.

The key point made was the Corporation's move away from the black housing associations approach to a 'needs' approach, from a 'narrow' to a 'wide' focus, together with an emphasis on local development of approaches. The Corporation found a lot of support for the 'needs' approach, but also nervousness about leaving black associations unsupported.

The Corporation saw the meetings as well-run and as effective public relations, as well as securing useful input from associations and others. Participants' views were mixed. There was no systematic attempt to feed back to participants the results of the meeting, although in some cases this did happen. In general participants were unenthusiastic about the influence of the meetings on the draft document. There was agreement between the Corporation and the participants that the most commonly expressed view was that the 'black associations' strategy should be maintained.

The consultation document

Following the listening meetings the Initiatives Manager coordinated the drafting of the consultation document, writing most of it. Submissions were obtained from the members of the working group on their perspectives on the proposed changes. The draft was sent initially to Corporation first level senior staff for revision and then (largely unchanged) to the Board itself on 7 November 1995. The draft was launched for consultation on 20 November, with a deadline of 8 January 1996 for comments.

Written responses

The draft is described by the Corporation as high-profile and controversial. Ninety written responses were received: from the Corporation's Regions, from housing groups, from black and minority ethnic housing associations, from other housing associations, and from local authorities and their associations. Regions circulated it to relevant groups in their own areas and sought to emphasise how important responses were.

The views within the written responses were broadly the same as from the meetings. In form, the written comments were more detailed than those given in the listening meetings, and also included proposals for solutions to issues and changes to be made. Most written responses wanted the second strategy to be repeated, and expressed the view that black housing associations were not strong enough to survive without support from the Corporation. However, many also supported the housing needs focus which the Corporation proposed.

The Corporation summarised the responses in an appendix to the final document. All of the respondents we interviewed felt that their views were represented in this summary, with the exception of one organisation which took the view that the selection of responses for the appendix was arbitrary.

Of those we interviewed, Ujima Housing Association, NHF and FBHO were clearly concerned at the ending of the black associations strategy. Ujima describes the draft as having no policy framework and no targets, and as vague. Ujima wanted continued funding of selected associations. FBHO's view was that all associations should be Corporation funded, as a right.

Whilst believing that smaller associations needed continuing support, Manningham Housing Association was by contrast very positive about the proposals, emphasising the need to work jointly in the locality with other major providers, and describing the stance taken by some groups as negative and unhelpful. But whatever their view on the new approach, three of these groups believed that the second strategy involved a fixed proportion of funds for black associations, and that this had been abandoned.

The new framework document

The framework document was written by the Initiatives Manager, with the help of the Head of Promotion and Advice and the consultant, in January and February 1996. The detail of the draft was revised to allow different concerns to be worked out at the local level. The review group did not meet to discuss the drafts, but received individual copies for comment. The Deputy Chief Executive also commented.

The Corporation's Board meets on a bimonthly basis and was therefore unable to consider the final version. A sub-group of the Board therefore agreed the final draft, and a copy of the final draft was sent to all Board members. The DoE also saw and agreed the final draft.

A new policy – *Black and Minority Ethnic Housing Needs: An Enabling Framework* – was launched in April 1996 at a special press meeting with Corporation officials. This policy was not a strategic approach as in the past, but, as its name suggests, a framework within which new developments could be worked out. Publicity was poor, and many black associations learned of it after it had taken place. NHF made a formal complaint about the Corporation's failure to invite them to the launch and received an apology. The document was received quietly in the press.

Respondents identified some improvements to detail, but saw little overall change between the draft and the final document.

Assessment of the process

The process itself was in general seen to be effective – although the tight timescale for comments was criticised. The lack of feedback from meetings was similarly criticised, more so by some organisations than others.

Some confusion was caused because the Corporation was carrying out a number of other consultations, more or less at the same time, and this made responses more complex than was ideal.

There was scepticism about the validity of the exercise, in that the decision to end the second strategy was not negotiable, and yet maintenance of this strategy was the preferred option of many respondents.

Resources

The Corporation's estimates of its total costs are given below.

Routine staff costs (core team, working group, PR, and including £3,000 research management)	£60,100
Listening events	£5,000
Print and distribution	£14,750
Research	£55,365
Conferences, Board etc	£10,000
Total	£140,215

With the exception of the research project costs – around £60,000 in all – all costs were an essential part of the consultation. In addition, the consultant was paid £7,000.

Management

The core team's brief was to prepare a draft report for consultation, to receive responses, and to produce a final document. The team's work began in Spring 1995, and the draft strategy was scheduled for September. However, an extension of the original timescale was negotiated following a group meeting in June at which the scale of the task was reassessed. The draft was not completed until November, and the process was delayed by several months, resulting in the squeezing of the consultation time into some seven weeks. However, this was not considered a major obstacle by the participants and respondents.

The working group discussed the issue of how to consult, and the idea of 'listening fora' was proposed by the Director in this discussion. The Regional Directors were initially opposed to the listening meetings, which they saw as consulting on an issue not yet agreed by government. These objections were overcome through negotiation and discussion. The Deputy Chief Executive became involved at the drafting stage, and several Board members were involved in commenting and advising on the draft.

This exercise was tightly and effectively managed and owned by the Corporation, which succeeded in meeting a difficult schedule (with one exception – see above), whilst sustaining an inclusive process both internally and externally. The Board and senior staff were kept in touch at the key stages of the work, and the final document was agreed by both. This was a difficult and demanding process for core team staff. The issue is sensitive and controversial, and there are strongly held differing views between participants. Managing the project therefore required in-depth knowledge of the sector, both the personalities and the issues. Patience and negotiating skills were also needed to ensure that both Corporation staff and others were able to consider the issues fully.

Impact of the process on its output

The Corporation considers that the use of the 'listening meetings' ensured that the detail of the consultation document was tuned to the concerns of the consultees. However, it is difficult to assess this view, given that most consultees were in favour of keeping the second strategy, and it was not within the Corporation's power to do this.

There is some evidence to suggest that the listening meetings were not an important part of the process for the consultees. In addition, the written responses were a repetition of the comments made in the meetings, emphasising the inability of the process to accommodate the main preference of the consultees.

The role played by the listening meetings seems to have been to prepare the ground for the draft in circumstances where its main proposals would be unpopular. As a method, therefore, it is difficult to assess its direct impact on its outputs separate from the issue of how substantial the consultation could be. This is explored below.

IMPACT

Direct

At the time of writing there has been no direct impact on the funding of associations, because of the timescales of the funding cycles. The framework document describes itself as 'enabling' and is being treated by the Corporation and some commentators as the beginning of a process, rather than a new strategy similar to the first and second strategies. The new framework is therefore permissive, and at both national and regional levels the Corporation has begun a process of development of specific proposals and ideas around the framework. The framework requires local development to take place, and this is still in its early phases.

In Spring 1996 the Corporation established a review team to monitor development, and the practical implications of the enabling framework are being considered by this group. This group monitors the action plan, and was chaired by the Deputy Chief Executive, until she left the Corporation in early 1997, with a representative from each region, plus headquarters staff. Nationally the Corporation has also organised a twice yearly meeting, with NHF, CRE, HACT, local authorities, and housing associations, both black and white, to monitor the new framework – a sort of external advisory group, which met for the first time in Autumn 1996.

NHF sees the new framework as very general, and identified 23 policy commitments in the document, all of them hedged, and fed these back to the Corporation. NHF also suggested to the Corporation that a steering group should be set up with strong terms of reference, and described the available monitoring mechanisms for implementation as very weak. NHF is critical of the lack of specificity in the framework document, of the Corporation's lack of clarity about its own objectives and what it expects the outcomes and impacts to be.

FBHO organised a conference to discuss the new framework in May 1996. The framework was not popular with the black associations who attended this conference.

Unintended consequences

The Corporation did not anticipate the strength with which specific groups – refugee and Irish groups – would express a wish to have their housing needs included within the framework. These groups mounted intense lobbying campaigns.

The future

FBHO will continue to lobby both government and opposition for a return to a black housing associations strategy.

The Corporation describes the process of change as still underway, with the review body developing new ideas around the enabling framework. The document is not seen as the end product, but as a framework for implementation which will involve further consultation, and 'bottom-up' rather than 'top-down' initiatives for change.

Assessment

Success of the project

There are differing accounts of the Corporation's funding approach prior to the end of the second strategy. There was no official policy to earmark a specific percentage of funds for black associations. However, there is a widespread perception amongst housing associations and even amongst some Corporation staff, that there was an allocation of a specific percentage – 9 per cent – of Corporation grants to black associations.

A number of changes in policy – for example a competitive framework for bidding between associations – are said to have begun to prevent the continuation of this earmark approach, even before the strategy review began. A further factor thought relevant is the decline in the Corporation's funds in recent years, including a real decline in funding for new provision for housing associations.

There is however, general agreement that continuation of the 'black associations' approach was not an option on offer during the consultation. Dissatisfaction arises both from this aspect, and from the desire to continue the second strategy. The Association of District Councils' (ADC) view was that in practice the Corporation could not change the new needs-based approach as the government had already effectively made the decision, and that the Corporation's resources had in any event been reduced, making it more difficult to continue to directly support black associations. Most housing associations seem to agree with the ADC view. A good contrast in responses is provided by Manningham, who took a 'seize the opportunity' approach, and FBHO, who will continue to seek a return to the old policy.

The Corporation's new framework is much less specific than its previous strategy, and one view offered was that the Corporation has ended up with a controversial framework document for which it has been, and will continue to be, much criticised. However, another view offered to us was that the Corporation would do well to be more upbeat about the role of black associations in the new framework, as the issue is not as sensitive as the Corporation sometimes appears to think.

Many involved in the consultation believe that a general focus on need is correct, in the main because most black tenants are housed by 'white' associations. The controversy was caused because it was feared that black associations would lose the support of the Corporation. At the time of writing, we do not know whether this is happening. The Corporation's view is that given that in practice the Department, the Corporation and local authorities work more closely now than in the past, black associations will have to adapt to this.

FBHO was concerned that differences in the level of support in the past for the black associations strategy in some parts of the Housing Corporation, particularly at a regional level, suggest that there will be noticeable differences between regions in their level of commitment to making the new strategy work. As a consequence, in some regions the development of black associations may be damaged.

Research methods

Interviews were carried out with members of Corporation's core team and working group, both regionally and centrally, and with a Board member. Interviews were also carried out with two black housing associations, one local authority association, FBHO, and NHF. We studied documents including both the draft consultation document and the final one, a number of individual written responses and the summary of these. The fieldwork took place in Autumn and Winter 1996.

Commentary

Overview

The Housing Corporation carried out a consultation exercise on the detail of its new policy for meeting the housing needs of black and minority ethnic communities in 1995. A new policy was needed, following the end of the second five-year strategy, which had focused on support to black housing associations. The Corporation used two methods: a series of meetings at which the principle features of the policy were explained and debated, and a draft policy document, written after the meetings, which was circulated in November 1995 to interested organisations for written comment by January 1996. The new policy was published in its final form in Spring

1996. The new policy was to provide a framework within which need could be met through local cooperation between providers.

We identify a number of key points which are examined in this commentary:

- When contextual purposes and explicit purposes overlap, consultation can lack substance.
- Consultees' purposes need to be considered carefully to ensure the best results.
- Organisations need control over the issues on which they consult.
- Internal consultation can be a useful purpose.

Contextual and explicit purposes

In seeking the Corporation's agreement to inclusion of this consultation exercise as a case study, we had thought that its purpose was to settle on a new approach to the housing needs of black communities. But this was not so. The new approach was settled before the first phase began, and the consultation was about detail only. The meetings phase had two aims: to increase internal regional understanding of the new approach; and to explain externally the purpose of the next phase, the written consultation, which was to be about the detail of the new approach only.

The consultation was not therefore as substantial in content as it may have appeared, and contextual drivers appear to have outweighed any explicit driver. In this case the contexts were the requirement to consult, and in our view a judgement about the importance of consulting on such a controversial topic. Because the consultation was carried through effectively as a process, this produced the rather odd situation in which the major comments made could not be taken on, and the outcome in terms of influence was slight.

The aim in using two methods was to seek to make clear to consultees what the new approach was to be, and that comments on details only were being sought. The responses received from the meetings phase were broadly the same as those received in writing – mostly seeking the maintenance of the original strategy (which was not possible). In that the meetings sought to help the written consultation to focus on the limited purpose, they were clearly unsuccessful.

Use of more than one method can be a decision based on different purposes, different audiences, or different types of products wanted out of the consultation. The written phase was the Corporation's routine approach, especially useful for detailed responses to detailed proposals, from organisations closely involved with issues. The meetings were an innovation. But for such a complex purpose, meetings would probably only be of use if they were discussions of some length, perhaps over an entire day, and with detailed feedback to participants. Here they seem to have been ineffective in shifting consultees' focus towards detail

Consultees' purposes

This case study was one of two where some of the participants wanted the consultation to be about something which was not intended. As a result, some consultees could see little substance, and although they appreciated the Corporation's attention to detail in the process, they felt that there was little change as a result.

We find it difficult to see how this could have been otherwise, given the strength of feeling and the dramatic shift which the new approach was seen as representing. The listening meetings were in part an attempt to deal with the difference in purposes, but were clearly unsuccessful in this.

Control over the subject of consultation

The Corporation's second strategy for meeting housing needs had focused on support to black housing associations.However, government policy and legislation prevented this 'organisations' approach from continuing. The Corporation is encouraged to consult on changes of this kind, and was therefore placed in the odd position of consulting on the detail of a settled approach which had arisen in part from the actions of government.

This type of difficulty is most likely to arise at an organisational level for non-departmental public bodies where the relationship to a department is subject to divisions between policy and operations. But difficulties of this kind may also occur when, for example, local authority councillors and staff are unable to develop a shared perspective on service or policy development.

Internal purposes

The Corporation needed to ensure that its regions, which would have responsibility for implementation of the new policy, understood the broad sweep of the policy, and contributed to the detail. Consultation activity was therefore directed in part at regional staff. Regional practices in relation to the meeting of housing need for black and minority ethnic communities were varied, and the new policy was founded on an approach based on local initiatives.

Controversy and consultation

Some of the limits to consultation are revealed in this exercise. Dissatisfaction amongst some consultees led them to talk of change through the political process, rather than through administrative, consultative mechanisms. In addition, some of the organisations involved had policy positions which they expressed in response to the document. When either or both of these is the case, consultation may not be a good use of resources. For example, if you already know what will be said, then policy documents and position papers already in the public domain might provide just as good an indication of the views of an organisation. And it is less expensive to get copies of these than to consult. If consultees will look elsewhere if they do not get the policies they want, then it may be sensible to wait until they have done this, if timing allows for it. The Corporation could not of course wait, for the reasons outlined above.

The relation of consultation to the political process is an underlying issue for most public services, and one which will continue to need thought for the foreseeable future.

CASE STUDY NINE

The Inland Revenue: Self Assessment

ORIGINS AND OBJECTIVES

The Finance Act 1994 made the main legislative changes necessary for introducing a new system for assessing personal tax for people who get tax returns. From April 1997, these taxpayers became involved in assessing their own liability for tax, thus bringing major changes to the way tax assessment is managed and operated.

To prepare for these changes the Inland Revenue carried out an extensive programme of research and consultation to establish how taxpayers, agents and employers wish to learn about the new system, and to inform the design of the new tax return. The commitment to an extensive consultation process was announced in the 1993 Budget, and work on it began that year. The final draft of the tax return was issued in September 1996. Information and education programmes which resulted from the consultation began in 1995 and are continuing into 1997, and possibly longer.

Origins

Self assessment affects the 8.5 million taxpayers who receive an annual tax return, primarily the self employed and employees who pay higher rate tax. It also affects some 70,000 accountants and other agents, and about 300,000 employers who provide expenses or benefits in kind to their employees.

Self assessment is intended to provide a clearer and more streamlined system for taxpayers, and to give them more control over and responsibility for their tax affairs. It is also intended to reduce the overall costs of running the tax system, both for business and for the Inland Revenue. These ambitions would not be realised if people did not understand the system or if there was a high incidence of error or omission in completing the returns.

The Inland Revenue had an established programme of customer service research before work began on self assessment. The preparation for self assessment built on this, but represented a major increase in the resources committed to research and consultation. Self assessment is a fundamental and far-reaching change to the tax system. It is essential that it should work smoothly and cost-effectively – the potential costs and political implications of failure on this are very significant. These considerations meant that serious attention was paid to the findings of research and consultation, at all levels within the Revenue.

Objectives

This case study explores two programmes among the many consultation activities which the Revenue undertook. Two parallel programmes were concerned with developing a well-designed tax return and establishing the information and education needs of agents, employers and taxpayers. There were strong links between these programmes and both were part of the overall approach to publicity and preparation for self assessment. This included, for example, extensive advertising campaigns in the media and the publication of a series of information leaflets.

The Revenue recognised that it needed to consult users in order to develop a tax return that they found as easy as possible to understand and to use, that they could complete fully with minimum error or contact with the Revenue, and that staff would be able to process efficiently. It also recognised that a cost-effective system would depend on providing information and advice to users in the way they find most helpful.

THE PROCESS

Methods

A number of different methods were used in each programme. Both used focus or discussion groups. For work on the return, these took the form of workshops, which included practical exercises. Consultation about information and education needs also included a feasibility study and satisfaction surveys. The programme of work on the tax return included trials of pilot versions, interview surveys, public consultation packs and usability tests. Of these, the Revenue had only the workshops and the public consultation packs in mind at the beginning of consultation period.

The overall approach was to consult all user groups, but to start with agents, then employers, followed by individual taxpayers. Previous work by the Revenue's Customer Service Division had shown agents and employers to have a key role in providing accurate and punctual tax returns. It had also shown them to be a good channel for disseminating information to taxpayers. The Revenue also recognised that agents and some employers would need longer to prepare for the introduction of self assessment than would individual taxpayers.

In both programmes, the plan for specific research and consultation activities evolved, rather than being drawn up at the outset. Decisions were made in the light of emerging findings and the perceived success of different methods and activities. Generally speaking, they moved from consulting small groups to wider exposure.

Work took place over a three-year period, with consultants and research organisations being commissioned to carry out substantial but discrete pieces of work, in partnership with Revenue staff. Where this happened, the plan for each project was generally developed in discussion between the Revenue and the contractor. The tender documents specified objectives but not methods. Consultants and research organisations were appointed through a tendering process for each major block of work.

Table 1 Developing the tax return for self assessment: main stages in consultation and research

Date	*Activity*	*Notes/outcomes*
Late 1993	Forum on self assessment	First meeting of consultative group drawn from representative bodies
December 1993 – January 1994	Focus groups of members of the public to examine first draft	Each group attended two or three workshops and were required to do 'homework' between meetings
	Two staff workshops (one for technical and one for more junior staff) to discuss and complete the return	
	Nine representative bodies asked for comments on plans for self assessment	
		Results in a report by Research International, April 1994
September 1994	More workshops of the public, including some who had previously been involved, to consider next version of return	Results in a Research International briefing to the Revenue in September 1994
Autumn 1994	Mock trial of the return in two regions	
	1,000 volunteers (taxpayers and agents) asked to complete the return, which was processed. 900 of them interviewed by telephone, three times each	Results in a Revenue report, March 1995
November 1994	Inland Revenue press briefing to publicise draft return and public consultation pack	20,000 distributed on request, 600 of the accompanying questionnaires returned
April 1995 – March 1996	Live trial in Leicester: interview survey	Pilot version of the return used 'for real'
	Taxpayers each interviewed three times: after submitting return; when received response from Revenue; when received statement from Revenue	
	Agents interviewed once	Results given in a Revenue press briefing, April 1996
June 1995	Live trial: further groups of taxpayers	
	Non-trial: further groups of taxpayers	
	To discuss/test latest draft	
November 1995	Second consultation pack produced and publicised	40,000 issued
Late 1995 – early 1996	Usability testing of return at National Physical Laboratory	Observation and video of people filling in the return
		Results in various reports, December 1995 and January 1996

Date	*Activity*	*Notes/outcomes*
January – March 1996	Self Assessment Forum	Worked in sub-groups with staff and specialists from outside the Revenue to provide detailed comment and raise technical questions
March 1996	Design consultancy and Plain English audit	
April 1996	Live trial, second year, Leicester and Southampton	
	Further group discussions and NPL tests	
September 1996	Final draft of return for 1996/7 issued, for information, to agents and staff	

The activities

Developing the return

Table 1 shows the main stages of the consultation and research work involved in developing the return.

The first stage was the setting up of a Forum on Self Assessment, a consultative group representing the self-employed. This was used as a sounding board for initial ideas and continued to meet at intervals throughout the whole development phase. A later group was set up to deal with queries from employers' organisations.

Qualitative research, December 1993 – January 1994

At the end of 1993, a market research company, Research International, was commissioned to carry out qualitative research to explore users' views of the first draft, with a secondary objective of testing initial reactions to the concept of self assessment. They convened six groups of taxpayers and agents. Participants were recruited over a short period, using personal contacts and snowballing. Participants were drawn from those who were already used to completing an annual tax return, thus providing a relatively experienced group for consultation in the early stages.

Each group of employee taxpayers (mainly those with complex financial affairs) and agents met three times; each group of self-employed taxpayers met twice. Inland Revenue staff were present to brief participants, to answer technical questions and to gain first hand experience of users' reactions.

The groups were described as workshops rather than group discussions because participants were required to do 'homework' between meetings of the group. The homework included completing the return (using mainly their own financial information) and providing a critique of the return. This arrangement made it possible to consider the issues more fully, and to practise completing the return in more real-life circumstances at home.

A key feature of the self assessment consultation process as a whole is a concern with consulting Inland Revenue staff as well as users. This was driven by the need to inform and train them, to test the system for operational ease and efficiency, and also to draw on their front-line experience. Consultation also gave staff the opportunity to voice any concerns about the impact of self assessment on their work and jobs.

Two staff workshops were held over this period, to discuss the draft return and to attempt to complete it, using case study information supplied by the organisers. One workshop was for clerical staff, the other was for technical staff.

The third element of this stage of the programme was a request to nine representative bodies (accountants' organisations, Confederation of British Industry (CBI), Federation of Small Businesses and so on) to provide written comments on the draft.

Further workshops, late 1994

Fourteen more workshops were convened by Research International in November to consider the latest version of the return, which had been developed over the summer and drew on the findings of the earlier consultation. The groups followed the same format as before, and included some of the previous participants who were thus in a position to compare the two versions. Groups of staff and agents were made up of people who were new to self assessment.

Mock trial

Quantitative research was carried out to complement the workshops. For this exercise, careful attention was paid to selecting a sample to be representative of the taxpayer population as a whole. One thousand volunteers, comprising both agents and taxpayers without agents, were recruited. The only reservation about the sample was that, as volunteers, the participants might be more competent and/or compliant in tax affairs than the taxpaying population as a whole.

The volunteers were asked to complete the return over a period of a month. These were then processed by the Revenue. The objective was to obtain the reactions of a larger sample of people, who would not receive the artificially high level of help given to participants in the earlier workshop. They were given the names of Revenue staff to whom they could refer for help.

Research International carried out a telephone survey of 900 of the volunteers. Each person was interviewed three times: when they received the return, after completing it, and when they had received their statement from the Revenue. The processing of the returns was also monitored for errors, for the need for repair (correction to obvious error) and the degree of completion.

Public consultation pack

The wider public was given an opportunity to comment when a public consultation pack was issued in November 1994. The Revenue issued a press release and held a press briefing to publicise the introduction of self assessment and the consultation process. The pack was distributed free of charge on request. Of the 20,000 people who requested a copy, 600 returned the enclosed questionnaire which sought views on the design and content of the form and guidance notes, and the ease of completing it.

Live trial

After this first research programme, the next step was live testing of the next version of the draft self assessment return. This was done as part of a full trial of self assessment where taxpayers participating in the trial paid tax on the basis of their completion of a draft version of the self assessment return.

The trial took place over a two-year period covering the 1994/5 and 1995/6 tax years, using a later version of the return for the second year. It was based in a Leicester tax office for the first year, but expanded in the second year to include a Southampton office dealing with large employers. It initially involved about 5,000 individual taxpayers, increasing to 17,000 for the second year. Participants also included over 50 accountancy firms, representing over 2,500 taxpayers and 30 employers. The participating employers agreed to provide their staff with the information they would need under self assessment.

Again, a sample of about 800 taxpayers were interviewed three times. Agents were interviewed once to obtain their overall views of the new system. (As many agents were handling tax for a number of clients, their interviews were not designed to focus on a single stage in the assessment process.)

In late 1995, five group discussions were held with live trial participants. These were not workshops, as they had already completed the return, but were a forum for discussing their views of the return and the ease of using it. Some participants had been involved in previous consultation exercises and were, by then, well placed to comment on the evolving design and to make comparisons between drafts.

During the trial, in November 1995, a new version of the return was published and press released as before. Forty thousand copies were issued. The enclosed questionnaire invited people to try completing the return, using a case study supplied by the Revenue, and sought their views before and after this exercise. A version of the return on computer disk was also piloted during the Southampton trial, following some focus groups carried out by Research International to explore the demand for such a product.

Usability tests

The Revenue was concerned that the research to date had not identified, with sufficient precision, the points which caused people difficulty in completing the return. They also found that people had forgotten finer points about their experience by the time they returned to the next meeting of their workshop, or were interviewed. It was also suspected that groups generated a feeling almost of euphoria and of mutual satisfaction at having finished the exercise, and that difficulties were then understated.

These concerns led to work at the National Physical Laboratory (NPL), where people could be observed and videoed as they completed the return, using mock data. NPL had previously used these techniques primarily for testing the usability of computer software. The sessions took place between late 1995 and October 1996, involving about 40 taxpayers on an individual basis.

The circumstances were still somewhat unrealistic as taxpayers would not generally complete the form at one sitting, and would go through the process of collecting information and talking to others over a period of weeks. However, the

NPL exercises did show clearly where and how people were having difficulties, and demonstrated flaws in the design very precisely.

Producing the final version

By 1996, the Revenue was concentrating on the production of the final draft. This needed to be available well in advance of April 1997, so that both staff and agents could prepare for self assessment. It was decided to continue the live trial through the 1996/7 tax year in Leicester and Southampton. This was to continue testing self assessment in practice, but there could be no further public consultation on the return itself during this period.

Design work at this stage concentrated on the physical appearance of the form and the 'signposting' assistance given to users in finding their way around the documents. There was also a plain English audit. A new draft was then produced, which differed in appearance and some of its language from earlier versions, though not in content or basic structure. This was tested again at NPL. The Self Assessment Forum studied this version in great detail by working in sub-groups on particular sections. They generated several hundred technical points for investigation. The final version of the return was published, and press released, in September 1996.

Information and education needs of agents, employers and taxpayers

The programme of consultation to establish the needs for public information and education about self assessment was shorter than that for the design of the return. For agents and employers, consultation resulted in a programme of seminars which began in June 1995. Consultation with unrepresented taxpayers took place in Summer 1995 and informed the approach to their education and information from then on.

Agents and employers

Table 2 shows the main research and consultation activities in assessing the information and education needs of agents and employers.

The team from the Inland Revenue's central Customer Service Division began by discussing possible strategies with local office staff. Consultants were used to facilitate this process. Together they worked with staff from five offices in a series of two-day seminars to generate ideas. The same staff then piloted 14 seminars and focus groups with the agents representing the taxpayers. They were then brought together to report back on the results of these pilots. This meeting culminated in a presentation to senior management to put forward their conclusions and recommendations for a programme of seminars for agents.

The acceptance of these proposals led to a feasibility study of a self assessment education programme for agents. PE International were commissioned and the work took place between November 1994 and January 1995.

The objectives of the feasibility study included exploring the differences within the overall target group and involving staff as fully as possible, in order both to draw on their experience and to ease the process of implementation. The project was

Table 2 Information and education needs of agents and employers: main research and consultation activities

Date	*Activity*	*Notes/outcomes*
Early 1994	Initial research by consultants to develop ideas for educating agents	
	Worked with staff from local offices	Resulted in recommendation to senior management that seminars should be used as means of educating/informing
	Pilots undertaken with agents	
November 1994 – January 1995	Feasibility study on education programme for agents	
	Involved: discussions with senior Revenue staff in 11 regions; 15 focus group meetings with local office staff in 10 regions; 5 focus group meetings with agents in 4 regions	Results in a report by PE International
June 1995	Information pack sent to 80,000 agents	
	Beginning of programme of 'launch seminars'	
July 1995	Information pack sent to all employers	
Autumn 1995 – April 1996	'Launch seminars' for employers	
Autumn 1995	Survey of satisfaction among agents and employers attending seminars	Contracted out to NOP
May – Sept 1996	Workshops for agents	
February 1996 – June 1997	Calculation workshops for employers	
September – October 1996	Update pack for larger employers	
October 1996 – January 1997	Tax return workshops for agents	

carried out by a joint Inland Revenue/PE International team, with the Revenue's Customer Service team taking a very active role, particularly in the meetings with regional and local staff.

The programme of work for the feasibility study began with individual meetings with senior staff in 11 regions, followed by focus groups with local office staff in ten regions, and five focus group meetings with agents in four regions. The staff focus groups involved a combination of written responses and group discussions. Written responses were analysed quantitatively. Groups covered staff attitudes to and experience of self assessment, what each education programme should include, communication tools and methods for delivering the information, the staff role in the programme and the skills and resources needed.

The consultation with agents drew on earlier group discussions (see above) which had considered the tax return in late 1994. Groups in the feasibility study covered the level of knowledge of self assessment, problem areas, the content of the education programme, delivery mechanisms and the type and form of help required from the Inland Revenue.

The feasibility study achieved a number of things: it quantified the target audience; set out a process for developing communication tools; and suggested an approach for assessing the competence of staff to deliver the programme and for identifying training needs. It put forward a strategy for educating agents and employers, assessed its likely costs and benefits, and recommended the steps needed to implement it.

At the time of this work, the legislative changes concerning the effect of self assessment on employers had not been made. This consultation therefore concentrated on agents, but the report includes some outline recommendations for an employers' programme, and suggested that these should be refined through market research. Further work did take place on this later.

Once the programme of information packs and seminars for agents and employers was underway, National Opinion Polls (NOP) was commissioned to carry out a satisfaction survey of those who took part. This provided an independent complement to the Revenue's own monitoring.

Unrepresented taxpayers

Table 3 summarises the activities in this part of the consultation programme.

Table 3 Information and education needs of unrepresented taxpayers: main consultation and research activities

Date	*Activity*	*Notes/outcomes*
June 1995	Workshops with unrepresented taxpayers	
	Four groups with triallists in Leicester, six with non-triallists	Part of Leicester Live Trial
		Results in a report by Research International September 1995
November 1995 – March 1996	Feasibility study with local office staff	
	Local office staff brought together to discuss plans for local actions. Process facilitated by consultants who advised on how to assess success of projects	

Qualitative research was commissioned to assess the education needs of self-employed people, employees and pensioner taxpayers who had no tax adviser. The overall aim was to assess the best method(s) of communicating and providing education and assistance on self assessment to unrepresented taxpayers.

Ten workshops were held, four of them with taxpayers involved in the live trial in Leicester, who had direct experience of self assessment, and six with people outside the trial. Again, Revenue staff were in attendance to brief participants and to answer questions. Following this, Customer Service Division staff, again with the help of consultants, worked with local office staff on a feasibility study of proactive approaches at local level. Various locally based activities were piloted, including the exploring of taxpayers' views by questionnaire.

Assessment of the process

The combination of different research methods is thought to have worked well, with each bringing a different type of understanding to the issues. The results of the different exercises were consistent, which was reassuring, and further illuminated one another.

The return

As we have seen, there were four main strands to this work: the workshops/groups, trialling the self assessment process and debriefing those involved, public consultation packs, and usability tests. This combination of approaches is thought to have worked well – the Revenue does not think it would omit any of these methods in a future programme of a similar nature. They would, however, make more and earlier use of the usability tests.

Each strand of the programme had a specific value. Workshops were useful to explore ideas at the beginning, and to help them understand the reasons for people's views and objections. The trials tested the return in use, by taxpayers and staff. A representative sample gave quantifiable results, enabling them to compare performance with current arrangements.

The main purposes of the public consultation packs were to inform the wider public and to give them a chance to comment. This exercise produced a wide range of views. However, it is not possible to know if these views are representative of the public as a whole, and it is difficult, therefore, to know quite how to deal with them. The Revenue is also aware that such a wide dissemination of working drafts will generate criticism, including press criticism. But they consider public exposure and input to be more important than avoiding adverse comment.

Usability testing, which was new to the Revenue, was introduced at a fairly late stage. This proved to be a powerful technique, which added a great deal to the development of the return in the later stages. But it does require the structure of the return to have been developed already, and this development was informed by the workshops and other consultation methods.

Education programmes

Again, various methods were used, though the main approaches were to use qualitative techniques in consulting small groups of staff, agents, employers and taxpayers and to pilot ideas with staff and customers alike. These approaches produced the type of in-depth understanding of attitudes and behaviour which was necessary for deciding on the approach to education. However, it is recognised that those who agreed to take part may be more confident with form-filling generally than the tax-paying population as a whole. They may also be less likely to have got into any difficulties with tax affairs in the past.

Consultants and research agencies were extensively involved in the work. Much depended on establishing an effective working relationship between them and the Revenue. Staff from Customer Service Division were closely and actively involved in each stage of the contractors' work, and consider that this contributed to the overall success.

Managing the process

Two staff from the Customer Service Division were appointed to run the research and consultation programme on self assessment. They also held the budget and commissioned work. They could draw on other Customer Service Division colleagues as necessary, to run the Feasibility Study, for example.

The development of the return was the responsibility of a sub-project within the Self Assessment Programme. At first, this unit was an internal customer for the Customer Service Division, which commissioned research and so on, on their behalf. In April 1995, the tax return project took direct responsibility for research on the return.

The Inland Revenue has a dispersed office network, organised along Next Steps lines, which give staff at regional and local level a greater degree of autonomy over the way in which they run local services. For these reasons, and because self assessment was introducing such fundamental and far-reaching changes, it was important to consult and gain the support of local and regional managers and staff throughout the programme. There was therefore a great deal of internal consultation within the Revenue, and this inevitably added to the cost and time involved.

The effective management of commissioned work was vital. Those involved report the value of flexibility by both sides: the Revenue was open to suggestions about how to carry out projects, and contractors were flexible in accommodating the constraints and changing timetable for the development of self assessment as a whole. Contractors valued the easy access to policy debates within the Revenue, which increased their understanding of the issues to be explored.

The Revenue felt a close working relationship with its contractors to be beneficial. In some instances they had a considerable degree of involvement in the design and carrying out of the work, and felt this helped to deliver an appropriate product to high standards.

Resources

Two core Customer Service Division staff were assisted by other colleagues from the Division and within the self assessment programme on particular projects, and by administrative and clerical support. The team developing the tax return contained the equivalent of five full-time staff over a period of two years. Numerous other staff, throughout the Revenue, were involved in the research and consultation and in the trials.

The Revenue has given the following figures for the work it commissioned:

Tax return workshops with staff, taxpayers and agents in 1993/4	£27,000
Tax return workshops with staff, taxpayers and agents in 1994/5	£30,000
Mock trial 1994/5	£125,000
Agent/employer feasibility study 1994/5	£120,000
Tax return research 1995/6, including Leicester workshops and usability testing	£200,000
Proactive approaches, taxpayer education 1995/6	£28,000
Proactive approaches, feasibility study 1995/6	£40,000
Employer education programme, customer evaluation, 1995/6	£58,000

Impact of the process on its output

The tax return went through seven versions during the public consultation. The final version differs dramatically in structure from the Revenue's original ideas and from the previous tax return. It is also different in content, style and design.

The proposals for a programme of seminars for agents and employers were a novel and radical departure for the Revenue. Although there had previously been some initiatives on these lines in Revenue offices, there was no precedent of using such an approach on this scale, and no experience of doing so. While it is possible that such an approach might have been proposed if the consultation had not taken place, the evidence from the consultation was essential in making the decision to go ahead and to inform the design and content of the programme.

The results of the consultation with taxpayers pointed in a different direction to those from the discussions with agents and employers. Taxpayers did not want to receive substantial, general information, such as would be provided in seminars and videos that used a formal lecture-style approach. Instead, they stressed the importance of communication and public information, the availability of assistance from the Revenue, and an easy to use return. Pilots organised by local offices also showed that some would benefit from informal workshops to help them deal with the new tax return. These views were accepted by the Revenue centrally and informed their approach to taxpayer education.

IMPACT

Acting on the output of the exercise

Customer Service Division staff reported to the Revenue's senior management, including Ministers, when decisions were needed on recommendations for major initiatives such as the seminar programmes. Contractors have commented on the clarity of reporting lines within the Revenue, and the effectiveness of a structure of working parties which gave careful consideration to all the consultation outputs. Extensive liaison mechanisms were necessary to put the consultation outputs into effect: for example, between form designers and those preparing the IT systems based around it, and between the form designers and technical specialists.

The Next Steps structure increased the importance of the internal processes of consulting and gaining support of managers and staff. Local office staff carried out locally planned initiatives, as well as being involved in the centrally planned programmes. They were assisted in this by Customer Service Division and consultants, who advised on the design and monitoring of local projects.

Direct impact

The tax return is reported to have been dramatically influenced by public consultation. It came into use in April 1997. The return is accompanied by a leaflet which summarises important information in a clear and accessible format, and was itself a direct outcome of audience research. Research had shown the leaflet to be of key importance in making it clear how self assessment affects the individual taxpayer personally. It provides a link with the general information they have previously been made aware of through advertising campaigns.

A disk version of the return is also being made available. Research on this had uncovered a demand for a new product, especially one which was produced by the Revenue itself and was therefore regarded as authoritative.

The trial results on accuracy and completion rates for the return are encouraging. On the basis of the trials and the performance of the old return, the Revenue has set targets for the performance of self assessment. Results have also helped to inform planning, of staffing levels, for example.

The programme of seminars for employers was publicised in July 1995. 34,000 representatives of employers attended the launch seminars between Autumn 1995 and April 1996. Calculation workshops started in February 1996 and continued until June 1997. By the end of January 1997, 41,000 individuals from 28,000 firms had attended. Feedback from participants is consistently favourable. Attendees are asked to rate different aspects of the seminars on a five-point scale. 80 per cent of responses are in the top two grades. Similar results were obtained by the NOP telephone survey of seminar participants.

Launch seminars for agents began in June 1995. The initial programme was attended by 32,000 agents. A series of technical workshops ran from May to September 1996. It was followed by a new programme from October 1996 to February 1997, to guide agents through the new return. The same feedback mechanisms are used for employers and for agents. Both produce similarly high levels of satisfaction. Very high levels of satisfaction were also found by the NOP survey of agents and employers.

The Revenue's provision for taxpayers includes a new Orderline, for ordering leaflets and other information, a telephone Helpline for those with queries about self assessment, and self assessment talks where demand is high.

Indirect impact

All involved report a new level of commitment in the Revenue to consultation and evaluation. More research is being done on form design, and not only on the tax return which has such a key role in the tax system. Staff are sure that they will employ usability testing again, and that other new procedures will be trialled in the future.

Self assessment is, of course, extremely unusual in the scale and scope of change it introduces. It is unlikely, therefore, that there will a consultation programme of similar size or complexity in the foreseeable future. But research and evaluation have secured a more central role in the more routine work as well.

The training of local office staff to deliver the seminar programme has tapped a stream of talent which was not fully utilised before. The staff have acquired new skills. A valuable side effect of training them to inform others about self assessment is their advanced state of readiness for its introduction.

Future work

Staff point out that the real test of the effectiveness of the consultation and research will be in the operation of self assessment. The performance of the tax return, and the levels and types of enquiries received, will all be monitored.

Assessment

The consultation and research programme has achieved its objectives. The influence on decisions has been obvious and direct. The activities have provided clear and robust evidence, which has been essential in securing both the decisions and the funding to go ahead with some novel approaches to Revenue customers, namely the seminar programmes.

The timetable for self assessment meant that there was always pressure to move ahead quickly, and a great deal was achieved in a short period. But this did not mean that quick decisions were made without regard to implications for the other parts of the Inland Revenue also preparing for self assessment.

The scale of the research and consultation was commensurate with the significance of the topic under investigation. It is felt that the whole programme delivered value for money. The tax return is an essential document and the core of the new system, and of the computer systems on which the Revenue will depend for efficient performance. Viewed from this perspective, it is notable that the consultation cost relatively little compared to the costs of developing computer systems, yet had a key role to play.

The organisational structure for delivering and managing the consultation worked well. A core unit of experienced staff from Customer Service Division reported to their own division, to the Self Assessment Programme, and to the top level of management, including ministers, when necessary. The programme of activities was developed as time went on, rather than being determined at the outset. This gave an appropriate degree of flexibility. The close working relationship with contracted consultants and researchers, and the collaborative approaches to drawing up project plans, also contributed to the success.

The ground had been prepared for self assessment work by previous Customer Service Division research and by efforts within the Revenue to develop a more customer-oriented service. The organisation was therefore reasonably receptive to further research and consultation, and to the customer-oriented activities which followed.

Whenever any organisation faces major changes to the traditional ways of working, it is important to involve and consult staff as much as possible. This should minimise the risks of raising false expectations and of creating dissatisfaction through misunderstandings. Customer Services staff were acutely aware of this and ensured that the staff consultation over agent and taxpayer education was of as high a professional standard as possible. This was a signal to local office staff that it was a serious exercise, in which their views counted. Staff saw their input lead to action within just a few months, and this was very helpful in securing support for the work.

Research methods

We interviewed staff from the Customer Service Division and other central functions of the Inland Revenue who had been involved in planning the introduction of self assessment and carrying out the public consultation. We also interviewed some of the research consultants who had been commissioned to work on the programme. It was not possible to contact members of the public who had been involved in any of the activities.

Reports of the different consultation activities were studied, along with successive versions of the tax return.

Commentary

Overview

The Inland Revenue carried out a major programme of consultation to prepare for the introduction of self assessment for personal tax in April 1997.

The key points on which we comment are:

- The scale of the project. This was a long project, and probably one of the most expensive public consultations undertaken. But this was easily justified by the significance of the changes for which it was a preparation.
- The involvement of the most senior people was evidence of the importance attached to it by the Inland Revenue.
- The size and structure of the Inland Revenue meant that involving staff was an essential part of the consultation process.
- The impact was considerable, but public and media attitudes towards taxation may mean that credit is given for this belatedly or not at all.
- The evolution of a programme of consultation, using a number of complementary methods, allowed the necessary flexibility to respond to findings as they emerged.

The scale of the project

The consultation programme lasted for more than three years, and the activities which resulted from it continued for longer than this. More than £600,000 was spent on commissioned work, in addition to the costs of staff time, materials and other costs.

This is certainly the most costly of our case studies, but the cost should be seen in the context of the scale of the overall project – the introduction of self assessment – of which it was just a small part. The consultation is concerned, essentially, with the design of administrative systems and the delivery of information about the way the systems operate. It is unusual for such resources to be expended on such subjects. It is generally the policy consultations, of which this is not one, which require the most intense participation and the most resources. But the change to self assessment has the potential of creating serious financial and political problems if it does not work smoothly, and this explains the scale of the exercise. It was necessary to design complex systems from scratch and important to test them in use.

The weight attached to the consultation

Associated with the scale and importance of the project was the involvement of politicians and managers at the most senior level.

The size of the Inland Revenue

The Inland Revenue has over 55,000 staff. They will be involved in running self assessment and could also be an invaluable source of ideas to those planning it. For these reasons, and to overcome any potential tensions between the centre and regional and local offices in an organisation structured along Next Steps lines, it was essential to include staff consultation as a part of the programme.

The impact

The impact of the consultation was considerable, in terms of both the design of documents and in the approach taken to informing and educating taxpayers, employers and agents. Both were significantly different as a result of the findings of the consultation.

Publicity given by the Inland Revenue to the tax return during its development attracted adverse comment in the press, but the Revenue accepted this as an inevitable part of inviting input. Criticism continues as the first set of tax returns are completed. While we are sure that consultation significantly improved the products, and contributed to a more positive attitude towards further research in the Revenue, it may well be that public and media criticism will continue. There are two reasons for this: people cannot know what the products would have been like without consultation, and the requirement to complete tax returns will always be regarded as onerous.

An evolving programme

A number of different methods were used. Familiar consultative approaches were complemented by research techniques. The depth of qualitative work was followed by larger scale quantitative studies. The programme had sufficient flexibility to allow new techniques, particular the usability testing, to be introduced. This was an innovation for the Inland Revenue and added a great deal to their understanding.

It would have been impossible to carry out an exercise on this scale without using consultants and other sources of expertise from outside the Inland Revenue. These relationships were carefully handled, with the Revenue maintaining control and continuity, while allowing their contractors to understand and contribute to the Revenue's plans and discussions on self assessment.

CASE STUDY TEN

The Lewisham Citizens Jury

INTRODUCTION

In Spring 1996 the London Borough of Lewisham (the Council) ran a citizens jury as part of a pilot experiment initiated by the Local Government Management Board (LGMB). The Lewisham jury was one of six in the LGMB project, and part funding was provided by LGMB. The project was evaluated by the Institute of Local Government Studies at the University of Birmingham. Within Lewisham itself, the citizens jury was one element in a wider programme known as the 'Democracy Project', or 'Lewisham Listens'.

The topic chosen by the Council was community safety/drugs/crime. A jury of 16 local residents, selected from a larger number to be 'broadly representative' of the population of the Borough, met over four days in one week in April. The jury's findings were discussed and voted on at a meeting of two of the local authority's committees in July. A proposal for a Community Drugs Education Project was accepted by the Borough at the end of 1996, and recruitment for staff began in April 1997. Members of the jury sit on the project's steering group.

ORIGINS AND OBJECTIVES

Origins

In the 1980s, in common with many local authorities, Lewisham Council developed a track record in consumer consultation with service users, through surveys and polls. This consumer approach has been superseded in the 1990s by an approach to involvement with local residents based on a broader notion of citizenship.

The Council established a Democracy Project known as Lewisham Listens, which addressed what has come to be thought of as the democratic deficit. The Project sought to examine and implement ways of improved interaction with the electorate, and of addressing such practical democratic problems as the low turnout in local elections. The Democracy Project itself arose from a number of trends, circumstances, and networks:

- the experience of the service user approach and its limitations;
- networking between authorities, academics, policy analysts and constitutional reformers about local democracy;

- the specific involvement of a senior councillor in the Commission for Local Democracy (CLD), which recommended consideration of the value of the citizens jury;
- active promotion by the Labour Party of experimentation with participatory and consultative mechanisms;
- since 1994, Lewisham has been effectively a single party Borough, and there was increasing concern on the part of councillors at the difficulty of testing policies and plans without an opposition;
- citizens juries had been used for some aspects of decision-making by state organisations in both the United States and in Germany.

The Democracy Project had been developing through a range of methods:

- Community/neighbourhood forums;
- focus groups;
- a video box;
- drama workshops for sixth formers to encourage electoral registration;
- DALI – a European-wide project involving eight cities which used interactive technology to provide local information.

When LGMB proposed a pilot project to test citizens juries, the Council was therefore already considering the possibility of a citizens jury.

Objectives

The Borough's first objective in convening a jury was to assess its usefulness as a particular method of consultation/participation within a framework of enhancing democracy. The aim was therefore to establish whether or not juries could be used to examine complex issues in a way which would be beneficial to the democratic process.

Specific policy outcomes of a citizens jury were not therefore the main objective. However, a citizens jury is a deliberative method of consultation, thought to be appropriate for certain types of issues, and testing the jury as a process did therefore involve testing its usefulness for identified types of issues. In this sense, the outputs and outcomes of the issue debated by the jury were part of the objectives.

THE CONSULTATION PROCESS

The method

The Council wanted a jury 'broadly representative' of the population of the Borough, and opted for selection of jurors to fit a model of population quotas. This was intended to make the jury 'representative' of the local population. Other models of jury selection are self-selection, and random selection, as in the criminal justice system.

The subject

Subjects put forward initially included internal issues such as members' allowances, and the Council's budget. But senior staff advised that an external issue was more likely to be of obvious concern to the community. Three external options were proposed:

1 caring for older people;
2 community safety/drugs/crime;
3 the environment/pollution/Agenda 21.

Drugs/crime/safety was selected as an issue on 9 January 1996, after some debate amongst councillors, officers and other agencies in the field. The details were refined later with other relevant organisations who were either consulted, or who took part in a Steering Group established to advise on the project (see below).

The drugs topic was selected for a number of specific reasons:

- opinion surveys of residents showed crime and fear of crime consistently a high priority
- drugs abuse was a very big factor in both family problems and crime locally;
- drugs/safety was a complex topic on which 'experts' were unsure how to proceed – an effective drugs policy is very hard to construct;
- the problem of drugs is not adequately discussed in the political arena, because politicians are nervous of it.

In addition, drugs was a field in which the local authority, health, police and others were already involved jointly, making it a suitable topic for a multi-agency experiment with a jury.

Finally, drugs was considered to be a topic about which the public was likely to have views based on popular notions unhelpful to policy formulation. Convening a citizens jury would test whether jurors could debate, learn, and reassess their views, making a useful contribution to policy formulation.

The activities

The jury was organised by a core group of staff, assisted by a wider Steering Group drawn both from within the Council and from other local organisations (see below – under 'Management'). A briefing was prepared based on guidelines from the Institute for Public Policy Research on the issues requiring consideration, including practical details.

Refining the topic

After discussions in the Steering Group about which aspects of drugs to ask the jury to consider, and during which a range of views were put forward, the Head of Finance and Support Services decided on a broad approach – covering education, criminal and health issues.

Education Directorate staff wrote a paper for the core team, giving an overview of drugs education work, both the practice and the philosophy behind it, to enable the team to organise these aspects of the jury process. The Borough also held two focus groups on drugs issues in late March, a month or so before the jury, one based on the same quota sample used for the selection of the jury, and one made up of young people, given the 18+ age limit on jury membership. The consultants (see below) carried out depth interviews with drug users, professionals and young people to help decide what issues should be covered in the jury.

Recruitment of the consultants

The core team decided to use consultants to ensure independent facilitation and jury recruitment, and in February 1996 the Borough contracted with a market research company to recruit, run and report on the jury. Concern about the consultants' knowledge about drugs led to the appointment of a co-consultant with drugs expertise from the Standing Conference on Drug Abuse (SCODA), who helped facilitate the jury sessions.

Recruiting the jury

Researchers in the Policy and Equalities Unit drew up a profile for the composition of the jury, the basis of which was a 'representative' sample from the community, drawn using a quota based on census data. The consultants approached 300 residents, and obtained the agreement of 16 within the quota. In this sense, there was an element of self-selection.

Actual recruitment took place between one and two weeks before the date set for the jury, to minimise the drop-out rate, although in practice potential jurors were dropping out right up to the last minute. The consultants also paid the jurors as part of their contract with the Borough, in order to help attract people.

Jurors' motives for agreeing to take part were of two kinds: those about speaking up for the community, and those which recognised the serious nature of the social problems around drugs and crime. It is unclear what the balance of these was at the time of recruitment. The offer of a small payment was welcomed by all, but was said not to be a motive. Two jurors reported agreeing to take part without knowing about payment. Jurors reported knowing from the start that there was a four-day time commitment to a jury.

A pre-jury briefing session was held on 15 April at which a number of points of concern were raised: exposure to the media; confidentiality of jury discussions; and that the video could be turned off if they asked. Jurors were reassured on all of these, although after the event jurors remained dissatisfied about aspects of these. Some jurors expressed doubts about the genuineness of the exercise at this stage: whether it would be a properly conducted exercise; and whether they would find that the decisions had been made beforehand. In both cases jurors reported their doubts were not confirmed by subsequent experiences.

Witnesses

Witnesses were selected by the Steering Group, advised by the Council's Community Safety Coordinator and the Education Directorate's Quality Assurance and Development Division staff. Witnesses were recruited to give evidence for a 15 minute period, in addition to responding to questions from the jury, and were asked to provide written points in advance.

The questions put to the jury

The jury was asked to consider one general question, which was divided into three sub-questions. The general question was: 'What can be done to reduce harm to the community and individuals from drugs?'

The three sub-questions were:

1 In what ways are the community and individual harmed by drugs?
2 Who can provide the most effective drugs education and what message should they give?
3 Can treatment options for dependent users affect drug related crime?

The hearings

The jury of 16 met for a total of four days, split into two weekdays and one weekend, allowing for a balance of the needs of people taking time off work and those of the unemployed. Evidence was heard from 14 witnesses, including police, doctors, various drug users, relevant Council staff, voluntary sector projects, and teachers. A ground rules session at the beginning sought to ensure that the rules of debate were adhered to.

At the end of the second day the jury asked to recall the Community Safety Coordinator, and also to hear new witnesses: a Home Office Minister, voluntary sector project workers, recreational as opposed to addictive drug users, and a secondary school head teacher. The Minister was unable to attend, but his office sent a supportive message. A secondary head teacher was not found in the time available. However, a primary head did appear as a witness.

The jury was chaired by the consultants. The sessions were taped and videoed, with the exception of two confidential witnesses, by a video unit from the London Borough of Hammersmith and Fulham which was there throughout the four days.

Core team staff took notes, which they typed up and gave to jurors the next day. Two questionnaires were given to the jurors by the consultants – one before and one after the jury. There was an external evaluation by the Institutute of Local Government Studies (INLOGOV), whose questionnaire was given to jurors to take away with them.

On the consultants' advice, discussions were held in two sub-groups of men and women, as some of the women found it hard to contribute in the larger group. However, jurors to whom we spoke did not understand the reason for this split and thought it unnecessary.

Publicity for the jury was for the Council an essential part of the pilot. There was considerable media interest, and Radio 4 was there for the whole of the first day. The jury did receive favourable publicity, and several jurors and the police witness gave interviews either at the time or subsequently. But this emphasis on publicity was upsetting for some jurors and there was clearly an unresolved conflict in this aspect of the jury.

There were difficulties over how to collate and summarise the evidence and the jury's views. Although Council staff had expected the consultants to facilitate this, the consultants were unable to do so, and the core team devised its own approach. This involved developing a series of yes/no questions for the jury to answer, based on the views expressed in the deliberations. The responses to these questions plus the notes of the deliberations were then sifted into a set of recommendations.

There is general agreement that the process overall was a success. Jurors participated willingly from the start, taking their role as 'community representatives' seriously, making an effort to understand the witnesses, and asking questions. Discussion was generally informed, and disagreements were conducted with mutual respect.

Other consultation activities

The Borough placed an advert in the Council's newspaper seeking submissions from any interested organisation, with two responses.

Managing the process

The Core Group and the Steering Group

The process was managed by a core group of staff – the Policy Officer and the Policy Team Manager from the Policy and Equalities Unit. This core team was led by the Head of Finance and Support Services, who had corporate responsibility for 'governance and democracy' issues, and assisted by a wider steering group of other Council officers, and staff from the police, the Health Commission and Goldsmiths' College.

Lewisham describes its approach as corporate working within the Council, and partnership with other agencies. The Steering Group was set up at the end of February 1996 to secure a multi-agency approach to the jury. Initial membership was an officer from Social Services, the police youth and community section, and Goldsmiths' College, and later included the Joint Development Officer for substance misuse, from Lambeth, Southwark and Lewisham Health Commission, the lead councillor involved in the Democracy project, staff from the Education Directorate's Quality Assurance and Development Team, and the Borough's Community Safety Coordinator.

The Health Commission representative and the Community Safety Coordinator were both involved in government-sponsored multi-agency groups and activities around the problem of drugs. In addition, several posts in the field of drugs are jointly funded by the Health Commission and several local councils.

The police were willing participants, as they had already prioritised drugs in their plans and supported drugs as a topic for that reason. By contrast, the Borough was aware that the Health Commission would find the exercise difficult as any new policy decisions were likely to affect their resources.

The Steering Group met twice only prior to the jury because of problems of time. Core team members found that the process of setting up the jury involved a lot of quick decision-making and reacting, with a heavy administrative load, and the phase of setting up the jury intensive and difficult. Some of the Steering Group participants felt that they were given inadequate notice of meetings, and were unable to attend. A longer preparation time was thought desirable.

Members and senior officers

The jury was owned at a high level by both members and officers. At member level within the Council, decisions were made through the Democracy Project Task Group. From Summer 1995 the Democracy Project was led at officer level by the Head of Finance and Support Services. She led the jury process through to the adoption of the report by the Council's two Committees in July 1996 and continues to have responsibility for outcomes implementation.

Resources

Staff time involved in setting up and running the jury was estimated at two months full-time for the lead operational officer, with the other core team member spending around one-third of this. Education staff spent approximately the equivalent of ten working days, but without any time budgeted for. Senior staff time was not accounted for.

Staff are mainly self-servicing, and have no internal separate administrative support systems in place, and no separate administrative costs were therefore calculated.

Direct costs

	£
Consultants	18,200
SCODA (consultant)	2,400
Witness Expenses	800
Venue/equip/food/print	1,700
Video recording	3,300
Less an LGMB contribution of	4,000
Net direct cost	22,400

Council staff now consider that it would be more efficient to buy in administration, and spend less on consultants.

Impact of the process on its output

The local authority, the police and the jurors all found that the jury as a process was an effective way to discuss and form views on the topic of drugs and crime.

At the outset jurors had fairly uniform punitive views on how to deal with drugs, and after hearing evidence most underwent substantial revisions of their views and reached conclusions very unlike their original views. Jurors report that they all took the exercise very seriously, worked hard at a very difficult and disturbing subject, and that as a result they were able to come up with considered and reasoned views which had practical applications. These elements confirmed the suitability of the method for a subject such as drugs.

The Health Commission representative took a different view, seeing the issues as inherently too complex for a citizens jury, and emphasising the jury's inability to distinguish between opinion and evidence. In his view, the jury did not serve a useful purpose, with evidence to the jury limited, and even in some instances biased. He disputed the jury's recommendations on drugs prescription, and cited findings from a drugs education programme in the United States. He also felt that although the education recommendations would do no harm, it was doubtful whether they would make any difference.

IMPACT

Acting on the output of the exercise

Jury recommendations

A report, *Lewisham Citizens Jury,* was produced by the consultants in July, listing jurors' responses to the questions put at the end of the process, and offering a summary of jurors' views. At the same time the jury's findings were also summarised by the local authority as 27 recommendations under four main headings – drugs education, drug-related crime, treatment, and wider issues.

In the case of education and policing, the jury's findings were broadly in agreement with the views of the authorities. In the case of the treatment of heroin addicts, the jury's views were different from those of the Health Commission.

The joint committee meeting

A report on the jury's findings was presented to a joint meeting on 10 July 1996 of the Community Affairs Committee and the Policy and Resources Committee. Presentations were made by the Head of Finance and Support Services and by Education Directorate Quality Assurance and Development staff. Jurors present were impressed by these presentations and felt that Council staff had put the jury's findings across very well. Representatives of the police and the Health Commission made brief statements.

Councillors debated and agreed the report, in the presence of the jury. Jurors contributed to the discussion, some of them challenging the views expressed by some councillors.

Publicity and promotion

A report on the jury was sent by the Council to over 100 opinion-formers, politicians and research organisations.

The Community Drugs Education Programme

Because they have responsibility for education, the local authority opted to focus first on drugs education. Initially staff were asked to produce a programme on the assumption that resources were not a problem, for a parent and community drug education programme. This draft was well received at a Steering Group meeting in mid-June, and was presented to jurors at a de-briefing session towards the end of

June, attended by the core team, plus police, education, community safety and the consultants.

By November 1996 the Education Directorate's Quality Assurance and Development Team had devised a four-year Community Drugs Education Project, costed at around £115,000 for the first year, rising by inflation in subsequent years. Staff posts to carry out this project were advertised in the national press in April 1997. A new Steering Group has been set up to oversee the project with representatives from health, the police, the Council's Education and Community Safety Departments, as well as three members of the citizens jury. This project has a new focus, in that it is aimed at the whole community and not only at schools, as in the past.

Drugs treatment recommendations

The jury's health recommendations were discussed at a meeting of the Drugs Action Team, which has a commitment to look at the issue of more flexible prescribing, and to research this. The Borough's intention is to press the Health Commission to have a continuing public debate on this and will try to get the Commission to join in a pilot prescribing project, funded by the Department of Health, building on the Home Office's supportive response to the jury's request for a witness.

Direct impact

Policies and services

Police policy and practice could not be influenced, as these were already in place. Health Commission treatment policy is described by the Health representative as being decided on a clinical basis and not therefore influenced by the jury's findings.

The Council has found the jury helpful in thinking through community planning when making budgets. A jury might be used, for example, to assess community views on charging for community care services if they are obliged to consider charging.

Multi-agency working

Multi-agency working was a feature of the topic chosen for the jury, and one of the aims was to organise the jury jointly with other agencies. This was only partly successful. The jury has built on existing good relations between the Council and the police and brought the two authorities closer in dealing with the issues of drugs and crime.

Disagreements with Health over aspects of drugs treatment were evident in the jury process, and a doctor who gave evidence was not happy with some aspects of the findings. Inherent in the jury method is the crossing of professional boundaries, and in the case of Health this was not welcomed. The health representative expressed serious reservations about the jury as a process, as well as about aspects of the jury's findings.

Democratic practices

The success of the jury as a deliberative exercise has confirmed and legitimised the process for the local authority and the jurors. Jurors interviewed expressed concern about an apparent lack of specific outcomes, although progress made in drugs education since then may mean that jurors now hold different views.

The Future

The Council is setting up a Community Affairs Division, located within the Education Department, as part of its development of democratic issues. Consultation may become part of this Division's role.

Senior officers are keen to repeat the exercise. Some members have expressed reservations, feeling that it could undermine representative democracy, but others are keen, including leading members.

The jury is resource intensive, and the Council would not be able to do more than one or two a year. For regular consultations, they are considering research panels. Officers have some ideas for future juries, but at the time of writing no specific proposal has been put forward.

Assessment

The success of the project

The Council's view

The local authority's view is that the both the process and the content of the recommendations from the jury were extremely successful. The main points which the authority stressed were:

- Internally the success of the project has enthused more members about the whole Democracy Project.
- Relations with the police were strengthened.
- The impression that the Council was trying to create, that they are seeking to make improvements, was enhanced.
- Consultation always comes up against professional boundaries, and the jury shows that 'ordinary' people can have a useful say on complex matters.
- In itself the jury, involving 16 people, all with relatives and friends, encourages the spread of the habits of citizenship.
- The jury showed that you can generate attitude changes in the public, and this demonstrates to politicians that the boundaries can be changed.
- For local authorities, one of the secrets of attracting resources is to achieve a profile for a project both 'internally' – within the authority – and 'externally' – amongst a wider audience. The jury did both.

What the Council also reports learning from the experience is that better forward planning is needed, with longer timescales and more effort put into partnership approaches. Council staff experienced some difficulties over the short timescale, and some dissatisfaction with notice of meetings and communication was expressed by Steering Group participants.

The method used to summarise the results of the jury had to be devised mid-process, and this was not ideal. Media intrusiveness, and crowded overheated premises were both practical problems which require improvement for future juries. Education Directorate staff would have preferred their experiences of working with Health to have been used to better effect, in order to seek to avoid the problems experienced between Health and the local authority.

The police view

The police assessed the jury as successful as a process, but expressed doubts about its practical outcomes. Police policy was supported by the jury, but could not have been influenced. Police want to see improved arrest/referral schemes and pilots around several aspects of the jury's recommendation, but are not optimistic that funds will be available. The police also doubt the Health Commission's commitment to support of experimental pilots. Both the local authority and the police want to pilot projects to try different approaches to treatment for heroin addicts.

The Health Commission view

The Health Commission representative had strong concerns about the questions the jury would address, the choice of witnesses, the process of witness selection, and the weight of the findings. His view was that issues around health and in particular treatment strategies were too complex and a jury would not have the time or skills to reach a useful view. In essence he did not think the jury a useful exercise.

The Health Commission also felt that the jury did not get a balance of all views on treatment, but only two varieties of essentially the same view on which drugs to prescribe. The local authority's view, by contrast, was that two doctors gave directly opposing views.

The jurors' views

The jurors experienced the jury as professional, well-managed, and profound. They expressed pleasure and surprise at how well it was run, and at how well people blended and interacted. They were personally affected by the evidence, and became more concerned as the sessions progressed. The jurors described the process as hard work, upsetting, and involving.

Jurors were impressed by the efforts Council staff had clearly made to conduct a proper jury and by the high level of ownership of the jury within the Council. They found the SCODA consultant well-informed and her contribution made a real difference. Jurors felt that the Council's motives were in part about being seen to be doing the 'new' thing.

In general, their assessment, that they began with certain ideas and then changed their minds substantially, agrees with the Council's assessment of this aspect of the process.

The jury also experienced a number of practical problems. The media were intrusive at times, the video team occupied a lot of space, and caused concern about privacy and confidentiality. In both cases jurors felt that the Council had not stuck to its agreement with them. Finally, the venue was too hot and cramped, and noisy if windows were opened.

The jurors found that there was insufficient time for witnesses and for deliberation – a view shared by the witnesses whom we interviewed. Jurors found witnesses with hands-on experience more convincing than experts. They expressed surprise at the vehemence with which some of the health views were expressed – describing them as 'warring camps' – particularly when it was self-evident that whatever was being done was not working very well. In particular, jurors were concerned that nothing was on offer for crack cocaine addicts, which they saw as the largest social drugs problem for the Borough. They also considered they did not have time to hear enough evidence on health issues.

The aftermath of the jury was less satisfactory for jurors, who at the time of our discussions with them were uncertain about both the specific outcomes of their recommendations, and about whether a video of the proceedings had been made. Two jurors had received a copy of a video, but were unsure whether it was a 'final' version. This was the jurors' main criticism – that little had come out of the jury at the time of our interview. The jury wanted the Council to create and promote a new strategy on drugs, and they felt that this had not happened. They wanted an active, local campaigning and 'marketing' approach to the verdicts, instead of which they saw lost momentum, a lack of funds, and declining motivation.

The drugs education project, which was established some time after this study was completed, has involved some jurors in further activity arising from the jury's findings, and it may be that their views have changed as a result.

RESEARCH METHODS

We interviewed the core team, the Head of Finance and Resources and the lead councillor. We also interviewed education and community safety staff, and the Health Commission and police members of the Steering Group. Two of these were also witnesses. We interviewed four jurors in a group. We studied the various policy documents, the consultants' report, the jury questionnaires and the local authority's report on the jury, plus press cuttings and so on.

The Health Commission provided a copy of doctors' letters about the jury. Tapes of the jury and access to the video were offered but not taken up. We attended the joint Committees meeting in July, and met the jurors and the Chief Executive at the reception after the event.

The fieldwork took place in early Summer and Autumn 1996, beginning soon after the jury completed its deliberations. Additional information on progress in implementation of an education programme was provided by the Council at the end of 1996 and in mid 1997.

COMMENTARY

Overview

The Lewisham citizens jury was an experimental exercise in participation in the policy process by residents of the London Borough of Lewisham. The experiment had two aims: to test the feasibility of the jury as a process, and to obtain input to a suitable aspect of policy and service development of importance to the Borough.

We identifed a number of key points which are examined in this commentary:

- As a process, the jury was a success, with one reservation about the jury's independence.
- Considerable resources are required to carry out a jury effectively.
- Partnership working with other statutory bodies must be carefully nurtured.
- A jury needs specific questions to answer, in order to be most effective.
- Making the jury work well in the policy process and in decision-making requires clarity of purpose, process, and outcomes.
- The sources of jury legitimacy require careful elaboration.
- The use of a jury as part of a larger 'democracy' programme must be steered with care.

The success of the citizens jury as a process

The feasibility of the jury process was satisfactorily demonstrated by the Lewisham exercise, in that the milestones of jury recruitment, evidence, deliberations, and findings were all effectively reached. We have reservations about the jury's 'independence', which was not sufficiently guaranteed. Specifically, witness selection was not independent, jury deliberation was not private, and the 'findings' of the jury were 'constructed' (albeit in good faith) by local authority staff.

This issue of juror independence is important for the notion of legitimacy which underpins the jury (see below). In our view, the commissioning organisation should not be involved in juror selection, witness selection, or results processing, if a jury is to be seen to be independent.

Resources

Juries are expensive, in terms both of direct expenditures and staff time, and should only be considered where there is a complete framework within which the jury can operate, right through to detailed outcomes. Jurors are required to devote a lot of time and effort to the jury, and it is unreasonable to expect them to do so without a very clear role, purpose and timetable for both for the jury and the use of its findings.

Partnerships

The issues under consideration by a jury may well range across the responsibilities of more than one authority. The Lewisham jury was not very successful in bringing together all of the important bodies involved, which contributed to the lack of commitment to the process from the Health Commission. Participants are in general agreed that development of partnership working requires more time and effort than is typically estimated. Whilst consultation exercises need to be steered by core groups, the use of the skills of the most relevant staff, who may well be in different departments, must not be inhibited by such a central approach.

Specific questions with specific answers

The second purpose of the jury was to inform/influence policy. For the Lewisham jury, the broad scope of the jury's remit and the lack of an identified role for the jury's findings both contributed to a lack of specificity about the jury's role in policy-making.

The questions asked of the jury did not have answers which would inform decision-making in specified ways. The jury's findings were used to argue for specific developments, aspects of which were already in favour amongst key professional staff, giving the jury's proposals a legitimating role (see below), rather than an innovative one. This raises the issue of whether the jury did in fact add to the policy options available.

Purpose – making a jury work well in policy and decisions

Because the Lewisham exercise posed very broad questions, producing one new initiative in one area of its deliberations, we are unable to assess the effectiveness of jury deliberations in creating policy and services. The issue of what sorts of policy, service or planning decisions it may be useful for an elected member of a local authority to delegate to a jury is not clear to us. The deliberative character of the jury suggests topics on which no easily obtainable public view is available, so that juries may be useful as arbitrators between differing expert views. But for this role, they must be accorded decision-making status, and on the whole this seems unlikely.

A jury demands a great deal of its members, and the resources needed to set it up and run it are more than slight. It seems to us that if this is the case, then a jury should only be used for specific decisions. To be both most useful and most cost-effective therefore, a citizens jury needs a framework which includes an understanding of why a jury is a key element in a particular policy or service development, and public agreement in advance on what will be done with the answers to the questions put to the jury. Using a jury to take 'soundings' or get a feel for public opinion, or the lay view, without an intention to feed this through into specific changes would be expensive and unproductive.

The legitimacy of the jury

As a method, the citizens jury is seen as useful for the obtaining from non-expert, non-interest group-related citizens, views on complex social issues which underpin public policy. It relies on an assumption that the views of 'ordinary' people, after an appropriate period of education and discussion, can make a unique and therefore useful contribution to policy development. This is said to be the source of the value of the jury's views in policy or service development.

Legitimacy lies therefore in the notion of the 'citizen', which the jury embodies. It is also thought that citizens juries can provide an indicator not only of the views of the citizen, but also of the wider community. This is just about possible, but it is equally clear that this is an assertion, and that it is extremely unlikely. Sixteen people cannot represent anyone other than themselves, no matter how many categories of resident are used to balance jury selection.

The legitimacy granted to a jury's views lies therefore in the role given to the jury within the decision-making process. It is therefore a matter of policy, not statistics, as to how legitimate the jury's views are.

Democracy initiatives

Citizens juries are most likely to be considered by public service organisations which are experimenting with broad approaches to citizenship, involvement, and a range of 'democratic' initiatives. When this is the case, it is essential that the specific role of juries in this process is assessed, and that the jury is carried through with all of the steps outlined in this guide.

A key element in securing the achievements of the Lewisham jury was the hard work of one or two key staff at a relatively junior level, and the management skills of one senior officer. Whilst commitments to democracy and citizenship played a part in starting the process, the doing of it was a grind: rushed, unsatisfactory, difficult. The temptation to present such initiatives as the result of great visions alone is hard to avoid, but if at all possible visions and hard work should be given equal credit.

CASE STUDY ELEVEN

The Science Museum: Consensus Conference

ORIGINS AND OBJECTIVES

The subject of this case study is the first and only national consensus conference to have taken place in the United Kingdom. It was based on a method of public participation in policy-making which has been developed in recent years in Denmark. The Danish model involved a panel of citizens developing its understanding of a complex and controversial scientific or technical subject, reaching a consensus about the subject and presenting its conclusions to a conference.

The subject of the UK conference was plant biotechnology and it took place over a period of three days in November 1994. It was organised by the Science Museum and funded by the Biotechnology and Biological Sciences Research Council (BBSRC).

Origins

The origins of the consensus conference lie in the coming together of two broad interests, both of which went on to be reflected in the objectives of the conference. Those involved in the public understanding of science had a specific interest in the model as a way of engaging the lay public in scientific subjects. There was also the more widespread interest in innovative ways of involving the public in policy-making. This interest had also led to experiments elsewhere with citizens juries, deliberative polling and so on.

The immediate background to the consensus conference was, first, the programme of consensus conferences which had taken place in Denmark, later followed by the Netherlands, since the late 1980s and, secondly, the policy of the UK government, introduced in 1993, that the research councils should fund activities which contributed to the public understanding of science. These different interests came together in a joint initiative by the Science Museum and the BBSRC.

Objectives

The initiative had two broad objectives:

1 to conduct an experiment in public participation, public debate and policy-making; specifically, to test the Danish model of consensus conferences in the UK setting;

2 to contribute to the public debate and policy-making on plant biotechnology by providing the perspective of informed lay people.

The respective weight attached to these two objectives was not clear to many of the participants or observers, who had a range of expectations and interests. Further, the 'public debate' objective raised important supplementary questions: was the intended audience the general public, scientists or policy-makers, and how were they to be informed and influenced?

A third objective, related to the other two, was to evaluate the consensus conference as a method of contributing to public policy-making and of informing public debate on socially sensitive areas of science and technology. This evaluation is continuing and has provided useful background material for our own research.

THE PROCESS ITSELF

Methods

The process was deliberately based on the Danish model of consensus conferences. A panel of 16 volunteer lay people is recruited, with the aim that they should control the content and key aspects of the whole process. The subject of the conference, but not the specific questions to be asked, is set in advance. The panel then receives briefings before going on to: decide the questions they wish to address; question experts; assess the information they receive and reach a consensus on the subject. The panel then produces a report which it presents to a conference which is open to the public and the press.

The panel worked between August 1994, when it received its first written briefing, and November 1994 when the actual conference took place. There were also two preparatory weekends for the panel, in September and October 1994. The decision to fund the conference had been taken in February 1993. The decision to focus on plant biotechnology was made at an early stage by the BBSRC. Biotechnology as a whole was thought to be too broad a subject, animal biotechnology too controversial and emotive. Early planning meetings were followed by the appointment of the Project Manager in February 1994 and the Steering Committee in March 1994.

Activities

In the early stages of planning, the conference decisions were made jointly by the BBSRC and the Science Museum. Once the Steering Committee and Project Manager were in place, they could take on this role.

Steering Committee

The committee's brief was to safeguard the credibility of the consensus conference by ensuring it was organised and conducted competently and impartially. It had key roles in the selection of the panel, organising the briefing and preparatory weekends for the panel, and suggesting experts to be invited to discuss issues with the panel. It also planned the timetable and selected the venue for the conference and oversaw the budget. The committee had six meetings of about four to five hours each during the organisation of the conference.

Members of the Steering Committee were selected by the BBSRC and the Science Museum. The Committee was chaired by Professor Durant, Assistant Director of the Science Museum and Professor of the Public Understanding of Science at Imperial College. The other five members came from the biotechnology industry, journalism, a university, a consumer organisation and the Parliamentary Office of Science and Technology. There was no representative of any environmental organisation or any member known to oppose the technology. The organisers were later criticised for this by some environmental campaign groups.

Recruiting the lay panel

A press conference in November 1993 announced the consensus conference. A second press conference in June 1994 called for volunteers, and was followed by advertising in regional newspapers and on radio for those interested in joining the panel. The advert specified the subject of the conference, gave its dates and outlined the panel's responsibilities. It set three criteria for volunteers: they had to be available on all the set dates; they had to be 18 years old or over; and they had to be without any previous experience of the subject. Interested people were asked to write a one page letter 'about yourself and why you want to be considered'. Almost 400 people responded. They were then sent a questionnaire to elicit further information. Of these, 341 were returned.

The organisers were not aiming to recruit a representative sample of the British public. They recognised that to do so would, in any case, be impossible with a group of 16. However, they did want to get a cross-section of people who varied in age, gender, education, life cycle (for example, with and without children living at home), area of residence (urban and rural), and level of personal interest in the subject. Using these criteria, a panel of 16 was selected by project staff and two committee members, and recommended to the whole committee.

Panel members reported a range of reasons for responding to the advert, including an interest in science. Others were explicit about their total lack of knowledge of science, but were curious about the idea of the consensus conference, or excited by the possibility of the intellectual challenge. One commented that all the panel members, who had a range of formal educational achievement, were very intelligent people. The fact that they had volunteered to take part suggests that they were likely to be aware of and interested in public policy issues and willing to take on new challenges.

A later exercise by the evaluator involved five students scoring all the application letters, including those of the (unidentified) successful applicants, according to the degree of support they showed for the technology. The results showed a significant difference between the panel and the unsuccessful applicants, with the panel members being more in favour of biotechnology.

Briefing and preparation

The preparation for the conference itself was intensive. It was necessary to equip panel members with a level of knowledge about plant biotechnology which would enable them to formulate the agenda, to pose questions to the experts who would attend the conference itself and then to reach their conclusions. There is an inherent tension in this process, between the intention that the panel should reach its conclusions as independently as possible, and the panel's dependence on experts to provide them with information, at least in the early stages.

The difficulties in providing the panel with comprehensive and impartial information manifested themselves in a disagreement in the Steering Committee about who should be invited to address the panel at the first weekend, and in what order. The question concerned the position of environmental groups, who later expressed some scepticism about the objectivity of the committee.

This phase of the process involved:

- a written briefing sent to panel members in advance of the first weekend;
- the first preparatory weekend at which the panel received presentations from five experts, who were in research, education, the industry, and environmental policy/campaigning;
- the second preparatory weekend, when the panel held discussions on different themes with small groups of experts and then went on to draw up the questions they wished to ask experts in the conference itself, and which experts they wished to invite.

The assessment of this briefing and preparatory process varies. Reviewing the consensus conference afterwards, policy-makers and others, including the experts who gave evidence, were impressed by the level of understanding acquired by the panel. The process had clearly achieved the objective of informing the panel sufficiently well enough to satisfy the knowledgeable participants. It is more difficult, however, to assess the level of knowledge which is actually necessary. This may depend partly on whether one sees the main objective to be improving the public understanding of science or to enable the panel to decide the issues which should be the subject of public concern and debate.

Panel members generally felt the process had worked well. Some experts had been rather patronising but most were very helpful. Members' criticisms concerned both the intensity of the process and, for some, the enforced superficiality of it. Members found the preparation to be very intensive, but this was generally accepted as inevitable. One member reported considering leaving the panel after the first weekend because the whole process was unreasonably demanding and exhausting. This was exacerbated, the member felt, by a personal lack of any scientific education. Members varied in the amount of 'homework' they did independently, but the general view was that it was not possible to read all the written material they were provided with.

The difficulties of coping with the volume of material were coupled with frustration, for some people, at not being able to explore the issues in more depth, and at the speed with which they had to decide on questions and invitations for the conference. There was a general view that the lack of time meant they were guided in these decisions more than was desirable. One solution, suggested by interviewees, would have been to focus on a narrower subject than plant biotechnology. Another would be to allow more time, possibly a third weekend, but they were aware that this would add to the expense and would mean asking volunteers for a commitment that many would find unreasonable or impractical.

The conference

The first session of the conference lasted for most of two days. On the first day, between one and four experts were called to answer each of the seven questions. On the second day, there was an open question and answer session in which the audience of between 300 and 400 participated. The panel retired to write their report in mid-afternoon.

The conference was opened by the Parliamentary Secretary at the Ministry of Agriculture, Fisheries and Food and was chaired by a well known science broadcaster. The conference was open to the general public and had been widely advertised. Most members of the audience had a professional interest in plant biotechnology.

It appears that most members of the panel took the conference in their stride, although one or two described it as 'daunting' or 'scary'. At this stage the process was less about receiving completely new information than about understanding the different experts' perspectives on the issues.

The conference produced some heated exchanges, which was felt to be healthy. The view of some, however, was that the overall content was rather predictable and dull. The experts would have liked longer to make their presentations, and more opportunity for a discussion with the panel. In effect, they had two audiences – the panel and the conference audience. Some felt that the setting and shortage of time pushed experts into restating their organisations' position rather than entering into discussion. It was somewhat frustrating that they could not contribute to the questions which were allocated to others. The panel impressed them with the level of knowledge and understanding manifested in their questioning.

Producing the report

The panel returned to the hotel in mid-afternoon to write their report. They completed it at 5am the next day, more than 12 hours later. They were working under pressure as the report was to be produced in time for it to be printed and distributed at the conference the following morning. The whole process was described as fraught and tense. The anxiety of the organisers was heightened by the panel's decision to produce the report completely independently, without the presence of either the facilitator or the Chair of the Steering Committee.

This decision was prompted by the panel's concern and irritation that their independence and objectivity was being questioned by observers. Some panel members had also become worried that the process could incline them towards a bias in favour of the biotechnology industry and the scientific establishment. The trigger for their decision to exclude all but themselves from the report-writing process was a radio interview given by a representative of an environmental organisation, in which their neutrality was questioned. Their report is prefaced with the following statement:

> 'We the lay panel of the UK National Consensus Conference on Plant Biotechnology state that total responsibility for the following report is ours. There was no undue pressure brought to bear on the panel by any party to the conference. We set the agenda of discussion, requested the relevant available experts as we understood them to be, evaluated their evidence to the best of our ability, and wrote the report with complete independence. The organising bodies, and those who initiated the conference, had no opportunity to read the report or any part of it before it was completed.'

With the aid only of a wordprocessing assistant and an editor, who would play no part in facilitating the process, the panel had to devise for themselves a way of agreeing on the structure and content of their report. They used a secret ballot to elect a chairperson who suggested and guided a process for producing the report. He was felt by the panel members we interviewed to have done a difficult job well.

It was decided to use the seven questions posed at the conference as section headings in the report. Each individual wrote their views on each question. They then worked in pairs and groups of three to produce a single piece of text on each question. A final round table session of all the members was then held to agree the final draft, question by question.

Members of the panel differ in their views of the advisability of producing a report to this timetable. It was accepted that the momentum of the conference needed to be maintained and that to have a break of a full day would have caused a problem in terms of continuity and attendance by the audience. Some members felt it was quite unreasonable to expect them to produce a report without a rest or a night's sleep, or a chance to reflect. Others thought it was better to go straight to the task while the information was still fresh in their minds and to simply work until it was done.

By the end of the process, it was generally agreed, people were becoming tired and irritable. Opinions differ about whether, given more time, they would have produced a better or substantially different report, or whether the difficult process of defining and then reaching consensus would have been any easier.

Presentation of the report

Copies of the report were distributed to the conference audience on the following morning. Panel members read out sections of the report and answered questions from the audience and the press.

Publicising the conference and the report

The report was produced as a published document after the conference. In appearance it is rather more glossy than the hastily produced version issued at the conference, but the content is no different. It was widely distributed to policy-makers, scientists and journalists.

The organisers were aware that achieving the objective of encouraging public debate depended on securing coverage by the media. Not only was the report publicised, but there was a series of press releases during the months leading up to the conference, the conference itself was advertised in the press and 8,000 invitations were issued.

Managing the process

The paramount concern of the organisers, and particularly of the Science Museum, was with the credibility of the consensus conference. They were aware that any doubts about their objectivity or independence would damage the potential for influencing policy or encouraging debate, as well as the reception it would receive as a successful experiment in public participation.

These concerns had influenced the choice of the Science Museum as lead organiser. The BBSRC, which funded the conference, took a deliberately low key role. It was aware that, as a funder of research into biotechnology, it would not be regarded as impartial. A member of the BBSRC staff attended the Steering Committee meetings but was not a member of it.

The Steering Committee had a central role in directing the project. The choice of membership did lead to some criticism because of the absence of any representatives of environmental organisations. Critics suggested that the Committee membership was not sufficiently broad or pluralistic and suspected that the conference was more likely to endorse the technology because of this.

The project had a full time project manager, with administrative assistance, and a facilitator for the lay panel. The project manager and facilitator were co-opted on to the Steering Committee.

Resources

The budget for the consensus conference was approximately £85,000. This is described by the organisers as adequate. They consider there is little possibility of reducing this figure. This total covers the costs of the project staff, all the organisation, the venues and accommodation, publicity, the conference itself and the production of the report.

In addition a considerable amount of time was spent on the conference by the unpaid participants. The commitment of the members of the lay panel was considerable. They received expenses but no fee. Their commitment included the two preparatory weekends and the conference itself. There was also an expectation that they would read and consider the issues in their own time.

Steering Committee members spent about six days in meetings and attended the conference itself. Those who gave evidence spent time preparing for and then attending the briefing weekend(s) and/or the conference itself. The conference lasted three days.

The impact of the process on its output

A number of features of the process may have influenced the nature and content of the report.

Seeking consensus

The panellists were advised by the organisers that they should seek to find common ground, but not resort to bland compromise. If they could not reach consensus, then a report which presented opposing or majority and minority views would be acceptable. In the event, a single set of views was presented. All concerned felt that the panel took the process and their responsibilities very seriously.

Certain points advocated by a single panel member were excluded, on the grounds that they were too detailed or insignificant. The process of agreeing the final draft became somewhat tense, according to some members. There was an element of conceding to the views of the most persistent in order to get the job finished in the limited time available.

The view of an independent lay panel

The panel's decision to work without assistance has been described above. This was a result of a concern, felt particularly strongly by some members, that they should produce, and be seen to produce, their report independently. Their decision demonstrates that they felt ownership of the process and responsibility for the product by this stage. The preface to the report is striking to those who read the report and to others who hear about it.

More generally, to produce an independent report, the panel needed to receive a broad and balanced range of information during their preparatory phase and to reach a point where they were able to decide on the questions, and the experts to be invited, for the conference itself. It seems to be generally accepted that they did receive a broad range of information. The pressures of time meant they felt more guided in their choice of questions and experts than they would have liked to have been.

Views of the report

It is interesting to note that panel members' assessment of the report is rather different from that of other participants, such as Steering Committee members and experts. Members were pleased with the considerable achievement of having produced a report on a complex subject of which they had known so little only a short time before, and of having met their very tight deadline. They felt it was well written and of a professional standard, but were aware that detail had been sacrificed and that more radical viewpoints had been eliminated. This may be the nature of consensus building: they had been given the task of weighing different pieces of evidence and points of view, many of which contradicted each other. However, there was some feeling amongst the panel that the report was rather a bland description of their discussions and their understanding.

The report was generally given a favourable reception by the organisers and other participants in the conference. This overall view was made up of a number of elements: admiration for the panel for having produced a report at all in such a short time; admiration that the report showed such a high level of understanding of the issues; and relief that the report was so balanced and did not recommend any radical policies.

Many participants described feeling nervous beforehand about the possibility of the panel coming to a radical or controversial conclusion, such as recommending either drastic restrictions or uncontrolled freedom in the use of the technology, and they were relieved that these fears were not justified. Some observers felt that the panel showed clearly, during the proceedings and in its report, that they were not totally convinced by the claims of either the industry or environmental groups. The result was a measured and equivocal report. Less positive reactions described the report as acceptable and unexciting, but better than anodyne. There were a very few inaccuracies and misconceptions about the science and, in some eyes, this slightly dented its credibility.

IMPACT

Acting on the output of the exercise

A widespread view of the first UK national consensus conference was that its impact was limited because it was not linked into an institutional framework that would take responsibility for at least considering it. Unlike the Danish model, on which it was based, the UK conference had no direct channel to parliament or to policy-makers. Another possible reason was the fairly non-contentious nature of the subject. This was a deliberate choice but may have contributed to the lack of impact.

The Danish model has developed over a number of years. The Danish Board of Technology (DBT) is an independent institution funded by parliament. The organisation and funding of consensus conferences is one of the tasks for which it is funded. These are held in the parliament building and usually concern topics currently being debated by politicians and in the media.

It is notable that it is parliament and not the Government or a government department which funds the DBT. The aim is to inform parliamentary processes, not the policy or actions of a particular government. Having funded the conferences, parliament is more or less obliged to take notice of them. Consensus conference reports have been followed by debates in parliament, and these have sometimes focused on specific conclusions in the reports.[1]

There is no exact equivalent of the DBT in the UK. The nearest equivalent is the Parliamentary Office of Science and Technology, but this has no specific or official remit to carry out exercises in public consultation or participation, and its work is very different from that of the DBT. There was, then, no obvious or established route by which the report could seek to influence decisions or views. Instead, a number of different activities accompanied or followed the conference, with the intention of gaining greater awareness and influence.

As described above, the consensus conference was publicised to the press before the actual conference took place, and the media were present at the conference itself. Members of Parliament, policy-makers and scientists were encouraged to attend the conference. The conference was drawn to the attention of relevant government advisory committees. An exhibition about the conference was mounted for several days in the Houses of Parliament. The BBSRC promoted the idea of consensus conferences to schools as an innovative educational activity. The evaluation of the conference has resulted in a number of documents which describe and analyse it, and draw attention to it as a method of public consultation.

1 Under legislation passed in 1996, the DBT moved to the Ministry of Research, as part of arrangements for setting technology assessment on a permanent institutional footing. This move into government was opposed by many in the policy community.

Actual impact

The consensus conference had two objectives: to test the model in a UK setting and to contribute to public debate. Any consideration of the extent to which it achieved these has to be prefaced with a reminder that this was the first such event in the UK, and there was no direct experience on which to base it.

The assessment of the impact depends on an understanding of the objectives. Amongst those interviewed, both experts and members of the lay panel, there was awareness of both objectives but a lack of clarity about the respective weight attached to them, and about ways in which their achievement could be measured. However, there was broad agreement that the first (testing the model) was achieved, while the second (public debate) was achieved to only a limited degree or not at all.

Extent of the impact

Press and radio coverage of the conference has been calculated by the evaluator as similar in level to that achieved by the consensus conferences in Denmark and the Netherlands. There were 128 articles and 25 broadcasts. About half focused on the process, the rest on the substance. There was no television reporting of the conference itself or the report.

Their impression of the media coverage led the panel and many others to express disappointment, particularly at the lack of reporting on television and in the serious or quality press. Some panel members thought the Steering Committee had been wrong to decide against allowing the BBC to make a documentary of them at work, as this would have increased coverage. This decision had been to protect the panel from additional stress and to avoid the danger of their thinking being influenced by the presence of the cameras. There was some sensationalist reporting in the tabloid press. A preponderance of the coverage was in the specialist or trade press. A balanced report did not attract the attention of the more serious daily media in the way that a more radical one might have done.

Some civil servants and experts who sat on various advisory committees attended the conference. Few Members of Parliament attended and a number of people commented on the concluding remarks by a member of the House of Lords which they thought were dismissive of the report's contribution. The report appears to have been discussed at one or more advisory committees within government, but there was no obligation to do so. Those involved report little interest in the exhibition in the Houses of Parliament. There are no known instances of any policy decisions being influenced by the report. The subject of the conference was not linked to any current policy debate or decision. Indeed, it is difficult to see how this could be arranged, given the time needed to organise it. It appears, however, that such timing is achieved in Denmark.

Other and less direct impacts which were reported included a general and non-specific influence in government. The report raised some new issues, such as the use of plant biotechnology in the third world and product labelling. The industry gained a valuable resource, a supportive and quotable report which resulted from a public consultation exercise. Others thought that both industry and pressure groups should learn from the fact that the public did not accept the views of either uncritically.

Two direct but small outcomes were a consensus conference in schools and the Food Future Programme by the Food and Drink Federation, the Science Museum and the BBSRC.

The future

No plans to run further national consensus conferences have been announced. However, based on the experience of the first one, there are two broad points to draw to the attention to those who might plan any such exercises.

The choice of lead organisation to run the conference is crucial. It has to be seen as impartial on the subject under discussion, and should have no role in the development of policy or the provision of services on that subject. In this case, in the UK context, where there is no neutral body charged with consulting the public about science and technology, the Science Museum was a reasonable choice. But even the museum can be seen as having a pro-science and technology stance. Ideally the lead organisation would have something currently absent from the UK – the equivalent of the Danish Board of Technology with an official but independent and neutral role in informing policy.

The choice of subject is another key decision. Some types of subject are better suited to the consensus conference method than others. Consensus conferences are best suited to subjects which are somewhat controversial with legal and ethical implications, including implications for everyday life. This means there exists no clear cut or obvious answer, even amongst experts. But the subject should not be so emotive that consensus or compromise is unlikely or impossible.

The timing of the conference within the development of the subject is also important. There needs to be an opportunity to influence development, so the development of the technology should not be complete. But it should be sufficiently well advanced for issues and implications to have emerged. There is also the possibility of using a consensus conference to address long established issues when new information emerges.

Assessment

How well did the conference meet its first objective of testing the method? It worked well as a self contained exercise and only minor changes would be made to the processes if it were to be repeated. The experience also seems to have had a significant impact on the attitudes of those involved. They were impressed with the ability of lay people to master a difficult technical subject and to produce a balanced report. Many had feared that neither of these things would happen. This paved the way for greater acceptance of the concept of the consensus conference.

However, no further national consensus conferences have been announced. Further, there are structural or institutional difficulties to be dealt with if their impact is to be enhanced and the second objective of public debate is to be achieved. This objective also begs the question of who is to be engaged in the debate – the general public, politicians and policy-makers, science and industry, or campaigning organisations? And what is the particular contribution a consensus conference can make?

The panel members we interviewed generally considered that the conference had less impact than did other interviewees. We can speculate about the reasons for this. They had little or no contact with what went on informally or unreported within plant biotechnology after the conference, so would have been unaware of subtle or 'behind the scenes' influence. They may also have had different expectations and were less likely to simply be impressed, as others were, that this innovative process of involving the lay public had worked at all.

Observers' assessment of the impact appears also to depend on their position in relation to the public understanding of science. The meaning of this phrase varies even between those involved in the field. Put simplistically, positions seem to range from a belief that the public needs to be better educated about science and technology, to a commitment to a greater debate between the public and those who hold scientific expertise and make decisions on science and technology policy.

For those who hold the former view, it was clear that the conference had educated the panel members, but had probably little influence on the public beyond this group. However, using £85,000 to educate 16 people about plant biotechnology is unlikely to be considered cost-effective. Those who emphasise the need for greater debate between public and science will have a different perspective on the conference's impact.

Reasons for the low impact

The institutional framework was a major reason for the lack of impact. It may be difficult to overcome this in the UK administrative and cultural context, where government has consultation structures which tend to be cheaper, quicker and more centrally controlled than a consensus conference.

Several interviewees commented also on a wariness, even suspicion, about the role of the consensus conference on the part of policy-makers and politicians in particular. A concern was that it may be a threat to their role as representatives in the democratic process and would encroach on the territory of, for example, select committees. Such concerns may stem in part from a lack of shared understanding of the conference's purpose and the type of contribution it could make. The panel was not a representative sample of the public or a guide to general public opinion. It could not be. But it could deliver several useful contributions – first, it could provide a guide, for those involved in the detail of the science, to what the informed lay public would be concerned about and likely to accept. Only deliberative methods of public consultation can deliver this. In summary, the conference could be a contribution to agenda setting, and not a substitute for decision-making or policy discussions in the structures established for such purposes.

The consensus conference could also provide a guide to the aspects of the subject that the wider public might be interested in, and could contribute to an increase in general public awareness. It was therefore disappointing for some, especially the panel members, that they had no impact on general public awareness and interest. Achieving this depends on the activities of the media.

Research methods

We interviewed: the chairman of the Steering Committee; the evaluator; members of the lay panel; members of the Steering Committee; and experts who gave evidence to the panel and the conference. The conference report and reports from the evaluator were studied. Fieldwork took place between the Spring and Autumn of 1996.

Commentary

Overview

The conference had two broad objectives: to experiment with the model of a consensus conference in the UK and to contribute to debate and policy making on plant biotechnology. As a first attempt to run a consensus conference in Britain, this was remarkably successful. It showed that the process, in particular, can be a successful one. There are institutional and structural issues to address if any future conferences are to have more of an influence on policy.

The key points on which we comment are:

- As a process, the conference was a success, and enabled procedural improvements to be identified for any future conferences.
- To make the conference work well in influencing policy, its role needs to be clarified and set in a policy-making framework.
- A consensus conference is expensive, so will only be cost-effective if procedures are reviewed and policy frameworks clarified.

The consensus conference as a process

Key features were that the conference itself was a public event, adding to the transparency and credibility of the process, and that the panel then retired to deliberate and produce the report themselves, without any involvement of the organisers. This is essential if deliberative methods are to be used to produce an independent view.

We consider that these three attributes – transparency, independence and credibility – are essential for a successful process and could be enhanced by considering the following:

- The selection process for the panel: A group of 16 people can never be representative of the public as a whole. But the process of selecting them would be less open to criticism if it did not start with the call for volunteers. Of course, participation should always be voluntary, but the recruitment process could begin by approaching a sample of people, using socio-demographic criteria, in order to have a more rigorous cross-section of the population. This would also avoid recruiting only those who respond to calls for volunteers.
- Composition of the steering committee: The absence of any representative of an environmental or other organisation with known reservations about the technology is difficult to understand. It damaged the credibility of the conference

before it began. Such representation would have been seen to be a balance to the presence of a senior figure from the biotechnology industry.

- Openness: The committee's brief was to safeguard the credibility of the conference by ensuring it was conducted impartially and competently. We consider that the organisers of future conferences could take further steps to demonstrate their openness and probity by, for example, making the minutes of meetings and their internal reports available to enquirers. This would reflect the spirit and practice of open government.
- The conference itself: The conference provided little new information to the panel, but repeated much which had already been heard at the briefing weekends. Adjusting the balance between the time spent on receiving information and considering it would make the conference itself more central to the whole process, and allow those attending to take part in something which was clearly part of the deliberative process.

The role of the conference

The concern of the organisers to provide the panel members with such a volume of detailed information seems to reflect their view that the panel members had to be enabled to reach a high level of expert understanding before they could make a judgement. This and the fact that they were consistently described as 'lay members' rather than 'citizens' reflects the influence of the ethos of public understanding of science on the conference.

The concept of a consensus conference assumes that there is a value in knowing what an informed panel of non-experts think about a complex issue, and that this can make a useful or necessary contribution to policy development. Acceptance of this by policy- and decision-makers is necessary if the conference is to be allowed to have an influence. The public understanding of science may not be the best structure within which to hold future conferences.

Further, a commitment and procedure for considering the conference report is needed to make the efforts of all involved in the conference worthwhile. The conference was not part of any institutional framework or decision-making process which was concerned with future policy on plant biotechnology, and this lessened its impact.

Cost

A consensus conference is expensive, both in direct costs and the time of all involved. It can be a cost-effective contribution to policy, where the views of informed citizens are valued. This will require the clarity about its role discussed above.

References

Simon Joss (1995) Evaluating consensus conferences: necessity or luxury? In Simon Joss and John Durant (eds) *Public Participation in Science: the role of consensus conferences in Europe,* Science Museum

Simon Joss and John Durant (1995) The UK national consensus conference on plant biotechnology, *Public Understanding of Science* 4, 195–204

CASE STUDY TWELVE

Tate Gallery Liverpool: Young Tate

INTRODUCTION

Since 1994 the Tate Gallery Liverpool has been developing a programme of activity and involvement in relation to younger audiences known as 'Young Tate'. The aim of Young Tate is to bring the Tate's activities closer to the abilities and preferences of young people in relation to art, thereby enhancing access.

In Spring 1994 the Young Tate coordinator (the coordinator) recruited a group of over 30 young people from across Merseyside, to form an advisory group for the development of youth-related Tate activity. This advisory group met at intervals and devised workshops which were then run in part by group members. The group has expanded into a large mailing list of Young Tate members, from which active participants in drop-ins and longer projects continue to be drawn.

In Autumn 1994 a sub-group of the advisory group was established to take part in making a display from the National Collection of Modern Art. A 'display' in the Tate is an exhibition of works from the National Collection of Modern Art, and we use the term display throughout this case study.

This group met weekly over a long period, and worked with an exhibitions curator (the curator) and the coordinator, to produce a display, *Testing the Water*, which opened in September 1995 for six months. A range of events was organised by the advisory group around this display, including dramatic presentations in the display space itself. The display was well-received by the public and the art world.

Young Tate activities were in part funded by the Gulbenkian Foundation, whose support included a measure of evaluation and the involvement of a cultural historian with an interest in young people and culture.

ORIGINS AND OBJECTIVES

Origins

The Tate Gallery is a non-departmental public body, funded by the Department of National Heritage. The Tate Gallery Liverpool was opened in 1988, and was the first of the Tate's two 'regional' galleries. The Tate Gallery Liverpool is supported by charitable trusts, foundations, donations and sponsorship. Its overall aim is to bring the National Collection of Modern Art to the North of England and Scotland.

The involvement of younger people in the Tate derives directly from this overall aim. Specifically, audience research which developed a profile of target groups had shown that although a large proportion of Gallery visitors are under 35, the Tate's only 'captive' audience of young people was school parties. The Tate therefore had a general aim of increasing the contact between younger people and the Gallery.

Young Tate – a programme of involvement of younger people within the Gallery – has been the Tate's approach to meeting this aim from 1994 onwards. Young Tate was preceded, and in part shaped by, the Gallery's earlier youth-related activities, including long involvements with young people's arts groups, a mobile arts programme, and a Youth Arts weekend held in Summer 1993. These are described by staff as 'external' to the Gallery. Young Tate marked a change in that it brought young people into the Gallery as participants. The shift to Young Tate was also part of a broader shift – from short-term projects to rolling programmes.

During the Youth Arts weekend, the idea was put forward in debate of developing an advisory group of young people to help with the development of the Gallery's activities aimed at its younger audiences. As part of the evaluation of the Youth Arts weekend by members of the Education Department, the Gallery's management group recommended the setting up of Young Tate.

The second part of this study – the display group, which contributed to *Testing the Water* – had precedents in a television series which followed an art project in a local community, and an exhibition in an art gallery in a nearby town which had similar involvements.

Objectives

The overall objective of Young Tate was to facilitate improvements in how the Gallery provided for its younger audiences. The project has two complementary specific aims: to bring more young people into the Gallery, and to improve the Gallery for those young people already using it.

The advisory group was to be an 'informed consultative body of young people' which would assist in meeting the overall objective. The effect of the display group would be both to widen the range of people who could work with the National Collection, and to promote a greater sense of ownership by young people. The display group would also test the influence young people could have on an exhibition. In all there were four targets of change:

1 young people who became involved;
2 the visiting young people amongst the public;
3 organisations who bring young people to the Tate;
4 the Gallery itself.

The consultation process

Methods

If the origins of Young Tate lie in the Gallery's aims, the method used arises in part from specific circumstances, but is also in part a 'recognised approach' to work with younger people, requiring some explanation in these terms.

The method was the recruitment of advisory groups of younger people, to perform a number of roles, including some leading roles, in the activities of the Gallery. The method is highly participative, involving as it did a degree of control of both process and products by the consultees. Involvement was also long-term, allowing for development of participation over time.

The timing of the start of Young Tate related in part to the period of working 'externally' with young people (see above), and in part to other local experiences of similar activity with young people, which were also influential as examples. The method was however shaped by philosophies of education and of the youth service, which favour peer-led activity and direct involvement, with interaction as a key premise of learning. This perspective was also reflected in an approach to art which emphasises that individuals bring their own knowledge and understanding to the works of art which they encounter. Perspectives from the cultural historian on the relation between young people's values and 'fine art' also exerted an influence on the method.

The method was seen as providing a mechanism which permits active, practice-based involvement of users, and which therefore promotes the matching or meeting of different cultures. The strengths of the method were thought to be that it would be of benefit to a user group whose culture was perceived as not immediately responsive to the culture of the service. Young people as a user group need to be both visible and active in processes which seek to enhance their involvement, and the group method would allow this.

The activities

Setting up the advisory group

An existing member of the Tate's Education Department staff was appointed as Young Tate coordinator. The coordinator held a series of meetings with local youth associations and the City Youth Services, followed by personal contact with a range of local schools and youth arts groups, including a special unit for children with learning difficulties. The recruitment of the advisory group then took place from these contacts.

The group was recruited over a period of two to three months in 1994. The aim was to recruit a 'representative' group of young people from across the area – around five individuals from each of Merseyside's five boroughs. Membership was however as individuals, not as representatives of the organisations from which they were recruited. 36 young people attended the first meeting of the group, with an age range from 13 to 25.

Meetings were to be held monthly, every fourth Thursday evening to fit around school and working hours, and meeting dates were planned for the whole year from the start. At the first meeting a set of aims was devised and agreed. The frequency of the meetings was decided on by the coordinator, who describes this decision as 'intuitive'. The idea of regular meetings, planned in advance, aimed in part to promote familiarity with the group amongst Gallery staff.

The coordinator emphasises the importance when working with young people of ensuring that specific practical matters – safety when travelling in the evening, parental consent, expenses – are all attended to. Each member was required to complete an information/consent form, which included details of any medical conditions.

A key factor in the success of the recruitment was the coordinator's previous youth contacts and knowledge of the organisations in the locality. She targeted schools and organisations with a track record in out-of-school activities, with the result that the selection procedure worked well, and was a good combination of targeting and self-selection. Local advice from teachers was also useful. The wide age range of members was beneficial, with the younger members culturally distant from the Tate, and the older members understanding the Gallery more.

Advisory group activity

The first three meetings were Tate-led, involving practical activities. The coordinator's approach was to create a framework in which group members would develop their own rules. This had some success, in that members proposed chairs, agendas, and minutes, although these were often rudimentary and late. Initially the group discussed how to improve access for young people, and was involved in the development and running of a programme of one-day workshops and holiday events at the Gallery. Workshops are one-day bookable events based on an exhibition or display. Advisory group members studied a particular display and then devised a workshop around it, jointly with the coordinator. The first of these was in Summer 1994 based on a Tate exhibition, *Africa Explores*. Workshops based on around ten exhibitions and displays have been organised with the participation of advisory group members since then. Advisory group members were also involved in events around the display *Testing the Water*. Other activities included events lasting several days, known as projects, also organised around an exhibition or display during the school holidays, and group members have taken part in the organisation and running of several such projects.

Keeping attendance up was a major task for the coordinator, with letters and phone calls each month. Initially the original 36 decreased to around 25, and for the first six months, 18 to 25 attended, but this settled eventually at between eight and ten. The reasons members gave for not attending were mainly other calls on their time – school, including taking examinations, and their social lives. The display group, with its weekly commitment (see below), also had an effect on attendance. There were also seasonal variations. Winter evenings proved unpopular, and by Winter 1994 the group had asked to change to Sunday meetings. Over time the advisory group membership stabilised at just over 20, although numbers attending meetings is not high.

A review of the Young Tate programme in 1996, which the advisory group played a key role in, has led to replacement of the Sunday workshops with drop-in sessions. Projects continue to be a feature during the longer school holidays. Drop-ins tend to last three hours, and consist of activities around a current exhibition, and practical work such as making prints and collages.

Setting up the display group

The display project was a joint venture between the Education and the Exhibitions Departments of the Gallery. An Exhibitions curator and the Young Tate coordinator were both heavily involved, although the group was initially set up by the coordinator alone. The display group was recruited from amongst the membership of the Young Tate advisory group to take part in making a display from the National Collection of Modern Art. Originally the display group was to have been part of a wider festival, which did not take place.

The display group was to involve itself in some way with the Tate's core work, rather than in additional, youth-focused activities such as those worked on by the advisory group. In deciding to create a display group, the Gallery was therefore developing a second strand to its method. The Gallery had involved outsiders in shows in the past, but until Young Tate these had all been other professionals.

The group was set up in Autumn 1994, and was recruited from the membership of the advisory group, again on the basis of two from each borough, selected by the group, giving a total of ten members. This mix of self-selection with a balance of individuals from the different boroughs, again using a notion of representation, was thought likely to produce the most effective group, and would ensure that within the group everyone knew someone else personally.

Membership of the group proved popular, and initially it had 13 members, rather than the ten intended. The cultural historian suggested a participant observer join the group as part of the evaluation, and a new member was chosen, making 14 in all. Most of those involved in the display group had some direct interest such as drama, music, art, in contrast to the advisory group membership, who were from a greater range of interests.

The Curator of Tate Gallery Liverpool, the Head of Education, the Exhibitions curator and the coordinator drafted a list of aims and objectives, and general ground rules for the group. One of the rules, whose purpose was to reassure Tate staff, was 'the curator has the ultimate say'.

A long timescale for the display group was needed for a number of reasons:

- Works from the Collection need early booking, and the Gallery wanted the display group to work with the whole collection.
- The museum's deadlines are six months in advance.
- The advisory group had only just formed, and teaching/familiarisation time was therefore needed for the display group.
- A proposal for a display had to go before the January 1995 meeting of the Tate's Loans Board.

Making the display 'Testing the Water'

The display group played an active role in developing a Tate display, *Testing the Water,* which was open from Autumn 1995 to Spring 1996. The specific nature of the group's involvement in a display was a matter of debate within the Gallery. A concrete outcome was thought to be essential for the maintenance of the group, given the need for a long period of involvement. Two alternatives were discussed: to re-present an existing show, or to devise a new one. The option of making a new display was chosen, with the sense that an open brief would give more freedom to the group.

Discussions then focused on the level and nature of their involvement – they might, for example, only select works, or they might be involved in every aspect. After discussion, staff decided to model what the group's members would do on a curator's tasks – drawing on past practice and on the curator's own current practice. Tate staff describe this process as 'organic'.

Between September and Christmas, Tate staff organised an induction schedule, and the evening education sessions were timetabled with talks by Gallery staff and outsiders, to prepare the members for their role in deciding on a display title or theme, and then on the works which would appear in it. Intensive week-long sessions were considered as an alternative, but there were practical problems about taking members out of school, or possible absences during holidays. It was also considered that over long periods it would be hard to keep members' interest. Staff also considered that the group would absorb the works best through repeated exposure at frequent intervals. In the event, two long Sundays were also part of the programme. This period included three trips to the Tate in London to see the Collection, including lectures and special access to the storage there. Group members' response to this was a strong feeling of privilege.

Decisions about the basis for the display were made in part from principles and in part from the wishes of the members. The aim was to bring the group to a position where they could make a selection from the Collection on a basis which made sense to them, and which at the same time would meet the Exhibitions Department's standards for displays. The group itself wanted to make a Tate display, selected by them, with the works in the display the main feature, rather than creating a display as the 'voice' either of the group or of 'young people'. The group wished to become curators, not representatives of 'young people'.

Helped by the curator and coordinator, the group suggested a range of themes and developed ideas through interaction with an exhibition in the Tate. The curator then spent several days at the Tate in London with the Collection, preparing large theme-based lists of works which would be available, and slides and photocopies of these. The organising themes focused on a single theme of a journey from childhood to old age, and drew on a work by Salvador Dali – *The Metamorphosis of Narcissus* – and a poem which he wrote about this work. Selection was made in discussion, over a three-month period, on the basis of these slides and pictures. This process was described by participants as one of compromises/agreement as to what to include. After the selection was made, time at the group's meetings focused on familiarisation with the works. The group also opted to write the catalogue.

Testing the Water was installed by the Tate's Exhibitions team and technicians. The display group worked on the physical layout of the display through a model, and played some part in the setting up of the display. Most saw the works before they were installed, some were involved in final discussions about placing, and some were involved in discussions about where to put the text and in the choice of colour for painting the room. Final decisions lay with the curatorial staff.

Advertising for the display was generic, except for a *Testing the Water* flyer targeted at young people through clubs, bars, and similar places. This was not available until October, and was not targeted at schools.

The display opened on 22 September 1995 with 23 works, and was open for six months, until March 1996. Entry was free. A private view attracted a large number of young people, through both the mailing list of the organiser and ten invitees each for each display group member. Interest in the display, including school visits, was considerable. Impressions were gained from the two audiences for the display: the public, who seemed to like it, and art specialists, who were surprised. Press coverage was favourable.

The education programme around the display

An Education Department programme of activity around the display involved both display group and advisory group members. Group members took various roles in sessions around the display, with teachers and other young people. As part of the weekend Young Tate programme, the advisory group researched works in the display, and devised an animated talk, known as *Taking the Plunge,* assisted by a drama specialist. Some of the performances were described by the coordinator as very dramatic, with audiences of 40 to 50, drawn by tannoy announcements, and curiosity. Gallery staff were said to be unhappy about these events being called 'performances'.

Group members were paid £5 an hour if they led face-to face groups as part of the events of the Young Tate programme. This rate was thought to reflect members' youth/particular skills/knowledge, and was set at a level higher than that for shop work, but lower than for freelance work. This was said to have caused some surprise in the Gallery for staff who saw the advisory group as volunteers.

The catalogue

The catalogue for *Testing the Water* is described by the curator as the largest contribution made by the group. Work on this took place around Easter 1995, and the Exhibitions Department was responsible for its production and the budget. A freelance researcher, who had in the past worked in education at the Tate, assisted with ideas and planning, and a designer met the group and heard their ideas.

The group wanted three things from the catalogue: it should be different, it should be written by them, and it should be cheap. They produced text which was edited down by the coordinator, and edited for style by the curator. The introduction was written by the curator, and an analysis contributed by the cultural historian – both seen as necessary by the curator to ensure that the product resembled a Tate catalogue. Neither of these contributions was welcomed by the group, and group members interviewed by us were critical of the length of the longest piece, which was contributed by the cultural historian.

Managing the process

Decision-making

Young Tate overall was established by the Gallery's management, as a joint effort of both the Exhibitions and the Education Departments. Joint work is described by staff as the norm. In practice the development of Young Tate has been in the main by the Education Department, and specifically by the Young Tate Coordinator. Key decisions have, however, involved a team approach, both at management level, and with the Exhibitions curator who worked closely with the display group. Indeed it was a team decision to set up a display group, seen through by a planning group of the Exhibitions and Education Departments.

Routine activity

The advisory group was run by the coordinator. Key activities were those aimed at encouraging attendance, through letters, telephone calls, and general chasing up. This was essential if attendance at group meetings was to be sustained.

The display group was run jointly by the coordinator and the curator. The dynamics of this group resulted in different roles being performed by the two staff. The coordinator found herself in the role of friend and cajoler, the curator in that of authority figure, with more control. Interestingly, the members perceived the curator as the coordinator's superior. This difference in roles is seen as reflecting real differences in perspective and function within the Gallery, between education and exhibitions staff. It seems clear that there were difficulties for both the curator and the members in adjusting to one another.

Monitoring and quality

Evaluation was part of the project overall, and was part funded by the Gulbenkian Foundation (see below). The advisory group itself has reviewed Young Tate regularly and annually, and the coordinator produces annual reports as part of the requirement of the funders.

The display project was evaluated intensively, using several approaches. There was a clear schedule for the display group. Every group meeting was taped and videoed, two ethnographic reports were produced towards the end of the display, and the curator wrote an evaluation of the display group. For the display itself, the Exhibitions Department used its curatorial indicators: timing of selection; budget; catalogue time/budget; installation; transport; 'looking good'; attendance; attitude of information assistants; feedback from the public; press attention; 'fit' with the Tate's programme.

Feedback from audiences, and profiles of audiences, were gleaned informally. There were no surveys of audiences, or of wider groups of young people, either through schools and similar groups, or through those attending the Gallery.

Points about organisation

The Young Tate coordinator drew out a number of points of practical guidance for this type of work:

- A pilot period is needed before developing an exhibition or display. Young Tate existed for four months before the display group and so avoided problems associated with starting from scratch. Build up a relationship with the group first.
- The group members did not like one-offs, they wanted a longer-term involvement and a clear understanding of how much of their time is involved.
- Work with small groups is probably the best way, but you must be aware of the need to cast a wide net at the same time.
- It is important when planning not to create too much of a specialist clique, but to bear in mind the long-term reasons for consultation.
- Pay travel expenses.
- Promote peer-led activity.
- Try to pay fees to young people when they help to lead a session.

Resources

A precise costing of Tate staff time spent on the two advisory groups has not been feasible, given that the programme overall is an integral part of the Gallery's work. The Young Tate coordinator worked almost full-time on the whole programme. The curator was working on four other exhibitions in 1994–5, but the display group occupied more than 20 per cent of her time. The Exhibitions Department set up the display, and Information Assistants staffed it for six months. Tate managers also spent time on project discussions and decisions, and on setting up the display itself, as did Tate staff who gave instruction sessions for the display group.

Overall, Young Tate always occupies a minimum of one full-time staff post, with further staff time needed according to activities.

Education Department

Direct costs consisted of the groups' travel expenses, including trips to London and food on Wednesday evenings for the display group. Fees were paid to advisory group members for leading sessions. The gallery also paid some outsiders to contribute to the induction programme.

Expenditures details provided show:

1994/5	£6,178
1995/6	£9,404
1996/7	£6,000 (budget – no expenditure figures available at the time)

In addition, designer costs for the catalogue and *Testing the Water* were an extra £2,500.

Income for the Young Tate was from donations and sponsorship, and amounted to £31,500 over 3 years:

1994/5	Gulbenkian	£6,500
1995/6	Ian Short Partnerships (local solicitors)	£5,000
	Association for British Sponsorship of the Arts	£5,000
	Gulbenkian (including £1,500 for evaluation)	£6,000
1996/7	Gulbenkian (including £3,000 for a publication)	£9,000

Exhibitions Department

Expenditures for the display were £16,626, for the costs of putting the display up, travel and entertainment for the display group, and £13,700 for the catalogue and posters. The allocated budget for direct costs for 1995–6 for the display was £10,000. 3,500 catalogues were produced and priced at £2.50.

Skills

The skills required to develop Young Tate are listed by Tate staff as knowledge of: the Gallery's internal policies and procedures, of the Collection itself, of how to work with educational groups and young people and local youth services, and of how young people develop. A youth service philosophy of looking beyond the formal curriculum, with an emphasis on peer-led activity, underlay the approach to the groups.

Both the coordinator and the curator have an arts education background, and the curator has experience of group work with young people at Millbank. Motivating group members was a key requirement. The style of the meetings of both groups emphasised flexibility, role play and enjoyment. Meetings trod a path between familiarity and formality. Keeping everyone informed had to be balanced by acceptance that young people do not read everything they are sent, and may not respond easily.

Impact of the consultation process on its outputs

The involvement of a group of over 30 young people has been visible and high-profile within the Tate: groups, education sessions, workshops, drop-ins, three-day projects, a display, a catalogue. But assessment of the influence of this particular method on what has essentially been an evolving programme is difficult. A specific difference for the *Testing the Water* display lay in the choices of works – described by the curator as a mini-museum, an eclectic group of works, spanning most of the 20th century, from different schools and styles, and different countries. This is something the Tate would not usually do, and Tate staff found it interesting to see it done, and are considering trying a similar approach in the future.

The display group achieved its specific objective of making a display which was visited by the public, and the media, and which was liked. The display also aroused interest in the art world. The process of involvement gave the display some specific qualities noted by Tate staff as distinctive.

The advisory group has influenced the Young Tate education programme for young visitors, in that the group has had a role in decisions about what to do and when, and in running workshops. But the impact on the workshops and other events themselves is not known. Whether the sessions were different as a consequence of the advisory group's involvement is hard to say.

Impact

Direct impact

The Young Tate overall is a developing programme which has no specific endings. As it has grown, changes have been implemented by the Education Department – shifting from workshops to drop-ins, and from an established advisory group to a mailing list and wider trawl for involvement. In this sense, the Education Department has responded to an evolving situation.

The presentation of the display as a Young Tate project stimulated interest in the media and the arts world, and amongst friends and family of the advisory group members. But information on other audiences and audience reactions remains at the level of impressions, and no clear information was gathered on this. For example, it is not known if the display attracted wider audiences of young people. The ground rules drawn up for the display group are offered as a model for such involvements.

The broader output implied in the establishment of Young Tate – bringing the Gallery closer to young people on Merseyside – has not been assessed in detail. The development of a large mailing list by the Young Tate coordinator may be seen as an expansion of influence directly attributable to the earlier Young Tate activities.

But the notion of 'young people' is in itself difficult, and we have not pinned it down very well in these projects. The age range of 13 to 25 meant that at least one Young Tate member was only a few years younger than the two Tate staff involved in the display group. The project premise was that 'youth culture' is distant from the Tate and that levers need to be applied in various places to bring the two together. With an age range of 13 to 25 it is not clear what 'young' means in this context, and distance from the culture of the Gallery is unlikely to be an exclusive attribute of a loosely-defined 'youth'.

Indirect or unintended impact

On the participating young people

The impact on the participating groups of young people has been dramatic, and this was an aspect of the project which has been extensively evaluated and written about. Some Young Tate members have become the focus of media interest. The display group became a group of 13 articulate artistic people. The members interviewed see themselves as having been furnished with an opportunity not often available, and many report improvement of their knowledge and abilities in art.

On the Gallery

As an institution, the Liverpool Tate seeks to innovate and to provide a model for research and development in its work. The view offered in this study was of an approach based on themes and innovation. This is contrasted with the more traditional Tate Millbank.

Tate staff seemed to have different views of Young Tate – some staff perceiving a sequence of one-off events, whereas for the Education Department the groups and activities were part of an overall youth programme. This is unsurprising, and is most likely to relate to how close to organising the Young Tate different staff were.

Working with an outside group was a precedent for Exhibitions staff, showing that it was not something to cause alarm. Understandable alarm at the thought of untrained members of the public 'ferreting around' in the National Collection seems not to have been triggered by the display group's activities.

The issue of impact on the Gallery is also influenced by somewhat different perceptions of the degree of influence which it is possible to exert. The curator saw the display as capable only of very limited influence on the work of the Exhibitions Department, because of the absence of a curating 'orthodoxy' which can be subject to general influence. Further, Exhibitions will not in any event be in a financial position to make another display involving young people. Education staff comment that their view is that curating relies in part on accumulated traditions and, whilst there is no orthodoxy, there are expectations of how things are done.

This may mean that the Education Department will be the main focus of opportunity for change in the Gallery, and that the bringing of the Collection to a wider young audience is itself an education activity, rather than Gallery-wide.

The future

Audience research is now leading to the revision of generic leaflets. The work of Tate Liverpool may influence the work of the new Bankside Tate, which has shown considerable interest in *Testing the Water.*

By 1996 the Young Tate as a programme had moved away from reliance on a constituted advisory group as its main source of involvement of young people. The Young Tate coordinator has developed a network of interested young people whom she contacts through a mailing list and Young Tate has a wider membership. Young Tate continues as a series of projects and drop-ins organised by the coordinator and involving different combinations of the advisory/display group members and others. An evolving approach to the programme is described by the Tate as a rolling programme. For 1997, an emphasis on focus group discussions with young people has been a feature.

Assessment

The view of Tate staff

The Young Tate advisory group played a key role in devising and staging a series of workshops, but has been less high profile since the display ended. The approach to Young Tate has changed, and it relies on a wider group of young people, contacted through a mailing list. The coordinator assesses this evolution as a success, and sees Young Tate as an initiative which has succeeded over a long period.

The timing of the display group is seen as less than ideal, and staff believe that the group may have been too early in the life of the Young Tate advisory group. The creation of the display group also caused a split with the advisory group, which felt cut off. The curator had some reservations about the display group. Two specific difficulties were highlighted. First, the curator felt under pressure to constantly create an 'orthodoxy' for the group, which did not really exist. Second, the decision to allow the group to make a new display, rather than re-model an existing one, was, with hindsight, a mistake. The curator had agreed to this at the time, but concluded later that the display group would have worked better with the limits set by an existing show. The Education Department took a different view, seeing the very open brief as offering more freedom. In the curator's view this gave the group less.

Group members' views

Members of the advisory and display groups experienced Young Tate as an important opportunity for them. Young Tate offered a privileged access to the National Collection of Modern Art, and an introduction to a range of skills and experience rarely available to anyone. Commitment on a regular basis was difficult for some of them, and they understood and appreciated the dedicated work of Tate staff who had encouraged and cajoled them into continuing involvement. They acknowledge the difficulty of getting a group of 30-plus together who did not know each other, and expecting them to work well together, and the huge effort made by the Young Tate organiser and the curator to keep them involved.

Some group members were over-awed by the 'sophistication' of some of the older people, and by the Tate itself. Some were daunted by the newness of the experience, and spoke of problems even with approaching the building and ringing the door buzzer. The group's members did not see themselves as representative of young people, but as individuals. Although they were aware that they were drawn from across Merseyside – from different classes, backgrounds, and interests – they did not see this as being 'representative'. This is an important comment on the link between participation activities and the wider aim of improving the Gallery's relation to younger people.

RESEARCH METHODS

We interviewed the Young Tate coordinator three times, the display curator twice, and the head of Education once. We also did a group interview with a small number of Young Tate members. We were provided with a copy of the catalogue from *Testing the Water*, and two sociological analyses – one by the observer, and a theoretical text written by the observer's supervisor.

We were given access to the tapes and videos of the meetings of the display group and selected one for viewing. We also had copies of the assessment carried out by the curator, and two Young Tate annual reports, and an article written by the coordinator and one of the members.

The fieldwork took place in Spring and Summer 1996, shortly after the display ended. We did not therefore see the display.

COMMENTARY

Overview

In 1994 the Liverpool Tate Museum began the development of a programme of involvement of young people in the Tate, as part of its work to improve access to the Gallery for specific sections of the population. Initially a group of some 30 young people was recruited to discuss, advise on, and take part in special events. In Autumn 1994 a sub-group of the advisory group was set up, to take part in making some sort of show in the Gallery. This resulted in a display in the Tate of works from the National Collection of Modern Art, open from Autumn 1995 to Spring 1996.

We identified a number of key points which are examined in this commentary:

- Methods based on long-term participation can bring intense interactions and produce intensive changes.
- Evidence of 'results' is less easy to measure with long-term participation.

- Long-term involvements are difficult to sustain.
- Consultees seen as belonging to one group may well be different in important ways.
- Consultation through evolving procedures requires goals which match this evolution.

Intensity and long-term participation

The Tate involved local young people in two related programmes of activity which spanned two years overall. The outputs from these involvements included a range of workshops, a major exhibition, and an expanding programme of youth-related activity which continues three years after its start. Some of the young people originally recruited made significant contributions to this process over a long period.

Evidence of results

The Tate's purpose in recruiting the Young Tate advisory group was general rather than specific: to fulfil its role as an institution. There was understandably therefore no specifically identifiable purpose of the type driving other case studies in this guidance which can be assessed for outcomes. The products of the advisory group – workshops and so on – are tangible. But the outcome in terms of the young population of Merseyside is difficult to assess.

This was not however so in the case of the display group, whose specific remit was to involve young people in making a display within the Gallery. The product of this exercise was a display which was open for six months. However, although this display was assessed for its qualities in relation to the Tate, impressions of its audiences were formed, and a larger than usual number of young people attended a private view by invitation, no systematic approach to understanding its impact on young people was attempted.

The detailed ethnographic and sociological writings around the projects focus on the dynamics of the specific groups, and the small-scale. The effect on the individuals, and the processes which produced these effects, are accounted for in detail through observation, tape recording and video. But the wider picture rests on impressions.

What this raises for participative involvements of the public is the need to develop more sustained ways of understanding impact and relating activity to outcomes. It would clearly have in theory been possible to, for example, survey the display's audiences, send a questionnaire to local schools, or convene young people's discussion groups around Merseyside to test awareness of the Tate and of the display. We do not know whether the Tate has the resources for such exercises, but a better approach to assessment would help inform future activity.

Sustaining long-term involvement

Long-term involvements are one method which can be of benefit to more complex organisational needs such as development of service strategies, and for policy and planning.

But long-term involvements can be hard to sustain. For the Tate, sustaining attendance for the advisory group was more difficult than for the display group.

We believe that there are a number of reasons for this. The display group was an exercise, albeit one which spanned a period of more than one year, and we would therefore expect that motivation would be clearer, and the appeal more obvious for the members of the display group. In addition, a clear positive outcome was one of the possible options for the group. The display group was probably the more attractive option for advisory group members who were keen, as it was a goal-oriented high status group, self-selected from the advisory group. It also met weekly, rather than monthly, creating more continuity, meaning involvement was therefore easier to sustain. This did nonetheless require a lot of hard work by Tate staff.

For a less focused, longer-term approach such as the advisory group, the coordinator worked very hard, through letters, phone calls, chasing and so on, to keep attendances up, but with less success than for the display group. This problem is likely to arise in long-term involvements of many types – in working groups, in committees, in research panels. Typically, an initially large group will dwindle in numbers, often leaving many less than had originally been sought.

What the Tate involvements show is the advantages of specific purposes and the possibility of positive outcomes in making a bridge between the lives of the participants, and the issues facing the organisations. In public service such a bridge may often be difficult to offer. For example, many public services face planning and policy decisions which involve choices between two or three less than ideal options, and the public may not find involvement in difficult options a very attractive prospect.

Differences between consultees

Service users have a practical and potentially understandable relation to public service organisations. Involving wider publics – those who do not use a service, a particular population group, or the general public – means accepting a less certain framework. The less knowledge there is about potential consultees, the greater the risk of inventing them, or at least inventing their characteristics. The Tate faced this difficulty, in its interest in a category described as 'young people', the age range of which was from 13 to 25. This group was thought to require special approaches, derived from youth service and other knowledge. 'Relevance' was a key bridge between the Tate and the young people, a bridge built by the Young Tate coordinator. A second, active link was sought when Tate staff laid down ground rules for behaviour designed to inhibit the less productive aspects of youth culture – instant opinions, over-confident dismissal of differing views, bad language – and so on. This worked to a considerable extent. Interestingly, the bridge was not needed at all times by all participants, some of whom saw the opportunity on offer, sought to learn about curating a show at the Tate, and valued the privilege this offered.

The age range within the original group was huge. This diversity was welcomed for its educative nature – the older members were described as more Tate-minded than the younger, and this helped the younger ones to understand. But despite this, we found it difficult to see what characteristics 13 and 25-year-olds might have in common. Tate staff did not describe this as a problem, and for the activities and tasks it may not have been. It seems that the bulk of members were clustered in a narrower age band, and the over 20s and under 15s were an exception.

Where the age range becomes a problem is in seeing the activities of these groups as having some link to the broad population of the area. If there is no obvious link between 13 and 25-year-olds, who might the wider links be to, and how might this be demonstrated? The fact that the Tate did not demonstrate it may in part be because of this spread, this too general category of the 'young'.

Evolving procedures and evolving goals

Although Young Tate had some goals which were specific, it has remained a general development project – an approach to involvement, rather than a primary goal with steps or sub-goals for its achievement. Consequently, there was something of a dislocation between a specific goal-oriented activity such as the display group, and the overall aim of Young Tate. Young Tate activities have been substantial and have developed effectively, but the relation between these and the Tate's general aims is not explicit. This is in part an inherent difficulty, but is also accounted for by the underlying approach itself, which casts Young Tate in a particular framework of ideas about young people, and which operates with high-level generalisations which may be of little help with planned development. A participatory philosophy has obviously been of help for the relations between the Tate and the involved groups, but it did not provide a means of assessing whether there was an impact on the younger population of Merseyside.

This problem might be addressed by establishing goals which themselves can develop as the nature of the participation develops, and which taken together provide an approach to the general aim. For example, planned development of involvement with the schools and clubs which the original advisory group members were drawn from might have been a second string to the start of the programme, combined with active monitoring of attendance at the workshops and thinking through what the next steps should be, based on these experiences and activities.

CASE STUDY THIRTEEN

Walsall Metropolitan Council: the New Art Gallery

ORIGINS AND OBJECTIVES

The subject of this case study is a public consultation programme led by Walsall Metropolitan Borough Council to inform decisions about facilities to be provided in a new art gallery for the town. The consultation exercise was also intended to gauge the level of support for the project, and to promote interest in it.

Origins

Plans for a new art gallery

There has long been a wish in Walsall to improve the town's existing museum and art gallery facilities and to build a new art gallery. In recent years this has become a major priority for Walsall Metropolitan Borough Council and forms an important part of Walsall's overall regeneration strategy. The New Art Gallery (NAG) project is a cornerstone of the Walsall City Challenge programme. Central to the vision of the NAG is the desire to provide facilities which are accessible to everyone and which encourage not only looking at exhibits but direct participation in arts activity. The development of the new art gallery is felt to be of major local significance: it is the first large public building to be built for a long time. The building of a new provincial art gallery is also seen as having significance beyond Walsall itself.

Walsall Metropolitan Council is the lead agency in the development of the NAG, working in partnership with a wide range of other organisations. In 1989 architects were appointed to design a new art gallery and developed it to First Design stage. It was then postponed indefinitely because of lack of finance. Success in securing City Challenge funds in 1993 enabled plans for the NAG to be revived.

The current Head of Museums and Galleries was appointed as Project Director to lead the new development. A feasibility study was followed by the development of a fund raising strategy, creation of a NAG Steering Group and an Implementation Team. Architects for the NAG were appointed after an international architectural design competition.

Funding for the NAG will come from a variety of sources which include the European Regional Development Fund and the National Lottery as well as City

Challenge. It was announced in October 1996 that Walsall had been successful in its lottery bid and was granted £15.75m for the new art gallery.

Tradition of consultation

The consultation programme has formed a key part of the process of developing the new art gallery. Those responsible place this in the context of a general commitment to consultation by the existing museum and art gallery and an enthusiasm for involving people in service development by the Council as a whole.

A belief in the importance of consultation is considered, by officers, to be shared by councillors. The current administration, which took control after the May 1995 elections, following a troubled period in the borough, is particularly keen to be seen to be consulting local people. Some participants in the NAG consultation contrasted this experience with their perception of the usual lack of consultation in Walsall, and expressed satisfaction at being asked to give their views 'for once'.

The existing museum and art gallery considers that it has long been much more in touch with public views than are many other galleries. The art gallery already had a tradition of active consultation, as part of its philosophy that 'people have rights to access'. All their projects, including exhibitions, educational programmes and collections are described as embodying this approach. The development of plans for the NAG on a site opposite the current Museum and Art Gallery was itself influenced by the results of a cultural audit in 1986.

Objectives

A number of very practical concerns drove the project. Previous local experience where a lack of consultation had been criticised reinforced the need for consultation. The project was also motivated by the need for a successful outcome to the application for National Lottery funds – a demonstration of local support for the project would be essential for the application to succeed.

Politically, it was important that the community was supportive of the project and had some sense of ownership of the new development. It was a high profile and very costly project, even though a large proportion of the funding was to come from outside the borough. It was crucial for the officers to be able to demonstrate to elected members that the project had the support of the local community.

The specific objectives for the consultation programme were to establish:

- the level of public support for the idea of the New Art Gallery for Walsall;
- people's ideas for the types of facilities that should be in the new art gallery in the next century;
- people's views on the nature of the services offered, such as opening times, charging regimes etc.

There were also explicit limitations to the scope of the consultation, and these were made clear to participants. Specifically, the aim was not to get views on the design of the building. This was to be determined by the architects who were appointed after an international competition. It was their job as professional architects to design the building:

> 'Design was not open to consultation, in terms of the basic ideas, which were the city tower, the big house, that it has a gallery square, that it had many different types of space within it. But it was totally open to discussion what sets of facilities this gallery might offer.'

THE CONSULTATION PROGRAMME

Methods

In developing the new art gallery the staff wanted to develop a more active involvement with the local community than they had achieved before. Consultation is described in the Detailed Project Description for the New Art Gallery as 'genuine dialogue, not window dressing'. This project was described as 'virgin territory' for the organisers. No-one had experience of an exercise like this, on the scale that was being proposed.

The document goes on to say:

> 'Consultation can often mean simply telling people what it is they are going to get, offering no opportunity for dialogue. This is not the case in Walsall. In Walsall we understand consultation to mean engaging with people at many levels, encouraging people to give their views, and, when it occurs, being open to criticism.'

The approach to consultation is seen as part of a wider attempt to challenge assumptions about the role of museums and galleries:

> 'Museums and art galleries have to move beyond the Victorian "missionary position", expecting to convert people to the good cause of cultural enlightenment.
>
> We do not expect 100 per cent of the population to be supportive of the project. However, we believe that there is a huge groundswell of untapped interest in, and support for, arts and cultural development and that genuine openness to the concerns of people, and communities, can only strengthen the project and ensure its sustainability in the longer term.
>
> We want people to believe that it is their art gallery, something that they can be proud of, something that will boost the battered self-image of Walsall, and something that is used by people from all communities.'

From the beginning, therefore, it was clear that an extensive and participatory consultation programme was needed. A number of methods were used to achieve the objectives of the programme. It was recognised that one method alone could not meet all the different objectives.

One consideration which influenced the choice of methods was the need to canvass as wide a range of views as possible and this suggested the need for several different types of consultation process. It was also recognised that there were a number of different groups with interests in the new art gallery – such as children and young people, members of the ethnic minority communities, and people with special needs. The methods of consultation had to be appropriate for finding out the views of these different groups. The same method would not be suitable for all.

With hindsight, the organisers are not convinced that a large enough number of people from ethnic minorities attended the workshop or responded to the postal survey to give an adequate picture of views held amongst this group.

The choice of methods was also guided by constraints on resources. The exhibitions and the postal survey were seen as relatively cheap ways of engaging with large number of people. Another consideration was limits to the time and involvement that members of the public are willing to commit to consultation.

It was also important for the consultation process to take account of the fact that Walsall comprises six quite distinct districts. Politicians were keen to hear the views of people outside central Walsall. The organisers of the consultation programme therefore had to think about ways of consulting people in the outlying areas.

Groundwork for the consultation programme began in 1994/5, but the organisers say they should have started the planning sooner as this would have made the work less intensive and less stressful. The deadline for the submission to the National Lottery set the date for completing the process.

The activities

Consultation had actually begun before the launch of the main consultation programme in November 1995. Disabled people's groups had been contacted in 1994/5, with the intention of gaining their contribution to a design that would make the building fully accessible to all.

The main consultation programme had four main strands. Most of this took place during the second half of 1995 and Spring 1996. The four strands were:

1 A series of exhibitions around the borough to raise awareness and support for the NAG.
2 A postal survey to establish the level of support for the NAG and to obtain the views of a large number of people about the facilities which should be provided.
3 A workshop event to explore ideas about facilities in more depth. This was the most innovative part of the programme, and the technique which was least familiar to the organisers.
4 Work in schools to explore the views of children – identified as a particularly important group of potential users.

A travelling exhibition

The exhibition concerned the plans for the gallery, and included a model of the site. It included activities for children. The dispersed geography of Walsall led to the idea for a travelling exhibition: the exhibition toured six town centres within the borough area during October and November 1995. It began in the shopping centre in Walsall town centre and then moved on to other locations, such as outlying shopping centres and libraries. The choice of locations was intended to reflect the intention for the gallery to be accessible to all. In each venue the exhibition was mounted for five days.

Mounting an exhibition was regarded as the very minimum that could be done by way of consultation. It was also seen as a relatively cheap way of communicating with large numbers of people. Visitors to the exhibition were invited to complete a questionnaire. People who expressed a particular interest in the project were also asked to leave details of their names and addresses and these details were used as part of the invitation list to the public workshop held at the end of November.

1,062 questionnaires were completed during the course of the exhibition, although staff estimate that a further 1,500 people visited the exhibition but did not complete questionnaires. The organisers did not always have sufficient people to staff the stands, to answer questions and to encourage people to complete the questionnaires, and this is likely to have reduced the response rate.

With hindsight, they think they might have organised the exhibitions differently. Time was a problem: there was only a short time for organising the exhibition and the displays were mounted for a limited period. A wider range and larger number of venues were needed.

Postal survey

The postal survey took place in October 1995. Questionnaires were sent to a stratified sample of 10 per cent (10,000) households in the borough. In addition, questionnaires were made available at libraries, leisure centres, council neighbourhood offices and local museum and art galleries.

Conducting a pilot for the postal questionnaire was seen as a luxury for which there was no time or resources. Questionnaires were distributed by a specialist company. Temporary staff were hired to help with the input of data, which were then analysed in-house.

A total of 1,590 questionnaires were returned from the postal survey, a response rate of almost 16 per cent. This was considered by the project team to be a very good response. A further 403 questionnaires were returned from those distributed at other venues.

The results showed considerable support for a new gallery: almost 85 per cent of respondents supported the idea. The postal questionnaire also asked questions about priorities for facilities, including refreshments, baby changing facilities, access for disabled people, voice information, visitor shop and larger exhibition spaces. The responses of different potential user populations (such as those with young children, single people, childless couples and residents over the age of 55) were assessed.

The postal survey was considered to be a success by the team responsible. For them, its value was due to the information it provided, fairly quickly, about the views of a large number of people who were representative of the borough as a whole, and which could be analysed easily and with statistical reliability.

Workshop event

A workshop event was held on a Friday afternoon and Saturday morning in late November 1995. It built on a tradition in Walsall of what they call 'big' or 'limelight' events. The purpose of the workshop was described as being: to involve major stakeholders, communities of interest, target groups in a forum to inform the design, facilities and programming of the new art gallery, and to establish a channel of dialogue that will enable progress on the scheme to be monitored in the future, and to act as a sounding board to ensure that the new gallery retains its focus during the construction and detailed planning phases of the project.

The planning for the two-day public workshop took place over a very short period of eight weeks. Emphasis during the planning for the workshop event was on securing a representative attendance. A tentative list was drawn up of the types of interest they would like to be present.

The invitation list was made up of local councillors, members of the steering group, local arts groups, ethnic minority groups, community organisations, local business people, local school teachers and students, some randomly selected residents who attended the exhibition or returned the postal questionnaire, gallery staff, people with disabilities and religious groups.

Around 300 people were invited to the workshop; 70 people attended, some of them for either the Friday or Saturday sessions rather than both. In the event the project staff realised that the participants could not be representative of the different interests they had identified. Instead, staff emphasised that people were there in their own right as individuals and not there to represent organisations, although they may have been invited through local arts groups, community associations and so on.

There are different views among the organisers of the extent to which partial attendance at the public workshop influenced the effectiveness of the event. Ideally, the event would have had continuous attendance over the two days. However, some of the organisers felt that making information available about the outcome of the previous day to those attending on the second day, helped these participants to become involved, and overcame any lack of continuity.

Participants would have preferred to continue later on the Friday to complete the programme, and not to have to return on the Saturday morning, when they felt they had lost some of the benefits of being immersed in the subjects under discussion, and were feeling distracted by their usual Saturday morning commitments. However, this was not a feasible option as the organisers required an interval in which to collate information from the first session for feedback to the second.

Delegates received brief information before the event about its purpose and other information was handed out on the day to facilitate the workshop. The advance information made clear to participants that the workshop was about the facilities and use of the gallery, and not about the development of other facilities such as car parking or issues to do with the bricks and mortar of the new gallery.

The workshop was structured around a series of activity sessions, workshop events and presentations. These methods were specifically chosen to complement the other strands of the consultation programme, as they would provide qualitative information to complement the results of the two questionnaires. The workshop included voting at key stages on different ideas to help build up a consensus view about the new gallery. The emphasis was on active participation of the people attending. This was clearly achieved, and very much enjoyed. Although a little daunted at first, any misgivings on the part of the participants were soon overcome by the welcome they felt they had received, and by the venue itself.

The venue was thought to be excellent: bright, well-equipped, spacious and modern. The layout suggested that everyone, participants and organisers, were on equal terms. The facilities provided, including the equipment and refreshments, were all of a high standard. The result was that people immediately felt that they were being taken seriously; name badges presented on arrival helped them feel of individual significance. Care, time and effort had evidently gone into preparing the workshop.

At the start of the session people were asked about their expectations of the workshop. The responses included: finding out about plans; to have a say; to meet other interested people; to put forward views; and to keep in touch with what was happening. In fact, they received far less information than they expected. The time was spent in a busy sequence of activities that elicited information from them. Their impression was of a fairly blank sheet of paper on which they could propose ideas.

The format of the workshop was appropriate for a Friday evening. The pace was fairly fast, requiring much interaction but not very much that was demanding or required deep consideration. The layout of the room and the structure of the activities quickly got everyone participating.

Work in schools

Walsall has a high proportion of young people relative to other authorities of a similar population size. One of the main themes of the project was to involve young people, as they would be important users of the art gallery and the citizens of the future. Schools offered a captive audience but they needed a different approach. It was realised that children would not respond to the other three methods which had been used.

During November 1995 six schools with a range of ages from infants to secondary schools were selected. Two independent artists facilitated the workshops where children and young people were invited to say what the new art gallery should look like, and the sort of facilities they would like to see. A questionnaire was devised for the children and young people to complete when they visited the gallery at weekends or in the holidays.

The organisers felt they got a tremendous response and enthusiasm from the children. A key message to emerge was support for a range of facilities, including a place to get messy in. They wanted the interior to be light, exciting and fun. The organisers would like to engage with more children if they were doing the consultation programme again. Six schools was not really considered to be enough. Time and resources were constraints and they need to establish more contact with head teachers and organise presentations for them.

Disabled people's groups

The processes of consultation also included discussions with people with learning disabilities, people with mental health problems and people with visual impairments. The staff realised, as they discussed the gallery with these groups, how diverse the needs were.

Feedback seminar

The staff also organised a seminar in March 1996 to provide feedback to those people who had been involved in the different consultation programmes and who had expressed a particular interest in being involved further. The architects attended the meeting and talked about the way the results of the consultation programmes had been used in terms of the facilities in the gallery, and also the design of the building.

Other aspects

To further the overall aim of involving the public with the new art gallery project, events such as the sending of the lottery application were staged as occasions which the public were invited to attend.

Working with the local press was an important element of the process. There are two daily papers which have a very large regional circulation, and four or five weekly free sheets. The project worked hard to build up good relationships with the local press, which has responded by being very supportive of the project. They have provided the project with a great deal of coverage in response to initiatives from the gallery, but have also taken the initiative to follow the latest developments.

Managing the process

The management structure for the NAG included an advisory group, an implementation team, and a design team. The implementation team and the advisory group were mechanisms for involving key stakeholders in the project and for using their additional skills. The main link person between the different teams was the Project Director, who was described as being the driving force behind the whole project. He had responsibility for taking the results of the consultation into the design process.

Implementation team

A decision was made early on by the Chief Executive that the development of the new art gallery had to be a corporate process, involving representatives of different departments and agencies. The aim was to ensure a widespread feeling of ownership for the project and to bring in the necessary skills.

The members of the team were handpicked in consultation with the Chief Executive. Requests to Chief Officers went from the Chief Executive to release members of staff to work on the project. Staff from economic development, planning and so on were involved, as were staff from City Challenge (the major funders of the consultation process) and members of the local Chamber of Commerce.

Everyone involved with the consultation process was on the implementation team during the course of the consultation programme. They continued to attend meetings for as long as their involvement was relevant to the development of the project.

Involving elected members

The advisory group included some elected members and there were also seminars for members, which were attended by about 40 of the 60 councillors. The project team wanted to be open and transparent about the project, especially as it felt that lack of communication had contributed to failures in the past. It was particularly important to ensure that local politicians were involved, as their support was necessary for the project to go forward. This was the key objective of involving elected members. Overall, the project team felt that the views and comments from councillors did not raise new issues.

Advisory group

As well as elected members, the advisory group also included local business people. The support of the business community was important: local business people have an interest in ensuring that developments will increase local employment prospects. There was also the potential for cash support for the project from local businesses.

Design team

The information from the different strands of the consultation programme was fed into the design team, which consists of the project director, the architects, the quantity surveyor and the project manager. In addition, the design team brings in other people with particular expertise at different stages of the project. The design team met every week.

Involving architects

The architects themselves were closely involved with many aspects of the consultation programme. The choice of architects was, in part, guided by the beliefs they shared with Walsall about the process of consultation. They attended the public workshop and, importantly, the feedback meeting four months later. This was considered to be very important by the public, and was taken as evidence that their input was valued and taken seriously.

Skills

Not all the skills that were needed for the project as a whole were available in house. The business plan, which was key to unlocking funds from the National Lottery, involved use of outside consultants. But for the purposes of the consultation work, skills were available in house – apart from employing a company to distribute the household survey.

Monitoring quality

The organisers did not set up any systems for monitoring the processes or the outcome of the consultation. This was partly because this was the first time they had carried out a project on this scale and it was difficult, therefore, to find yardsticks or benchmarks against which to assess the work.

Organisers and policy customers consider that the degree of interest (for example, the rate of return of the postal questionnaire) shown by the public is a guide to the quality of the consultation processes. There were evaluation sheets at the end of the consultation workshop for participants to complete and these showed a high level of satisfaction with the workshop.

Resources

It has been possible to collect only a limited amount of information about the costs of the consultation programme. Not all aspects of the consultation programme were separately budgeted for. There was no specific assessment of the amount of staff time that would be involved, or the indirect costs of this. It is difficult for those involved to judge the amount of staff time, especially as some staff were pulled in to the project from other departments. However, it is fair to say that those most heavily involved in the consultation process committed a considerable proportion of their time over a period of months.

Information is available about the costs of the consultation workshop and the household questionnaire. Together these amounted to around £15,000.

The resources devoted to the consultation programme were very small compared to the overall capital spending on the project. This puts the cost of the consultation programme into perspective. This small part of the overall project is considered to have been very important.

The impact of the process on its output

The consultation contributed to decision-making about the gallery over time; as the results of each stage of the consultation phase became available they were added to the information being considered by the different groups, particularly the design team. There was no specific stage or process of reviewing all the results of the consultation and their implications for the work on the NAG.

However, all those involved in these decisions are clear that the consultation, by contributing information over a period, had a definite influence on decisions that were made about the gallery. In many ways, the findings reinforced the ideas that the officers had already formed about the gallery, and informed the detailed decisions. Participants in the workshop were certain that their input had a definite influence on the plans for facilities in the gallery. The workshop and other consultation activities generated great enthusiasm and support, and the continuing flow of information after the event contributed to a sense of involvement.

IMPACT

Acting on the output of the exercise

Different members of staff had responsibility for analysing the information gathered from different strands of the consultation processes with which they had been involved. This information was then fed into the design process, undertaken by the design team. The outcome of the different consultation programmes was also fed back to councillors through council committee meetings on a regular basis.

The consultation programme was written up as a report in March 1996 which formed part of the application to the National Lottery for funding.

Direct impact

The greatest impact of the consultation programme has been in demonstrating a level of support for the project and in informing decisions about the way the building will be used and the facilities to be provided. The use of the results was made easier by the similarity between the messages which were received from the different consultation exercises.

Both the organisers of the consultation and those responsible for implementing decisions consider that the consultation programme has informed a large number of people about what is being planned, allowed them to express their views, and made them excited about it. A key outcome of the consultation process was a clear statement of support for the new art gallery, which includes the support of those who do not use the existing gallery. This is thought to be an encouraging sign for the future success of the new gallery.

The project team is confident that it showed that a genuine and full consultation had taken place and produced a mandate from the public to go forward. Without this, it would have been much more difficult to get approval from councillors. The team also feels that a great deal of interest and enthusiasm was generated and that people's views have shaped the final look of the gallery.

The views on facilities and access were used by the architects and the design team as they worked on the gallery's internal details: 'The information we got back... is genuinely helpful and was taken on board.' One example was the clear demand for facilities for children. As a result of this demand, the architects included a three-storey children's house in the gallery, described as a clear physical manifestation of the impact of the consultation programme. People's concerns about access ensured that the architects made access an integrated design feature of the new gallery.

Local politicians have greater confidence in the project as a result of the consultation. Indeed, it would be difficult now for local politicians not to give support to the project or to argue that the new art gallery is not wanted by local people. The consultation process has also increased the confidence felt by the project team.

Indirect or unintended impact

The programme has encouraged a sense of cross-departmental working, and this has other spin-offs. Territorial attitudes have to be minimised if the gallery project and the consultation programme are to succeed. They depend on people with different skills being able to work together.

The consultation process has allowed the mechanisms to be set up to develop future relationships with users. This will be useful in terms of marketing the gallery in the future.

The future

The project team expected consultation to continue through the next phases of the project, and to form an important part of the ongoing running of the new gallery. For example, consultation on access is continuing and being managed by an independent consultant who will be talking with particular groups on the detail of the design as it develops. One of the project team is setting up an education forum which will involve teachers, education providers, and retired teachers and provide a means of consultation about a whole range of issues, such as marketing. They also want to have further consultation with members of the Asian and Caribbean communities.

Assessment

As explained, the consultation was not intended to find out views about the design of the building or its materials. It was to explore levels of support for a new gallery and to consider the facilities and access arrangements. It has certainly enabled those responsible for the project to go ahead with confidence. They can demonstrate both that there is a level of enthusiasm and interest in the project, and that people have been consulted. The organisers and policy customers feel that the project has been very useful and achieved its objectives: to get a wide range of views and a public mandate for what they are doing.

The consultation techniques involved in the workshop were relatively new to the project team. The workshop event was often described as a 'white-knuckle' event during which the project team had to be flexible, respond to circumstances and take risks. They did not always feel completely in control of this process. People were prepared to learn and take a certain degree of risk with this, and with the questionnaire survey (there was a certain nervousness that this might produce a 'no' to the idea of the gallery). This approach contributed to the success of the programme.

The different strands of the consultation programme fed into each other and this was part of their success. So, for example, information from the exhibition and the postal questionnaire was used to identify people to attend the workshop event. Results from the exhibition and survey were explored in more depth in the workshop.

The staff realised they could not meet everyone's needs although they did want to 'try and keep as many people happy most of the time but it is impossible to please everybody.' They accepted that they had to have the confidence to say, during the consultation, that they were not able to do certain things, and to give good reasons for these decisions.

Research methods

We interviewed staff of the local authority and others involved in organising the consultation and planning the gallery. We also carried out a group discussion with members of the public who had attended the workshop. Reports on the consultation and background documents on the gallery were studied.

Most of the fieldwork took place in the Spring and Summer of 1996, the group discussion took place towards the end of the year.

COMMENTARY

Overview

The public consultation over the new art gallery (NAG) for Walsall had two main objectives: to inform decisions about facilities and services in the gallery, and to establish the level of public support for a new gallery.

The key points, on which we comment below, are:

- The two objectives were pursued concurrently through the same consultation activities, raising doubts about whether both could be met fully.
- The combination of methods produced a useful range of types of information, both qualitative and quantitative, which complemented one another.
- Limited resources meant that some of the activities were not as effective as they might have been.

Objectives

The consultation programme took place while the plans for the gallery and the bid for funding were being drawn up. Detailed plans and evidence of public support for the gallery were both needed for the funding bid. Such evidence was also needed to gain the support of elected members. Another driver for the consultation was a belief in its value per se, and a desire to counteract criticism of the borough's record on public consultation.

A strong element in the programme was, therefore, the promotion of the idea of building a new gallery, and the creation of support for it. One of the ways in which Walsall chose to do this was to involve people in discussions about what the gallery should provide. The advantage of this approach was that people were invited to contribute their ideas and not simply to support an outline proposal over which they had no influence. The aim of securing public approval was also behind efforts to generate the interest and support of the local press, in the hope of encouraging favourable comment there.

There would, however, be a strong case for separating the consultation on the two issues: first, is there support for the new gallery, and, secondly, what should it provide? This would have given a more thorough and objective assessment of the level of public interest. It is not surprising, given the strong impetus behind the proposal within the organisation, and the demands of the timetable, that the first question, to establish the level of support, was not pursued as vigorously as the exploration of ideas about facilities.

The reaction to the results of the postal survey illustrates this. Although 85 per cent of those responding to the postal questionnaire supported the idea of building a new gallery, the response rate was only 16 per cent. The consultation team was pleased with this rate of return but we suggest that the non-response by 80 per cent may suggest a degree of apathy. This may not, in fact, matter except in that it could be misleading to suggest widespread public support, on the basis of such a response rate.

There was a genuine openness to ideas about the services and facilities to be provided. Clarity about the remit of this part of the consultation, and the fact that it was not about the design of the building itself, was strong and helpful.

Methods

The dual objectives demanded a combination of methods. The exhibition and survey served the purpose of ensuring that a large number of people were made aware of the NAG project and were given an opportunity to express support or otherwise and to say what they wanted the gallery to provide. The workshop involved more in-depth engagement with a smaller number of people, some of whom had already expressed interest in the NAG, and were able to develop detailed ideas through discussion.

Thus the combination of methods met the different objectives, and, importantly, provided complementary information. The workshop design was able to draw on survey results, for example. The use of more than one method can be invaluable for many consultation projects.

In using this range of approaches, it was necessary to assess the extent to which they provided 'representative' views. This case study neatly illustrates the two different aspects of 'representativeness' which those consulting the public have often to address.

First, there is the issue of sampling and statistical representativeness. Questionnaires returned by those who chose to visit the exhibitions were not representative of a wider group and the results could not, therefore, be used in quantifying views. The survey allowed a stratified sample of the borough's population to be approached and could therefore give a more reliable picture of public opinion, but the value of this was limited by a low response rate.

Secondly, there is the question of individuals being able to represent the views of others. A cross-section of groups who might be thought to have different interests were invited to the workshop. Initially, it was thought that individuals would be able to represent those interests. The workshop, and all deliberative methods, involve contributing ideas as they develop in the group. Individuals could offer their personal reactions, therefore, not the views of others.

Resources

The resources (especially staff and time) were not really adequate to the scale of the activities undertaken. The exhibition was not fully staffed all the time, thereby missing the opportunity to maximise contact with the public. There was no time to pilot the questionnaire. Good practice suggests that it would have been useful to do so and to perhaps have done some qualitative research beforehand (such as group discussions) to inform the design of the questionnaire. As a result, the value of the exhibition and the survey were not maximised. Additional resources would probably have made both more cost-effective.

CASE STUDY FOURTEEN

Waltham Forest Housing Action Trust: Tenant Participation

ORIGINS AND OBJECTIVES

Waltham Forest Housing Action Trust (HAT) was set up in 1991. Building on a tradition of consultation by the local authority, and on the overall HAT objective of tenant involvement, it has developed a range of methods of consulting tenants and an organisational structure which includes many tenant representatives, some with voting rights.

Origins

Housing Action Trusts

Waltham Forest is one of six Housing Action Trusts, non-departmental public bodies set up by government to address problems of poor housing and environmental conditions in urban areas. The objectives of Housing Action Trusts, in general, are laid out in the 1988 Housing Act. These are:

- to secure the repair or improvement of housing accommodation for the time being held by the Trust;
- to secure the proper and effective management and use of that housing accommodation;
- to encourage diversity in the type of accommodation occupied and, for rented accommodation, diversity in types of landlord;
- generally to secure or facilitate the improvement of living conditions in the area and the social conditions and general environment of the area.

The Housing Act 1988 also specifically states that the HAT's role is to carry out its programme of renovation 'in consultation with the residents'.

HATs had their origins in a central government initiative. They were at first politically contentious, as they entailed the removal of housing from local authority control. The Housing Act stipulated that tenants should be balloted before a HAT was designated by the government. The first attempts to designate HATs failed, due to the objections of tenants and to political opposition. Waltham Forest HAT was the second HAT to be designated, in 1991.

Previous consultation

There was a local history of consultation with tenants, carried out as part of attempts to improve housing conditions. The local authority had, since 1987, been trying to raise the money to remedy serious structural problems on four estates built in the 1960s and 1970s. A survey of tenants was carried out, which included interviews with between 80 and 90 per cent of tenants. This showed that the vast majority of tenants supported redevelopment and more tenant control.

The local authority produced two successive schemes to redevelop the estate, but these failed because of difficulties in agreeing funding mechanisms with the Department of the Environment (DoE). The HAT was an alternative structure.

As part of the preparations for a HAT, negotiations took place to produce a Tenants' Expectation Document, a written commitment to the ethos of involving tenants in decision making, working together in partnership towards completion of the project.

Participants in these negotiations included a Joint Steering Group of tenants, the local authority, the DoE, and, from February 1991, the Shadow Chair and Acting Chief Executive of the HAT. The local authority and the DoE shared the cost of funding the Joint Steering Group and consultants and legal advisers to the tenants.

Steps were also taken to inform tenants more generally about the issues at stake in the ballot on the HAT. For a month before, a one-stop shop was open on each estate, staffed by those involved in the consultation. Tenants could also see models of each phase of the redevelopment and talk to the architects. Information sheets on 20 different aspects of the HAT's operation were produced.

There was a 75 per cent turnout for the ballot (compared to a 41 per cent turnout in local elections). Just over four-fifths (81 per cent) voted in favour.

Objectives

The overall objectives of HATs obviously apply to Waltham Forest HAT. In addition, in Waltham Forest, consultation or involvement is given a particularly important role. This is more than a means to an end; it has its own aim of empowering the tenants.

'Empowerment' is defined by the HAT as tenants being able to take decisions or make choices themselves. It is one of seven indicators chosen by the HAT to gauge its success. As HATs are temporary, short-life organisations, it is particularly important that tenants can continue the work themselves once it has ended. The HAT's vision is that it should leave behind 'neighbourhoods of high quality homes occupied by people who have been empowered to take key choices about ownership and management...' A senior HAT official described the role of the HAT's officers as being 'guardians of the empowerment objective'.

THE PROCESS

Methods

The empowerment objective is said to 'run through everything we do'. Tenant empowerment and choice, and consultation and communication with tenants are amongst the core values selected by the HAT to underpin its work. The HAT goes on to say that tenant empowerment is to be achieved by ensuring that they have the necessary skills, knowledge and support to participate. Training is therefore very important.

The HAT has a community development department, responsible for funding and servicing the tenants' groups through which consultation takes place. There are also community development officers based on each estate, who help to get people involved by, for example, encouraging tenants to join the Estate Steering Groups (ESGs), arranging training and supporting members in their work.

However, consultation is not solely the responsibility of the community development department. Instead, empowerment is regarded as part of the working ethos for all parts of the HAT, including day to day management, and the design and redevelopment of the estates. Directors of different departments within the HAT consult tenants on the subjects within their area of responsibility.

Activities

Tenant representatives on the Board

Participation of tenants in the HAT's decision-making is formalised through the presence of four tenant representatives on the Board which controls the HAT. Tenants elect these representatives. The remainder of the 11 seats are taken by local authority and non-resident members, the latter proposed by the HAT Chair and approved by the DoE.

Board Members also attend area committees, sub-committees, and ESG meetings. Part of their role involves supporting and training the ESG, for example, helping it to communicate effectively with the HAT. They also attend public meetings. Tenant Board members said that they involved tenants in formulating policy by holding meetings on specific issues, before they were discussed at the Board.

Estate Steering Groups

Each of the estates has an elected representative body, the Estate Steering Group, which acts as a channel of consultation between the HAT and its tenants. All policy documents for the Board are circulated to the ESGs before meetings and their comments included in each report. The HAT gives each ESG an annual budget, their own premises and office equipment.

The ESGs are responsible for running their own financial affairs, and have been equipped to do so. The HAT has provided the ESGs with training in group work skills, equal opportunities, community representation skills and financial management. The HAT also paid for nine ESG members to go on a certificated course in tenant participation.

Being on the ESG also entails attending two ESG meetings a month and ESG sub-committees. Members also attend a project control meeting once a fortnight for their estate, which is attended by a manager from the building contractor and HAT officers, and at which they are given an update on progress. The number of meetings is a factor in the high turnover of ESG members.

Other activities include helping to produce the HAT newsletter, sitting on recruitment panels for HAT staff, sitting on panels to make appointments of consultants and contractors and being on working groups to discuss partnerships with the business community. The ESGs have been consulted, for example, about working hours for the contractors, to arrange what type of work could be done when and for traffic control.

Area committees

There was an important change in the committee structure in 1995/6 which increased tenant control. The functional committees (for example, for housing, development etc) have been replaced by area committees, which deal with policy and planning for all functions at an estate level. The committees are made up of equal numbers of HAT Board members and ESG members. The ESG members have full voting rights, whereas previously they exercised their influence through consultation only.

Consultation on redevelopment

Tenant involvement in the design of the redevelopment predated the establishment of the HAT. The local authority had already adopted a 'community architecture' approach and much of the design dated from the local authority's previous two schemes. The HAT continued this process of consultation, holding a programme of public meetings to inform tenants and allow them an opportunity to influence the design. The masterplan takes account of tenants' preferences for house types and street layout.

Consultation on other issues

Consultation has been held on subjects such as allocations, general progress on site, and the Tenants' Choice scheme. This scheme allows tenants to customise their new homes as far as possible. They are able to choose from a range of colour schemes and interior and exterior fixtures and fittings. Public meetings were held to discuss this. The organisers have found that tenants get involved readily in design meetings, as they are motivated by the opportunity to influence the design of their own homes. 20 or 30 tenants attend meetings where design is discussed and on occasions attendance had been up to 50.

Consultation takes place on specific, one-off issues. An example is the redevelopment of Leyton Orient football club; the HAT saw this as an opportunity to provide a community centre. Two options were put to tenants, either to build a stand-alone community centre or construct new facilities as part of the stadium. A series of discussions and an exhibition on the issue were held on the estate, and the developer addressed a public meeting to answer questions. Tenants also gave feedback through questionnaires.

Some decisions need a more comprehensive process of consultation than others. For some important issues, special working parties are set up. The Allocations Working Party is an example: this subject was also discussed at public meetings and an 'allocations road show' toured the estates.

Communication with tenants

Routine communication is an important part of the overall approach to consultation. The building contractors appoint tenant liaison officers based in drop-in premises. The HAT also produces a regular newsletter to tenants, a Tenant's Handbook and an Annual Report to tenants. Separate editions of the tenant newsletter are produced for each of the four estates. Key information for tenants is available translated into seven community languages, available in print and audiotape. English language documents are also available on audiotape and in large print. Staff have been sent on plain English courses.

Assessment of the process

Two groups of participants were interviewed; tenant members of the HAT Board and members of an estate steering group. Their roles and perspective are slightly different, and so are dealt with separately here.

Estates Steering Groups

Estates Steering Group members had taken part in small-scale community activities before getting involved in the ESG. They were motivated to take on the responsibility by the possibility of improving the estates, for others and for themselves. They feel that meetings are the main way in which consultation takes place, both where they get information and put their points across. Area committees were a welcome innovation; formerly the ESG had to send representatives to all the functional committees, but now everything is dealt with at the area committees. ESG members are sent papers beforehand and usually have a pre-meeting to decide on their response. The area committees are felt to encourage tenant participation because they have a local remit. The HAT senior management were concerned that Area Committees might lead to loss of coordination or delays. The structure is now thought to be working well, although staff now have to attend four meetings instead of one. HAT staff believe that Area Committees help tenants feel more in control and able to hold the HAT accountable.

Level of influence

To their surprise, ESG members feel that they are consulted on everything that affects them. They find it easy to contact the HAT, including the Chief Executive and Chairman.

Members consider that their involvement does make a lot of difference. One example was the decision to design the estate so that everyone could have a garden. Contractors are told that it is the tenants who are the clients. Everything the contractors do has to come for approval to the ESG.

This approach to consultation was contrasted to the attitudes prevalent when the estate was built: 'If they had consulted with the tenants in the first place, these tower blocks would never have been built', said one tenant.

Increasing tenant involvement

ESG members felt that other tenants did not participate as much as they should. Few people, for example, attended the meeting with the developer of the Leyton Orient stadium scheme and there was a poor response to the ballot on this subject. They attribute this lack of involvement to apathy. They also felt people were used to being told what was going to happen by the local authority, not asked for their views. People only came to meetings if they had a direct, personal interest in an item, such as allocations.

The ESG had discussed how to increase involvement. They are trying to produce their own tenants' newsletter to inform people what has been done and ask for their views. One initiative which they felt had been successful, but which they said had been stopped by the HAT due to lack of funds, was the employment of tenant information workers who went round from door to door giving people information.

Level of commitment

ESG members find problems in combining their role with other responsibilities such as child care and family life. As a result, a small number of people do most of the work. Of the ESG whose members were interviewed, about seven or eight members were active out of twelve.

The ESG members interviewed did not appear to resent the fact that they are not paid and did not suggest that they should be. They do gain through training and experience, valuable for personal development and for finding employment. Indeed, people finding jobs which use their newly-acquired skills was cited as a reason for people dropping out of ESG work.

Tenant members of the Board

Tenant members of the HAT Board are active participants in decision-making. The members have a long record of participation in attempts to regenerate the estate. They had been involved in Estate Steering Groups and in the earlier negotiations led by the local authority to raise funds for redevelopment. It therefore seemed a natural progression to them to stand for election to the Board.

The tenant members felt that their views were legitimised by the fact that they lived on the estates, and therefore, they felt, had an accurate understanding of tenants' views. They were aware that they were now 'experts' rather than ordinary tenants, but felt that they would not lose touch with those they represented. They were also democratically accountable through the ballot box.

Board members described their motivation as a desire to share their experience and knowledge they have gained. Part of their role is to make sure that commitments made to the tenants are honoured. Like the HAT officers, the Board members were concerned with empowering tenants so that they could continue after the HAT ended.

The tenant members felt that consultation had been constantly evolving. The establishment of the Area Committees marked a further stage in giving tenants greater control in decision making. One stated that the relationship had started as one of consultation, but it was now more of a partnership. However, they saw the process as still having some way to go if tenants were to have complete control.

Level of influence

Tenant members were worried that they would be outvoted on the Board, but this has not happened in fact. The other Board members listen to and rarely oppose them. They are felt to represent the people on the estates; this role, the tenant Board members implied, gives their views legitimacy and authority.

Acceptance of their views has changed over time. One member suggested that, at first, the other Board members might have felt they had to accept the tenants' recommendations, but later came to accept the authority and good sense of their views. It was recognised that the tenant Board members had a good understanding of the estates and could provide a reliable input to the Board's decision making. Now, tenant Board members feel that they and other members have a shared understanding of needs.

Commitment to consultation

The tenant Board members voiced some criticisms of the HAT's commitment in practice to consultation. They were more critical than the ESG members of this, perhaps because of their greater closeness to decision making or because of their greater experience. They felt that their role was needed to ensure consultation does take place. For example, they ensure that real attention is given to the section on consultation contained in each document to the Board.

Not all departments in the HAT had the same level of commitment to consultation. The development department, which works to strict schedules for budgetary reasons, was felt to have difficulty in allowing adequate time for consultation. Indeed, a general criticism of the HAT's consultation programme was that the timescale for consultation was sometimes too short.

Potential conflict of interests

Tenant Board members attend ESG meetings, and this can lead to a perceived conflict of roles. Other tenants were not always clear whether tenant Board members were representing tenants or the HAT. Tenant Board members were sometimes asked to leave ESG meetings, while the ESG held their own confidential discussions. The involvement of tenant Board members in confidential HAT business was sometimes viewed with suspicion by other tenants, although in fact it was limited to the award of tenders.

Training

The Board members were critical of the training they had been given. They had no proper induction at the start of their work, while now, a lot of the training available was no longer suitable because of the extent of their experience. A recruitment and selection training course, although adequate, was given to them too late, after they had already been carrying out the work for three or four years.

Managing the process

The HAT recognises that it is not always easy to measure the impact of consultation, as it produces qualitative rather than quantitative changes. However, the HAT monitors the consultation programme in a number of ways. It monitors complaints and carries out an annual survey of about 450 tenants, selected at random. This includes questions on whether the tenants feel they are kept well informed and also gauges their level of knowledge about the way the HAT is managed.

The HAT does have methods of monitoring its contribution to the development of sustainable communities – it monitors targets which it feels can be used as surrogates for this, such as the number of people getting jobs, or going on training courses, or using the community centre. One performance indicator directly linked to tenant involvement is the percentage of tenants voting in ESG elections.

However, there is no formal way of monitoring the impact of consultation on decision making. Indeed, this would be hard to measure, especially as officers' recommendations are felt to be increasingly in tune with tenant preferences. As a result, the HAT receives less and less feedback from the ESGs on its proposals.

Safeguards exist to make sure that consultation takes place. All papers should include a paragraph on what consultation took place and its outcome. The tenant Board members and ESG members will question any lack of consultation.

Resources

It is not possible to identify the costs of tenant participation accurately, as the consultation approach is expected to be integral to all the HAT's activities.

Grants are provided to the ESGs under Section 71 of the Housing Act 1988. Grants given to the four ESGs over the past three years amounted to:

1994	£69,006
1995	£41,815
1996	£66,102

Source: *Annual Report and Accounts 1994–5, 1995–6*

Tenant Board members are paid a salary. At the time of the research, these amounted to £5,000 each for the three ordinary Board members, and £9,000 for the Vice-Chair, a total of £24,000 a year. Like the ESG members, the time spent on HAT work fluctuated a lot. One estimate was that it was about 20 hours each week. The salary for ordinary members was not felt to be adequate, in view of the time and responsibility involved. Tenant Board members can also claim expenses.

An immense amount of unpaid time is contributed by ESG members and other tenants taking part in the consultation exercises. The HAT obviously relies heavily on the willingness of tenants to make this contribution without payment. The workload of ESG members varies. One estimate was that it takes about two full days each week, but only expenses are paid.

Impact

Social benefits

Many of those involved in the HAT consider the effect of involvement on individual users themselves to be at least as significant as improvements in housing design or management. In fact, social benefits were given more weight by many interviewees than more practical matters. There is a feeling that there is a change in the 'dependency culture' on the estate, and that the tenants with leadership skills have been identified and helped to develop. Social networks have also improved and isolation decreased.

One of the most important achievements of the HAT is the increase in confidence and skills it has given to the actively involved tenants. Tenant representatives are now able to deal with far more complex matters – such as negotiating a private financing deal with the Peabody Trust – than when the project started.

ESG members feel that they gained skills such as public speaking, organising, computer skills and the ability to take part in meetings. The control they are able to have, and enable others to have, over the design and fixtures of their houses, gives a sense of satisfaction. It has also given them confidence to deal with people in authority. They had discovered that they could make a difference, both as individuals and as a group. This gave them the motivation to carry on.

Better housing

Tenants appreciated having a say in the design of their houses. They also mentioned the improved record on housing management since the HAT took over (and which is confirmed by customer satisfaction ratings in the annual survey). They felt that this improvement was due to consultation.

The HAT officers felt that, although consultation makes housing management more expensive, it also makes it easier. It allows them to deliver the outcome that tenants want and will support. It was also suggested that in the long run it would lower maintenance costs, as people felt more of a sense of ownership and pride in the estate.

Board members and ESG members agreed that HAT tenants were not generally well-informed about what's happening in the HAT. However, they felt that they were better informed than tenants usually are, in non-HAT estates.

Disadvantages

None of those involved found it easy to identify disadvantages of the process of consultation used at Waltham Forest HAT. The extra time and expense involved was raised, although these were not felt to be as significant as the benefits of consultation. One issue was the strain on the limited number of tenants who became involved. The workload could have a serious impact on an individual's life outside the HAT and a conflict could arise with family responsibilities.

The future

The HAT is scheduled to be dissolved in 2002. Much attention is now being given to how the gains of the HAT can be maintained. The housing redevelopment will be finished, but tenants will need to be able to tackle other social issues.

One of the main immediate issues, however, is the choice of landlord that tenants must be offered before the HAT is wound up. One option is to go back to the local authority. However, the HAT set up a Community-Based Housing Association as an alternative to this. This is described as being 'controlled by tenants' and one of its aims is to encourage tenant and community participation. Ten of the 15 members on the CBHA Board are tenants. At first the tenant representatives were nominated by the ESGs, but from 1997 they will be elected. In preparation for the ballots, the CBHA took over the management of the estate from the HAT from April 1996, acting as an independent contractor. It may also be possible to get another housing association involved as a third potential landlord for the landlord choice ballot.

Assessment

Limits to the effectiveness of consultation

Those involved identify a number of problems which might limit the effectiveness of consultation. One of these was the involvement of only a relatively small number of committed tenants and the consequent burden of responsibility on them. The tendency of ESGs to have pre-meetings and decide matters in advance was also felt to be limiting opportunities for real participation.

ESG members themselves felt that they should try and increase participation. They felt that people were cynical and apathetic because they were unused to having an influence and that it may be unrealistic to expect many people to get involved unless they had a specific personal interest in the issue under discussion. A lack of appropriate training also inhibited participation.

Elements of successful consultation

The public commitment made to participation, as an objective in itself, and as a method of working, has been important. It has been made explicit in the key policy documents and in the requirement for consultation to be considered in all papers to the Board. All those interviewed had a strong personal commitment to that policy. The structure of the HAT helps to ensure that the commitment to consultation does not get overlooked. Tenants are not only consulted, but are themselves at the centre of decision making, through their membership of the HAT Board and the ESGs.

Resources have been provided to allow tenants to gain the skills and experience necessary to participate (despite some criticisms) and to run their own offices. The HAT's budget allowed this and other community development initiatives such as the employment of the community development workers to provide ongoing practical support.

The finance provided for the redevelopment of the estate also helped to convince sceptical tenants that, for once, something was going to change. This helped to dispel some apathy; the fact that users were to get new homes was a big motivating force. The enthusiasm generated by this has been channelled into other spheres of community development. Tenants have set up a number of new projects, such as After School Clubs.

The approach was thought to suit the tenants on this particular estate, for various reasons. The approach to participation worked here, but might not elsewhere. One officer thought it was very important that community development workers had paved the way by working at Waltham Forest for at least two years beforehand. The HAT did not have to start from scratch with community participation, as tenants had previously been active for some time in the earlier redevelopment schemes. Leaders had already emerged and some experience and skill had been built up.

The HAT has made an effort to provide information in a form that can be easily understood, although users still had some criticisms of the accessibility of papers for meetings and the short time to consider them. The HAT also feeds back information to tenants about decisions. Officers were felt to be accessible.

One element, which both derived from and contributed to the success, and which was generally remarked upon, was the good relationship between the HAT and its users, the lack of an 'us and them' mentality. In fact, in the context of the HAT, where tenants sit on the Board and where staff housing management devolved to a tenant-controlled association, the divide between management and users becomes blurred.

Users felt that the HAT officers had become very well-attuned to the needs of tenants. HAT officers in their turn seemed to have great respect for tenants' reasonableness, ability and hard work. This good relationship seems to have derived from users' confidence that the HAT really is committed to consultation. They feel that they are listened to and will not be overruled.

Research methods

We interviewed: staff of the trust; members of the Board and tenant representatives on the Estates Steering Groups and Board. Reports and other documents about the HAT were also studied. Fieldwork took place between Spring and Summer 1996.

Commentary

Overview

Waltham Forest HAT's approach to improving housing and environmental conditions was characterised by a particularly strong emphasis on consulting tenants.

We comment on the following points:

- A range of methods were used, some involving limited contact with large numbers of tenants (such as surveys and public meetings) and others involving intense participation by a small number of people over a long period (representatives with decision-making powers).
- The structure of tenant representatives requires committed individuals, and the resources to support them.
- Representatives are motivated by the desire to bring improvements to the estate as a whole. Personal gains, such as the opportunity to develop skills, are also important in sustaining their involvement.
- There is a possibility that representatives may themselves become distant from tenants as a whole, and that the distinction between user representatives and service providers becomes blurred.

Methods

A range of methods served different purposes. The overall approach was to consult as widely as possible on issues which affected people directly, and to give tenant representatives a full role in the decision-making structures. Our case study focused on the latter, as this was the most participative method investigated by the research.

Clear distinctions were made between those who chose to become actively involved, and the majority of tenants, who showed limited interest in attempts to involve them. Tenant representatives were themselves mindful of the gap between the degree of their own participation and that of the majority of tenants, and had views about the reasons for this. This case study therefore suggests some of the motivations and conditions that influence the degree of participation. These are discussed below.

A large commitment

The commitment and skills required of representatives are considerable. Their commitment could probably not be sustained without their strong personal motivation, the organisational resources to support them, and an environment which valued their role.

The HAT also illustrates the importance of taking time to creating the right conditions for such a structure to succeed. Many tenant representatives had emerged through earlier community development and consultation initiatives of the estates.

Motivation

Representatives were motivated by the desire to make improvements to the estates. Previous experience had given them the confidence that they had a contribution to make. Their commitment was sustained, in part, by seeing that they could and did make a difference. The development of new skills and experiences, which brought benefits to them as individuals, was also a valued result. Improvements in their own living conditions were also a motivating factor.

The tenant representatives considered the level of interest shown by the majority of tenants in consultation exercises to be unsatisfactory. They attributed this to an underlying scepticism that their input would influence decisions. It seems that the experience of the tenant representatives had only limited impact on changing the attitudes of the tenant population more generally.

The user/management distinction

Associated with the distance between the most and least participative tenants, is the possibility of a narrowing gap between tenant representatives and other policy makers and managers. The very success of representatives in influencing policy and practice and changing attitudes makes their influence less visible. This creates the possibility that representatives themselves will become less conscious of their distinct role.

Contacts

Michael Trickey
Director of Policy and Planning
Arts Council of Wales
Museum Place
Cardiff CF1 3NX
01222 394711

John Coles
Business Excellence Team
Benefits Agency
Room 2S 25, Quarry House
Quarry Hill
Leeds LS2 7UA
0113 2324636

Mike Barnett
The Research Section
Strategic Management Unit
City Hall
Bradford BD1 1HY
01274 752221

Graham Davey
Devon and Cornwall Police Authority
PO Box 229
Exeter EX2 5YT
01392 438781

Anne Lynch
Director of Planning and Contracting
Eastern Health and Social Services Board
Champion House
12–22 Linen Hall Street
Belfast BT2 8BS
01232 321313

Mrs Jane Graham
Chief Officer
Eastern Health & Social Services Council
19 Bedford Street
Belfast BT2 7EJ
01232 321230

Keith Rimmer
Head of Transport and Communication
City Development Department
City of Edinburgh Council
18–19 Market Street
Edinburgh EH1 1BL
0131 469 3781

Mr Chris Pope
Highways Agency
Toll Gate House
Houlton Street
Bristol BS2 9DJ
0117 987 8635

Adrian Moran
Head of Innovation and Good Practice
The Housing Corporation
149 Tottenham Court Road
London W1P 0BN
0171 393 2000

Sally McDonald
Inland Revenue Customer Service Div.
Room 621, Bush House SW Wing
The Strand
London WC2B 4DR
0171 438 7695

Brigitte Ghodes
Policy Manager
London Borough of Lewisham
Lewisham Town Hall
Catford Road
London SE6 4RU
0171 695 6000

Toby Jackson
Head of Education
Education Department
Tate Gallery Liverpool
Albert Dock
Liverpool L3 4BB
0151 709 3223

Professor John Durant
Assistant Director
Science Museum
London SW7 2DD
0171 938 8000

Peter Jenkinson
Project Director
The New Art Gallery
The Project Office
139–143 Lichfield Street, 2nd floor
Walsall WS1 1SE
01922 653159

Mike Wilson
Chief Executive
Waltham Forest Housing Action Trust
4th floor, Kirkdale House
7 Kirkdale Road
Leytonstone
London E11 1HP
0181 539 5533

John Seargeant
Policy Studies Institute
100 Park Village East
London NW1 3SR
0171 468 2216

Jane Steele
Public Management Foundation
252B Gray's Inn Road
London WC1X 8JT
0171 837 9600